P9-AFB-188

DISCARDED

Hiking the Horizontal

3500

Hiking the Horizontal

Field Notes from a Choreographer

Liz Lerman

GV
1785
L435
2011
c. 2

Wesleyan University Press

Middletown, Connecticut

EL CAMINO COLLEGE
LIBRARY

Wesleyan University Press
Middletown CT 06459
www.wesleyan.edu / wespress
© 2011 Liz Lerman
All rights reserved
Manufactured in the United States of America

Wesleyan University Press is a member of the Green Press Initiative.
The paper used in this book meets their minimum requirement for recycled paper.

Book design by Dean Bornstein

For text permissions, see page 297.

Library of Congress Cataloging-in-Publication Data
appear on the last printed page of this book.

5 4 3 2 1

To Jon and Anna

. . . .

Contents

Acknowledgments

To the dancers who have found their way to me and to the Dance Exchange, I am indebted. I list those that stayed awhile, but even those not mentioned here brought their hopes, their ideas, their bodies, and their histories to our mutual endeavor: Harry Belanger, Marty Belin, Jeff Bliss, Kimberli Boyd, Mary Buckley, Debra Caplowe, Adrienne Clancy, Sarah Cohen, Reggie Crump, Beth Davis, Peter DiMuro, Ami Dowden-Fant, Amie Dowling, Thomas Dwyer, Clark Ebert, Diane Floyd, Bob Fogelgren, Keith Goodman, Margot Greenlee, Jeffrey Gunshol, Betty Harris, Louise Haskins, Vee Hollenbeck, Elizabeth Johnson, Ted Johnson, Judith Jourdin, Deborah Lamb, Pamela Lasswell, Sarah Levitt, Anne MacDonald, Matt Mahaney, Kevin Malone, Gesel Mason, Pene McCourty, Paloma McGregor, Cassie Meador, Vanetta Metoyer, Celeste Miller, Christopher Morgan, Kazu Nakamura, Sally Nash, Jim Patterson, Michelle Pearson, Tamara Pullman, Rome Quesada, Helen Rea, Jess Rea, Seymour Rosen, Hannah Rosenthal, Charlie Rother, Shula Strassfeld, Vincent Thomas, Andy Torres, Tom Truss, Thelma Tulane, Bea Wattenberg, Marvin Webb, Ben Wegman, Boris Willis, Martha Wittman, Colette Yglesias, and Don Zuckerman.

It is a special group of individuals who are willing to support an artist and an art form that is so ephemeral. I am thankful to all of the amazing individuals who have served and continue to serve as board members for the Dance Exchange and the many people whose major gifts make it all possible, including Diane Bernstein, the Drescher Family, Ron and Diane Eichner, Sandy Frucher, Lorraine Gallard and Richard Levy, Marti Head, Martha Minow, A. J. Pietrantone, Betsy Raymond, Stan Reinisch, and Elliot Rosen. I am grateful to the institutions that have sustained our experiment, including Boeing, the Exemplar Program and the Animating Democracy Program of Americans for the Arts, Covenant Foundation, Nathan Cummings Foundation, Doris Duke Charitable Foundation, John D. and Catherine T. MacArthur Foundation, Andrew W. Mellon Foundation, MetLife Foundation, Eugene and Agnes Meyer Foundation, and Wallace Foundation.

I thank the institutions and government agencies that gave me time to write, even though my first language is movement, and that have supported the Dance Exchange consistently. These include the Rockefeller Foundation, whose support through a residency at the Bellagio Study and Conference Center allowed me to take the first decisive steps on this book, Haystack Mountain School of Crafts, New England Foundation for the Arts, Arts and Humanities Council of Montgomery County, Maryland State Arts Council, and the National Endowment for the Arts. My thanks go also to the editors who helped guide some of the original writing that informs several of these essays: Don Adams, Linda Frye Burnham, Karen Clemente, Michael J. Crosbie, Arlene Goldbard, Cathryn Harding, and Nancy Stark Smith. I am also indebted to Special Collections Librarian Vin Novara and his colleagues who helped me with photo research in the Michelle Smith Performing Arts Library at the University of Maryland, which houses the Dance Exchange Archive; to Kelly Bond, who managed the considerable task of securing photo permissions; and to all the photographers who graciously agreed to have their work reproduced in these pages.

I am very grateful to Suzanna Tamminen at Wesleyan University Press for her guidance, enthusiasm and great capacity to question. Her presence has somehow made the whole process more gracious and graceful. I have come to love sitting in her office, chatting quietly and looking out the window over the simple Connecticut landscape. The extraordinary Pamela Tatge helped me find Suzanna, and many others at Wesleyan had a hand in this work, including Anne Greene. As we completed the writing process, I had the pleasure and security of working with copy editor Bronwyn Becker.

We have had wonderful partners in the United States and in countries abroad, including Canada, England, Ireland, Poland, and Japan, who said yes and then worked so hard to make our presence on their stages and in their communities have value. Some have brought us more than once, including Elise Bernhardt, Philip Bither, Dominic Campbell, Carolelinda Dickey, Kathie de Nobriga, Susie Farr, Ken Foster, Emma Gladstone, Arnie Malina, Judith Marcuse, Toby Mattox, Sam Miller, Ritsuko Mizuno and Norikazu Sato, Sharon Moore, Macek Novak, Jordan Peimer, Carla Perlo, Michael Reed, Charles Reinhardt, Andrea Rogers, Colleen Jennings-Roggensack, Ivan Sygoda, Pamela Tatge, Liz Thompson, Douglas Wheeler, Jed Wheeler, and David White.

I have had a wonderful cadre of friends over the years who have walked with me, talked to me on long-distance calls, and helped to shape ideas and action in my life. I am in debt to them and mention here Rachel Cowan, Liesel Flashenberg, Arlene Goldbard, Sally Nash, Wendy Perron, Linda Caro Reinisch, Sherri Rose, Holly Sidford, and Michaele Weissman.

I am grateful to the staff of the Dance Exchange who made it all possible, most especially our Managing Director Jane Hirshberg, whom I met when she was director of development and education for the Portsmouth Music Hall, the organization that put together the Shipyard Project. Since then, I have watched in amazement at how she takes on the widest possible range of issues, from human happiness of the employees of the organization to the extravagant vision that the Dance Exchange employs in the world. She partners with the board and funders with an honesty and integrity that are her hallmark. She listens to the dancers for their complaints, their ideas, and their personal dramas as they try to lead the complicated lives of artists. She thinks about the Dance Exchange all the time and is able to problem solve while in the shower, while running, while talking to state legislatures, and while just being the great mother she is to her two school-age daughters. But what I truly appreciate most about Jane is that we can work together through long periods of inspiration while spar with full hearts and intelligence—while maintaining a mutual respect that runs very deep.

I thank John Borstel whose help on this book was immeasurable. He manages to get the grammar right as well as the ideas. He asks great questions when necessary and did some hands-on work when I just couldn't get the sentence to work. Most importantly, he cares about the ideas emanating from the Dance Exchange and sees it as part of who he is to make sure that others have access. And because he is also an artist, he brings to our partnership a sense of beauty, an awareness of rhythm, a profound depth of communicative power. I am grateful for the effort and the enormous impact he has had on my ability to bring anything to the public. Without him this would have been a different book.

I want to thank all of my family, from my wonderful stepmother, Sarah Dean, to the newest children, Leo, Ezra, Lilly, and Maya. My brothers, Richard and David, are a source of inspiration and refuge, and remind me every day to fight the right battle with intelligence and good humor. I have many sisters-in-law, all of whom have been great companions in my evolution. Particularly instrumental in the preparation of this book was Vicky Spelman, whose sharp mind and sympathetic ear have helped me find language for difficult concepts as well as support for just how to live in the world. And my endless gratitude goes to Jon and Anna and the animals we share a house with, who provide support, comfort, and on many days a challenging question too.

Hallelujah (2000): Pene McCourty, Margot Greenlee, Martha Wittman, Marvin Webb. Photo: Lise Metzger.

Prologue

I Am Interested . . . *

I am interested in remembering why I started to dance and how happy I was at that moment; in what we dance about; in who gets to do the dancing; in performers who look like people dancing, not dancers dancing; in the idea that dance is a birthright; in keeping professional dancers alive as human beings; in what dancers have to learn from people who have been in motion for over sixty years; in how much dancers know and how little we share it with the rest of the world; in how much dancers know and how little the rest of the world knows we know it; in the moment when people who are too fat, too clumsy, too old, too sick to dance actually step out and dance, and how transformed the dancer and the watcher are in that moment; in how my choreography is a vehicle for me to learn about anything I want; in the continual hunt for interesting movement vocabulary that satisfies performers, watchers, and the subject matter; in the aesthetic, physical, and social implications of combining young and old; in making an environment that somehow leaves room for individual and collective participation but stays loyal to an artistic idea and focus; in the continuing challenge of making personal expression valuable to me, the dancers, and the lady next door.

---

*Artist's statement used in Dance Exchange press kit, early 1990s

Hiking the Horizontal

This book is a personal history of ideas and actions that emerge from making dances. It is also a description of the Dance Exchange, a place I think of as think tank and action lab, a place that has been my home and home to many others since I established it in 1976. I wanted to record the events that led me to think and act in the world in a very particular way. I wanted people to understand that art is powerful, that dance can make a difference. I wanted to document ways of seeing and being that have the power to change the environments we live and work in, and the encounters that we have with each other.

The phrase "hiking the horizontal" is the most recent and encompassing terminology to express the underlying philosophy of my work. Before I found the words, hiking the horizontal was a physical gesture. It took me a very long time to understand the full implications of what was so simply accomplished with my hands. But the movement came first as a way of explaining why I wanted to live in a non-hierarchical world. Imagine for a moment a long, upright line that runs from top to bottom. At the top is art so separate from the rest of culture that its greatness is measured in part by its uselessness. Other characteristics arguably include emphasis on personal expression, crafting aesthetics, and a commitment to purity of form. At the bottom is art so embedded in its culture that no one thinks to call it art: here reside sacred rituals, healing ceremonies, objects made beautiful by their functions, people meeting and moving through the stories and needs of the calendar of festivals. Or your perspective might lead you to put culturally embedded art at the top and the art for art's sake the bottom. Either way, the forms of art are ranked from top to bottom according to a system of values. This is the kind of hierarchy of ideas that I grew up with and that continues to prevail in many worlds.

Now imagine turning this line sideways to lay it horizontal. That way each of these poles exerts an equal pull and has an equal weight. Of course, the line is not completely flat and the poles are often not equally heavy. It is more like a seesaw and that is why dancing and art-making provide sustenance for the hike ahead. If we are lucky enough, we can actually take the long highway between the sometimes opposing forces, discovering information that can feed our artistic impulses all along the way. It is hard work, but those of us wandering at one end or the other can begin by trying to find something to respect at the opposite pole. And if for a moment you take this continuum and bend it into a circle, you will see that the two ends can lie close, like next-door neighbors.

As I truly began to understand this idea of the horizontal, I recognized how frequently I was thinking along a spectrum of multiple perspectives. I knew I was hardly to first to notice the value of spectrum thinking. I was just reenacting an ancient idea with my simple hand gesture, because many have walked this path before me. Philosophers who admire paradox, rabbis and priests who seek union in opposites, artists rejecting dichotomy, business executives looking for a synthesis, educators hoping to foster learning communities that embrace multiple forms of knowledge and discovery: all of these reflect a desire to find meaning within ambiguity, common purpose amid individual vision and action. Once I had found the phrase, "hiking the horizontal" became my shorthand for a whole series of behaviors, practices, and beliefs that I have been working toward for most of my life.

At its essence are several concepts:

Allow for multiple perspectives *and* recognize that making distinctions is a creative act and worth doing in order to understand the nuances of our efforts. In a hierarchical order, the only way to make a distinction is to literally put the other idea "down." There is only room for one idea. But in hiking the horizontal, many ideas can coexist. Distinction is important, clarifying, useful. Distinction does not have to be about right and wrong.

Make the walls permeable between these distinctions.

Find a way to respect something that lives at the end of the spectrum farthest from where you are comfortable or from where you are doing your work at that moment. The respect has to be authentic, but it doesn't have to be uncritical.

Name where you are on the spectrum at any given moment, because the actions slide fast between multiple worlds. Some are more adept than others at making this slide, and it is hard to keep everyone aware if the walls are porous.

Consider when either/or thinking is useful and when it isn't. Tolerance, generosity, nimbleness are helpmates to hiking this path, but they are also outcomes from moving along it.

Recognize that finding the essence of an idea need not be an exercise in reductionism. The task is to discover the enormous potential for application that lies in the essential.

Before hiking the horizontal, I had many ways of stating what the Dance Exchange was and what we were doing. Even before we were incorporated, I was trying to explain why I was teaching dance in senior centers, government agencies, and downtown offices at lunchtime, all while rehearsing and working as a graduate student. "Keep one foot in the professional world and one in the community," I would say. "I am not fragmented. I live like this because the world is fragmented. I am just being the whole person that I want to be."

Thus I started by describing the relationships between art, the artist, and society. This sketch evolved into varied articulations, often under the pressure to make my case in a world where I was both advocating for the central role of art and bucking many of the conventions of the art world itself. As I was called upon to speak—either because of the necessities of survival or because someone had invited me to address a group—I began to notice ideas settling down. Things that might have swirled for months or even years took shape in one sentence, though not so much from writing, because I didn't write the speeches out, but from talking to real people sitting in front of me, listening. Formless shapes in my mind became essential phrases.

"Dance is a birthright," I would say, "and as we know about birthrights, they are easily stolen." But I soon discovered that I needed to elaborate a bit, so I rephrased as "Dance is for everyone (and that means Liz Lerman too)." And sometimes I would draw the circle wider with this: "Art in general, dance in particular, is too powerful to keep in the hands of only a few."

"Why would I want to live in a world where I would have to choose between concert or community, between nurture or rigor, between abstraction and representation?" I asked. When we wanted to assert why the Dance Exchange was making dances about the defense budget, getting sick kids to dance in their beds at Children's Hospital, and refining its own choreographic tools in master classes for dance majors, we would express this same idea by stating: "The Dance Exchange reintegrates the multiple functions of dance."

When I was asked to speak before Congress on behalf of funding for the arts in 1988, I brought with me something I had been musing about for a while. I said: "There was a time when people danced and the crops grew. People danced and that is how they healed their children. They danced as a way to prepare for war. With so much on the line, how did they decide who got to do the dancing? Who did they trust with the best part? Maybe it was given to the oldest person, the one with the most wisdom. Maybe they gave it to the fattest, the one who carried the most weight. But," I said with a lot of emphasis, "it did matter, and it still does."

For a while I observed a phenomenon that I called "colliding truths" and entreated people to be willing to "embrace paradox." These were phrases I used as I hunted for ways to maintain my commitment to the excellence of the concert world in a balance with the dynamic, meaningful, and equally challenging world of communities.

So the laboratory of doing has always been partnered with the rigor of articulating. It is through this process that I and the Dance Exchange eventually found our four questions: Who gets to dance? What is the dance about? Where is it happening? Why does it matter? Saying that our mission was to ask and answer these questions became one of the perennial means of expressing what the Dance Exchange is about. I don't think these questions came into existence at once, but they were rather the result of a long process that included many of the attributes of evolution: natural selection, extinction, adaptation, and mutation. Eventually, after all the trials and errors came a realization that who was dancing mattered, that what the dance was about made a difference to me and to those gathered, and that where it was happening changed things. The nature of inquiry and the framing of the first three questions constitute chapters 1 through 4 of this volume. I hope that the final question, about why dance matters, pervades the entire book.

My earliest memories include dancing. My big brother and I would beg Mom to put on the phonograph our favorite, "From the Hall of the Mountain King," and then we would do some kind of wild weird running/skipping pattern up and down the short corridor that connected our small bedrooms to the tiny living room. When friends of my parents were over for dinner, someone would inevitably say, "Why don't you dance for us?" and I would. I shake my head in bemusement now as I think about how it must have looked: probably a lot of twirling and jumping and, if I was lucky, some interesting falling down and getting up. I was at most three years old, and I was very happy.

I recently met someone who had known the family in those years. "Liz, you used to talk constantly," she said. "Words, words, words." This encounter makes me think that my need to understand the experience of dancing and my will to convey it in language go back a very long time.

I am fortunate that I have been able to hone that practice of understanding and articulation in such a wonderful living laboratory. The fantastic dancers who have made their way to the Dance Exchange, who put up with its messy and ecstatic framework, have all made contributions to our knowledge and to the body of work that has engaged audiences for so long. The staff, who slog away at the details and paint the big picture too, make it possible to think and re-think the ideas. And the amazing partners who have made available their homes, their laboratories, their houses of worship, their military plants, their stages, their young ones, and their ancient ones . . . all of this in order to make dance matter.

Here are some of the stories and some of the theories that have aided us along the way.

. . . .

How to Read This Book

Sequencing is a provocative activity for a choreographer, a fact that proved to be applicable in organizing this book. I gave a lot of thought to and experimented a bit with the order of ideas and categories. So feel free to read from the beginning to end. But you may also find yourself skipping around, and I think that can make sense too. Some ideas reappear, taken from a different angle, and some ideas simply repeat because they make sense all over again within the context of the subject of another chapter.

It is also possible to find some of this same information in different forms online at the Dance Exchange Web site. Please visit and let us know what's on your mind.

Ferocious Beauty: Genome (premiered 2006, photo 2009): Cassie Meador, Matt Mahaney, Elizabeth Johnson, Ben Wegman; biologist Harris Lewin in video projection, background. Photo: Andrew Hoxey, courtesy of the *University Daily Kansan*.

Questions as a Way of Life

Fueling the Imagination

I was visiting with my friend, the biologist Bonnie Bassler at Princeton, when she took me down the hall to meet her colleague Eric Wieschaus, a Nobel laureate who works with fruit flies. By that time, my dance *Ferocious Beauty: Genome* had already premiered, and I was eagerly fixing it. I was particularly interested in the part we called the fugue because of its complex relationship between video, text, and movement. The subject of this particular section was the myriad ways in which science and artistic research overlap. It starts with the scientist Aaron Terkowitz from the University of Chicago saying, "How do I ask myself a question?" followed by five minutes of dance and media that address just that query.

So I asked Dr. Wieschaus how he asks himself a question. And he responded, "I am fueled by my ignorance."

The precision of his answer thrilled me. "Nobel Laureate Fueled by His Ignorance" would make a great headline, I told him. Artists and scientists have a keen understanding that not knowing is fuel for the imagination rather than fuel for humiliation. There is nothing to hide.

Asking Questions as a Way of Life

Twice when I was growing up I asked questions so stupid that they brought the class to an absolute standstill. The first time I realized what I had done almost instantly. The second time I was clueless until the laughing started. You would think that after experiences like that I would never ask another question. But no. It seems that asking dumb questions paved the way for asking better ones. Or maybe at a very early age I just got over the embarrassment of not knowing.

"I wonder if this is the only way it has to be. Maybe it is changeable. In fact, Liz, you could change it." That would be my father talking passionately at dinner about almost anything political, but most especially about civil rights. Or it could be my mother, whispering about self-knowledge while she drove me to dance lessons. They both had their methods for making me think about my responsibilities and role in the world, as well as about the nature of change. But either way, to make change at all, you first have to notice what is going on around you or inside you. If you are a child or a young adult, noticing frequently takes the form of complaining. It took me a while to see the connection between that infernal crankiness and a method of inquiry.

So in the sacred space of the ballet-school dressing rooms with young dancers bemoaning the fat that will forge their fate, crying as they measure the full circumference of their waist with their own two hands, I am watching and thinking: Isn't there a better way for us to be sharing our precious time before class? Or an even more radical question: Is that skinny frame actually so beautiful? And by the way: Why are my feet bleeding just so I can stand up on my toes? Whose idea was that?

In the chaos of Hebrew school with little learning, less nurturing, and confirmation as our only goal, I am thinking: Can't the adults see that we are wasting our time here and some of us actually might like to speak this language? Do they even care what we think? Why don't they?

Or standing at an anti-war demonstration at the Vermont state capitol in the winter, freezing and wondering, Is this really helping anything?

The questions trip over each other. They never stop.

It took a while to understand that this could be a way of life, a way of making art, a way of making space for others to engage in the conversation, of naming things to encourage dialogue, of reordering ideas, or of making something useful or beautiful or both.

It can be destabilizing to think like this. The constant questioning implies a lack of knowledge. And the ambiguity of so many of the kinds of answers I could come up with didn't always serve as an antidote. I tried to make a virtue of "not knowing," which often proved difficult—in part because in our culture, in the media, and in many educational establishments, smartness is defined by the ability to have answers in a hurry, stated well and without complication.

Oddly though, this "not knowing" has become a bridge to good conversation and friendship not just with artists but with clergy and scientists too. There is kind of a shared delight, and sometimes misery, in the recognition that this source of inquiry can be an engine. And besides, I eventually learned that I can pull myself out of most disasters through methods that emerged long ago in processes of endless repetitions and trial and error. I can count on various means of discovery so that moments of not knowing are more like guideposts than endings.

Slowly I began to recognize many kinds of questions, reasons to question, and even ways to harness the act of questioning. I developed my capacity to distinguish between questions that required research as opposed to action or rehearsal or conversation, and to see how these modes overlap and lead into each other. The easygoing relationship between needing to know and then discovering answers based on reading, searching the Internet, trying an idea in rehearsal, and gaining insight through dialogue makes for a lively intersection of mind and body.

An Early Teacher

It was Rush Welter, a history teacher at Bennington College, who taught me how to be utterly absorbed by asking something and who gave me the overarching tool of inquiry as a way to address my ignorance. His course consisted of a set of six questions and a list of primary sources. At the end of every six weeks, we had to turn in a paper answering one of the questions. The questions themselves were based on historical dilemmas from pre-revolutionary America. One was about the colonial-era civil-liberties maverick Anne Hutchinson, and another asked which colony had led the revolution and why.

What was unique about the course was that the "textbook" consisted only of the list of primary sources and that the instructor didn't lecture. Instead, he would meet us twice a week to answer any of our own queries, and he let those questions determine what he actually talked about with us. Over the course of the year I learned to choose among contrasting positions of thought as expressed in the primary sources. I found my way around different versions of truth as I sought to both discover agreement with and establish my individual voice among the various directions my classmates were taking in their own quests to solve problems our teacher raised. It was exhilarating. Looking back, I think his methods were transformational and helped me to see how to choreograph, especially if I were to make the kind of dance that interested me: the open-ended, trying-to-understand-something kind.

Getting Help

Early on I learned that people like to be asked to help make a dance. Dance seems such a romantic and exotic activity that when I ask for help, especially help from a conceptual sphere, folks really step in. This became clear to me when I met Gordon Adams while we were both fellows at the Blue Mountain Center. He was director of the Defense Budget Project and author of *The Iron Triangle*. We actually began talking about the piece I was working on at the time, *Nine Short Dances About the Defense Budget and Other Military Matters*, while sitting on the swimming dock. Gordon gave me lots of help during my research, and he stayed engaged throughout the making of the dance. He introduced me to others in his field and provided me with facts and information that would underpin the rigor of the piece.

This is an important dynamic to understand. When you ask people for help with some special questions in mind, they in turn take an interest in your activity. They will of course come to see the concert. More importantly, they will become a partner in shaping the work. What might be considered a solo act of making a dance emerges as something quite different because of the dialogue. It is not that the advisors come into the studio embodied, but more that they are present in my mind as I work. It's as if I have a team of shadow champions in the rehearsal hall, encouraging me to continue even when I feel tired, or scared, or just plain dumb.

Turning Discomfort into Inquiry and the Beginnings of the Critical Response Process

The recognition that inquiry allows for better communication, better feelings, and even better outcomes became clear to me with increasing force as I began teaching and using the principles of the Critical Response Process that I developed in the early nineties. I discovered that this multistep process for work-in-progress dialogue also held some practical tools for pursuing the inquiry itself and some guideposts for intuition. This began with my awareness of the lengthy apologies from artists that preceded a showing of any unfinished work. I noticed that I too often had a litany of issues disguised as nervous excuses before I showed something. And when I thought more about them, I realized that these excuses were often the problems I myself was having with what I was making. At first I didn't realize they could be posed in question form. It wasn't until I started talking with loved ones (first my husband, Jon Spelman, and then others in a small orbit of very trusted friends) that I realized that what I said in introducing a showing was often the first thing that came up in the discussion as soon as it was over. So I began to wonder whether, rather than apologize, I could ask a question—ask it with dignity and want to hear the answer, whether useful or not. The principle of "turn discomfort into inquiry" begins with the things we make.

More Questions

I know my incessant restlessness started young, but I think some critical junctures along the way helped to guide it. Thankfully I found respite in choreography, in partnering with others with similar questions, and with a group of people who were willing to help figure out what is interesting in all of this.

I think it was my mother's death that forced the questioning to become a way of making art, because I really did wonder why she had to die so young, and why she had to have that ignorant rabbi she had never met come into her hospital room and rub her in all the wrong ways, and how I had the courage to give her the daily morphine shot and walk her to the bathroom and back in the middle of those last nights, and where my own strength came from—and so the questions flowed.

I think it was the dogma of the contemporary art world that made asking questions the stance of a gentle rebel.

I think the act of putting old people onstage constituted a series of questions all on its own. Did they really even belong up there? Would the audience look at them? I remember one woman who was half blind and couldn't see or hear her cues as I watched in awe of her teetering around in what seemed a very interesting little dance. I wondered if it could be art.

I think it was the political work that forced the questioning to become a way of making art, because to tell the whole story from my perspective was just plain too simplistic, too narrow, too yesterday.

But none of these realizations started as questions. They all started as complaints, opinions, awareness of discomfort, internal monologues looping around in an obsessive brain. It took a while to figure out that by changing the tone and letting my sentence end with an upward tilt, I could actually get back to the material at hand and go to work. Inquiry became liberating.

Two Dances: The Oldest and One Not Yet Made

My nephew, who is among many other things a writer, asked me about the difference between my earlier work and my newer work. After thinking for a long minute, I said, "I am cursed to always overreach. But in the later work the gap between my ideas and what I am capable of actually producing is smaller. In the early work, the gap was sometimes a chasm." I know that most artists overreach. That big vision is magnetic, an oasis in the distance during years of insomnia, and often just as illusive. I don't think this is the provenance of artists. I just think we are foolish/happy and obsessive/persistent enough to keep trying.

Here then are stories about two dances. I consider *New York City Winter*, made in 1974, to be the first dance of my adult life. As a solo, perhaps its scale was such that it didn't suffer too much from my penchant for overreaching. (By my third dance, I would definitely be in over my head.) *The Matter of Origins* will premiere in fall 2010. Inquiry is a constant companion in both, but does not always appear as a question.

. . . .

Author's Note: The Matter of Origins premiered on September 10, 2010, at the Clarice Smith Performing Arts Center at Maryland, College Park.

New York City Winter

When I moved to New York City in 1973, I had saved up enough money from a teaching job in Maryland to live and study for almost a year—live poorly, but live. I was housed in a six-floor walkup with the bathtub in the kitchen, but I had my own room, a lovely loft bed overlooking Second Avenue, and a roommate I could tolerate. I felt as though I had enough money to do what I wanted until I walked past a shop in the East Village that had in the front window a hand-embroidered peasant blouse from Eastern Europe. It cost thirty-five dollars, which in those days and my circumstances was very expensive. I used to walk past it just to visit. But I could not afford it without taking some extra work.

I was studying ballet with Peter Saul and modern with Viola Farber. I took acrobatics mostly with Broadway and television hopefuls who kept me informed about the other aspects of our biz. I also made contact with Daniel Nagrin, who had guest taught in my senior year of college. He asked me to be in his company. I went to see a performance at NYU and watched with interest for a while. The dancers were terrific. The audience, mostly friends of the performers and other dancers, seemed into it too. I, however, struggled. I wasn't finding the things I was looking for in dance performance, as much as I admired the abilities of the performers. My discomfort was about the dancers' inner focus and the nature of the relationships onstage. The dancers were having fun, but the audience was not a part of it.

A very strange thing happened. All winter I had been getting nosebleeds, and in the middle of this concert I felt a small one starting. I held my hand to my nose and continued to watch the dance. I had no tissue with me, and I was in seated in the middle of the row. There was no way for me to walk out easily. The dance continued, and the nosebleed stopped. But my hand was caked in blood. As I watched, I slowly licked the blood away. I felt I was inside a ritual of grief and sorrow, of liberation and decision making. I knew I couldn't accept being in this company. I knew that I was looking for something else—something bigger for dance, for the dancers, for the art form. Something that mattered.

Meanwhile, I wanted that embroidered blouse. I had no money. I was miserable in my dance classes, and I couldn't find anything to love in the theater. Then I learned something at my acrobatics class while standing in line waiting for my turn to try to do a backflip (with the teacher's help, always accompanied by a sarcastic remark). The girls were all doing various forms of go-go dancing to make a living. I was intrigued, as you could make thirty-five to fifty dollars a night depending on where you were and what you did. They told me where to go to find out about it.

I went to a building somewhere in midtown and found the office. I met with a woman whom I took to be the secretary, but I realized later she must have had more authority than that. She looked me up and down. I was wearing a black patent-leather raincoat with cherries on it. She made a lewd comment about the cherries. I never wore the raincoat again. But I took the information, and in a few days she called me with my first job.

Go-go dancing was a liberation for me. It was also very subversive. And, I concluded after my first night, I would learn a lot about performance. Everything that had bothered me at that dance concert at NYU was countered by the go-go experience.

For example, I was by myself. A true soloist making it alone in the complex and slightly dangerous scenes, including the bus ride to New Jersey, the bar, and the late-night return to Manhattan. Perhaps I felt it was a test of my ability to make it alone in the world, but I think the real satisfaction was in the relationship of the dancing to the audience, in the development of a movement vocabulary that worked in this context, in proving my own sexual attractiveness.

What was the relationship to the audience, and why did this interest me so much at the time? For one, and a very important one, I had to focus on the people I was performing for. I couldn't pull the modern dance stare or the inner-directed movement gaze. They demanded a relationship with the dancer. I found this intriguing, challenging, and difficult. And I felt it a worthwhile problem to solve. Over time I developed ways of talking with the guys while I was performing, a dialogue that reached its apex when I was able to get some of the men to actually choreograph my moves. I have always felt less sure of myself in relation to inventiveness. I trace this to my classical roots.

The dancer in me loves my classical training. The choreographer in me has been trying to escape it forever. When my mother was dying, I was thrilled to go back to ballet class. I loved knowing what was expected of me. I loved that my body knew what to do even when I was in such chaos. But when I step into the studio to find movement, develop physical approaches, or just let loose, I almost always have to make myself move away from the classical choices my body makes first.

I remember feeling particularly lousy when I was in high school that I had spent so much time in dance class but couldn't do the popular forms of the day. All I could do was my ballet. It drove me crazy, because whenever I was on the dance floor, people watched expecting me to be able to do anything. And I couldn't. I think I was trying to change that history while I was in the bars, and to do this day I am curious about and envious of true contemporary and pop forms of dance. They have, of course, their own orthodoxy requiring hours of training and practice by people willing to put in the time. I put in my time in the bars in New Jersey over the winter of 1973–74.

I have a complicated relationship to sexuality and dance. Sometimes I think of it as all context and history. Born midcentury to a woman who hid her own sexuality behind a stoic and aloof intelligence, I grew up in a house where female sexuality was not celebrated or even discussed. (My father did talk often about my ability to have children. This he did both verbally and nonverbally, as he took swipes at my hips while saying "good for childbirth" whenever he felt like it.) I have no memory of learning dance in any way that suggested its sexual potential. So it continues to shock me how often men, in particular, change their tone of voice, their stance, and where they direct their eyes when they learn I am a dancer. Leering and suggestive comments continue, even as I enter my sixties. Go-go dancing was a counterattack to these experiences. It was all about sexuality. And since at that time I was sewing up the wounds from an early marriage and divorce, in some ways it was a comforting place to go.

I am a quick learner. I figured out most of this after only three or four outings. I made enough money to buy the blouse (which I still own), and I noticed that I was trying to figure out how to be the best go-go dancer ever. Always competitive, I was keeping an eye on the appropriate level of this urge. One very mean night in a bar, the guys pulled the shades, began to bang on the tables, and offered me much more money to strip. I left. That was the end of it. I never went back.

Within days of quitting I realized that I might make a dance about the experience and try to pull some of these ideas onto the stage. The dance, which would become *New York City Winter*, was autobiographical. It included some of my ridiculous inner musings as I entered the go-go world. It was self-deprecating. I talked, told stories, and related my experience in dance and text form. I borrowed for the dance all the accoutrements of my real-life experience. I found that very satisfying and felt that, for the first time, stage life and real life were merging. One section of the dance looked at a ballet vocabulary and the slight changes required to reveal the sexual provocation latent it its classical form. I liked that section, as it marked one of the first times I was able to translate an idea to the stage. I think the dance also conveyed my loneliness and my cockiness.

I premiered it at St. Mark's Church as part of a poetry series that a friend of mine ran. I left New York the next day. I continued to perform the piece for a very long time—my last performance at Dance Theater Workshop was in 1988 when I was one month pregnant. I continued to edit the dance and was pleased to note that by the sixth year I had cut about six minutes. I decided that if you could keep a dance around long enough, you could count on losing one minute a year.

While making *New York City Winter* I discovered something critical, if quite by accident. It has to do with storytelling and embedding the ideas and points of view inside the action and the telling rather than in the theory. I learned that humor could make an audience stick it out longer. Later, others commented on the quiet feminism that the dance exposed in my work. I didn't set out to make a feminist statement, but I was proud to read that people thought it was there. I was just making a dance that had to be made. The positive response I received about including the very real thoughts, no matter how absurd, inside the mind of the performer showed me that an audience was interested in my brain and my body. And making the dance about this young girl and her quest for acceptance made it okay for the dance to be sexy as well as about ideas.

I stumbled into a few ideas about choreography that are still with me.

Use objects from real life. In my first dance I used the bag and coat I wore at that time, and the original costume I had made for dancing in the bars. (Actually, I made one change in the costume. I cut a big hole in one side of the bra in order to reveal a naked breast on which I painted a happy face during the dance. I did this to accentuate and exaggerate the situation for its hilarity as well as its provocation.) Even the makeup case and the makeup I put on during the dance came from my own daily use. I have continued this practice when and where possible. It connects my life off stage and on in a way that I find comforting, and lets one inform the other.

Tell stories. In one moment in the dance I just stepped forward and began to talk. It was short. Later I talked and moved a little. Later still I talked to a character who was not onstage with me. So the dance had various levels of text.

Recreate images. I was very poor in New York City that winter. When I got home from the bars it was usually around two or three in the morning. My little sixth-floor walkup was freezing. I would light the oven and sit there with a cup of tea to get warm. I used this image at the end of the dance.

When I finished the dance, I felt that I had found a way to reflect back on my brief stint in New York City. But I still had questions that remain with me to do this day. There seemed to be so many unwritten rules of behavior that the legions of young dancers were expected to keep.

I was feeling a great need and desire to step outside the dance world. I loved my dancing. I still wanted it. But not under these terms. So I said goodbye.

New York City Winter stayed in my active repertory for over a decade. After I last performed it, other dancers took it on. Around the time of its thirtieth anniversary, we revived the piece in a duet version for my fifty-something self and Cassie Meador, a dancer who was then approximately my age when I had choreographed it. We haven't performed this version yet: it proved too confrontational for the dance-festival gala for which it was originally planned. But we're still sitting on an invitation to bring it to a midnight series at home in Washington. So maybe soon the piece will return to its late-night beginnings.

The Matter of Origins

It still amuses and amazes me when things come together in a rehearsal. Such disparate ideas, movement sequences, and images get laid out individually, then connect in ways that completely surprise me. I know I am the person doing it, thinking it, imagining it, ordering it, telling people what to do, and yet so often I feel like I don't really control the situation. Something happens.

I am working on a new piece right now. The signals that convince me that it will become an actual work for the stage come from many different directions. Here is a short synopsis that captures a brief span of time in a rehearsal process where change is constant.

Gordy Kane, from the University of Michigan physics department, comes to one of our "Animated Keynotes" presentations, where the company and I talk and show live excerpts from the Dance Exchange's work. This one features excerpts from *Ferocious Beauty: Genome*. Gordy responds to this dance about genetics by asking, "How about one for physics?" I think, No more science. But then I meet with him and some of his colleagues, and we have a really interesting discussion about beginnings, about matter, about mystery and math. One thing I notice about this meeting is that everyone is on time. I wonder to myself if physicists and dancers have a similar respect for time and all that it can mean. And I challenge them to make an equation that explains how we partner on residencies, which leads to lots of laughing and good feelings. Then Gordy talks about CERN in Switzerland and its Large Hadron Collider and convinces me that I should make a visit while in Europe later in the spring.

My husband, Jon, and I go to CERN. What a cool place. With its scale, organization, and sense of purpose, I am reminded of the Portsmouth Naval Shipyard. I get back to the company, we do some rehearsing, and we unearth plenty of physical ideas. A few months later several of us go back to CERN to shoot video, talk to a few people, and try to make enough connections so they will want us and the project. They do, but there is not enough funding around to carry some of our biggest ideas forward, at least not yet.

A key piece of patronage arrives in the form of a commission from Susie Farr of the University of Maryland's Clarice Smith Performing Arts Center. She is the first to step out and say to me, "Make the next piece." She was the first to say to her staff, "Let's find a way to get Liz back onto our stage." Exemplifying a rare breed of presenter-as-patron, Susie's support includes ideas, technical resources, rehearsal space, and a kind of intellectual matchmaking. In preparation, you could see the two of us striding across the large green in the center of the campus as we went to meet faculty who might help in the research; under our umbrellas, marching up one portico after another looking for connections. "Let the dreaming begin," she might be saying, although with Susie the message is more subtle and a bit sly, and tinged with a challenge too: make it well.

I start reading a lot of books on the history of physics, especially in the twentieth century. Dennis Overbye's *Einstein in Love*, David Lindley's *Uncertainty*, and Gino Segrè's *Faust in Copenhagen* are all very engaging, and I find my imagination drawn to the intense group of mostly men described in these books who changed human thinking in such a short amount of time. I learn about Heisenberg's uncertainty principle, which posits that between position and momentum the more precisely one property is known, the less precisely the other can be known. Like many artists before me, I am fascinated by this paradox and recognize its potential for metaphor and for movement. I think Keith Thompson, an experienced dancer/choreographer who has come to Dance Exchange to be part of this piece, defies the uncertainty principle because when he dances you can see both shape and momentum.

Reading Kai Bird and Martin J. Sherwin's *American Prometheus*, I come across a reference to Edith Warner, who served meals at her teahouse to Robert Oppenheimer and his Los Alamos colleagues. During a big rehearsal phase I ask the three older women in the company to go in another room with teacups and chairs. They make something. It is all right but I want to fix it immediately, give it more charge. I tell them to put the teacups on their laps, take the gestures from what they made, and see how fast they can do them. The teacups rattle like crazy, and one drops to the floor. I leave them to problem solve. Later they show us a trio that contains one extraordinary event. They make the teacups rattle as they hold them, and suddenly all of Los Alamos and what it meant exists in this one image. I am so grateful.

The idea of tea has now taken hold. After rehearsal we experiment with different ways of staging it, with different dancers taking charge (one group even serves tea and gives massages at the same time). I begin to talk about Act One happening onstage and Act Two as a large-scale tea in the theater lobby, with a possibility of using tables as projection surfaces. I add that an undercurrent to tea is the idea of service, and that idea in this context could encompass who is serving whom, what happens to the experience of being served if the dancers you have just looked up to onstage are now pouring your tea, and how science (or art) is called into the service of utilitarian needs as the main justification for existence. I particularly like the idea of developing material not only for stage but for tables, for small spaces between tables, for video that might accompany the tea projected on walls or on the ceiling or a draped cloth just below the ceiling as a softer reception for the images or as a way to match with the tablecloths.

I often get unsolicited CDs from music publishers, which I love. These usually consist of various composers loosely linked, and the accompanying letter encourages me to think about using some of this music for dance work. One day a CD arrives with a collection of fanfares, and the first selection on it is terrific. I decide to use its energy to try to get the dancers to make the music completely visual. It is fast and furious and it occupies us for a while. Later, when we send our CERN contact a DVD of our process with some footage from our visit, we include one small piece of this fanfare.

At this stage, sometimes structure helps distill ideas, and sometimes it moves the dancing forward. With this in mind, I begin to consider a series of fanfares throughout the piece. I am cleaning up some CDs at home and come across Janacek's *Sinfonietta*, which opens with a big fanfare, and decide to try that too. Jim Ross, my conductor friend, comes to the studio to help us with the complicated rhythms. We discover that conducting is a little more like choreography than just normal "reading" of the music. In researching, I discover that Janacek wrote this piece for the Sokol Gymnasium and that it premiered one year before Heisenberg first posed his uncertainty principle. I wonder if a structure might be something about fanfares introducing the substance of the piece, or at least various scientific breakthroughs.

Meanwhile, I am trying to discover the right question to ask, so I am doing a lot of research and occasionally getting into the studio with small groups of dancers. We are generating material from a variety of sources. I still think that the concepts will emerge by following my own interest in the particular questions the scientists at CERN are trying to answer. This idea of beginnings begins to morph into questions about endings. If scientists discover what they are looking for, that means the end of the line for some theories. And as they understand the beginning of the universe, they keep wondering about its ending too, or the possibility that it has already ended once before.

Bob Dylan puts out a new CD, and I love a few songs on it that I listen to a lot. One of them makes me think of Jon and me in bed, just looking up at the ceiling, listening to the music, with the smallest of touching going on. I wonder about mattresses in a parking lot with hundreds of old couples of all kinds in various states of sleep, touch, wrapped up together. I think this is another dance. It will be months before I realize that I can just go to work on this image and let it seep and see if it was part of the CERN piece too. I think that the Dylan music and the question of endings are feeding each other and allowing both to stay in my mind. Once I opened up this connection, new structural elements made their way into my planning and our rehearsing.

I start trying to figure out what else besides beginnings is going on with the CERN guys. Matter and antimatter are attractive to me, but because they're overused in the popular press I give them scant attention. Then there is supersymmetry, which at first I dismiss because I don't like symmetry. Then I begin to notice how the scientists use artistic terms to defend their thinking, as they do when they talk about supersymmetry. It is a curious sensation to find art being used to justify ideas. I start to get into this a little with Gordy on e-mail. I explain that symmetry is often a sign of a new choreographer, and it can be a dead giveaway for amateurism of the worst sort. He takes it well, and we exchange some thoughts.

The physicists are looking for a unified theory, which I find odd since I like chaos so much. I learn that at least part of their reason for this search is to unify the classical model of physics with the quantum world. But I sense their quest for an overarching theory expresses a kind of yearning. I can't be sure about this, but I find the physicists' puzzle begins to underpin my own ongoing musings about accidental beginnings, faith, truth. It's not that I think this dance will "discuss" these ideas, but more that these perceptions may have a hand in its shape.

The Dance Exchange and I help plan a three-day symposium on sustainability and the arts in Houston and are invited to put on two teas in a small art gallery at the University of Houston as our part in the actual implementation. We learn so much about how this tea structure can work and how much to facilitate—not enough rules on the first try, more on the second. We lose some of the chaotic energy by adding rules, and it's a tradeoff I am not sure I want to make.

My daughter, Anna, spends her junior semester abroad in Spain, and soon after the Dance Exchange completes its almost-last tour of the year, I go to see her. We take a road trip through the south of the country. This is fun and inspiring and includes visits to several Islamic sites where symmetry was essential to the art and architecture. I recognize that when symmetry is actually part of life it has a certain magnetic beauty, so I buy a book on Islamic design in which the author suggests that since Islam forbids the depiction of God in art (just as Judaism does), design in this culture turned to mathematics and symmetry to create the imagery for God, as well as for the inner structure of all things. This is just like trying to see inside the atom: if you want to understand the beginning, you should not go backward, but inward. I'm inspired to return to rehearsals and submit all of our phrase work to symmetrical physical statements, which is completely new for me, although not for many choreographers. This makes the movement that has already been constructed look quite different, so we also try setting up tea and other dances around tables in symmetrical fashion. It is all a little odd and makes me think I might structure most of the first act with symmetry in mind.

I know that this piece needs a few "conceptual" scenes, and I am still hunting for them when I come across a long article in the New York Times about the Bush administration's reasons for not halting its torture tactics. What officials said was something like, "If we had known that these techniques had begun with the Communist Chinese, we would never have used them." This strikes me as a strange use of origins for justifying action. And then it happens: in my mind I have an immediate image that might give form to an abstracted idea, in this case torture. (I think this phenomenon happens all the time; what makes it special on this occasion is that I notice.) I translate torture as a quintet for four dancers and a chair: one dancer stands on the chair, and then—without reason or signal—the other three pull the seat away and the person on the chair goes flying. Taking this idea into rehearsal produces a series of great catches and more and more exploration of how to surprise the standing dancer so she does now know when or how the chair will go. The whole thing is very interesting and even more curious when done with a second group in almost complete symmetry. The additional group is minus one key dancer, and the absence paradoxically amplifies the impact of strictly symmetrical patterns. I think that if can get this all to work I will eventually ask a physicist to explain how we might measure what is happening in terms of velocity, mass, and contact, and thus use the scene to challenge the idea of measurement, which is another theme evolving in the dance.

The justification of torture that runs "If I had known _____, then I wouldn't have _____" is interesting to me, so I have the dancers do a long freewrite with this concept as the structuring device for their litanies. As they read them, they add up exquisitely; some are very funny, some so sad, and all are tinged with regret, which draws me in especially, since I have been feeling a lot of regret this year but only talking about it at ritual events like the Seder or New Year's Eve. I decide to work it a little and see where it goes. This is on my mind when I'm in a phone interview with *Symmetry*, a magazine that covers particle physics. The interviewer asks me what I talk to the physicists about. I reference the regret and then tell her about a conversation I had with Gordy and another physicist at Cook's Branch in Texas, asking them what it was like when a discovery is made and it disproves your life's work. What do you do and feel? Do you feel regret? There's a pause, and the interviewer says, "No one talks about that . . . ever."

I decide to try the mattress idea with lots of bodies lying down in a row sleeping, and I also decide to try a monologue while lying in bed looking up at the camera. It is a monologue about my beginnings. Right now it is too long for the piece, but it strikes the right tone, and I wonder if most of the spoken language can be delivered this way. What if I put Gordy and his wife, Lois, together, talking upward, or an Islamicist and a supersymmetry theorist together, talking under the covers and looking up as they float in space? I like the thought and consider that it might be a way to carry the narrative forward.

My monologue:

So you want to know my origins, my beginnings? It's hard to know where to begin. I guess you could start with Catherine the Great, who was great but who was responsible for putting all the Russian Jews in the ghettos, which made my grandfather's grandfather so angry and that must have been where the idea to come to American began, which my grandfather eventually did, bringing with him a love of opera. But then his wife died in the great plague, leaving my father and his twin sister, who were only six months old, which is why I think his relatives who took care of him gave him so much to eat because they felt sorry for him, so they fed him and fed him, and so when he became a soldier he was still unmarried, which is why he went to the classical music room at the USO in San Francisco just before he was shipped out.

In the meantime, my grandfather on the other side left his wife, my grandmother, to become a Rosicrucian in Alaska, which is why she was raising my mother and her sister alone. She wanted them to be very cultured, so she made sure they knew classical music, but she also pressured my mother so much to be smart, and she made her work in the artificial flower store in the Sir Francis Drake Hotel that she ran, and my mother hated that, which is why she was probably so unhappy. This doesn't explain why the man she was supposed to marry was one of the first people to jump off the new Golden Gate Bridge, which is why my mother was still single when she went to be the DJ in the classical music room of the USO in San Francisco.

Now this explains how my older brother came to be, but you have to wait till the war is over to get to my birth. My father was with the ski troops in Italy, and when they won that war they put all these soldiers on boats to send to the Pacific where the statistics for death were quite high, and so the guys all thought they had survived one front only to be killed in the other. So my father always said to me: "You are on this earth because of the bomb."

I think there might be a monologue like this about CERN too, because its existence is due in part to Los Alamos. The monologue could begin with anti-Semitism as well, since the exodus of German scientists between the wars is an incredible testament to the role of impending doom as a motivating factor for many of the Jewish scientists gathered at Los Alamos. And as the people at the Human Genome Project and the people at CERN like to say, "Big government means big science." The Manhattan Project taught us that.

I try to figure out how much to tell the staff and dancers as I muse among these ideas. I know that many explorations will give way to further developments, some will disappear altogether, and some may be saved for a later work. I do talk with presenters who are interested in the piece, including Jedediah Wheeler at Montclair State who has an interest in the science work. It is always a pleasure to engage with him as he sees things from an interesting historical perspective and possesses keen artistic sensibility. In this case he asks lots of questions, then ends with his odd and wonderful combination of berating me and encouraging me by saying, "Go back to CERN, keep us in the present." It is a good idea.

As of this writing, the piece is still eluding a structure. Once it's found, many of these early ideas will fall away. Meanwhile, the movement metaphors arrive with ease and the dancers are tackling the problems with gusto. Where it ultimately goes I can only surmise. But I have research time ahead in the studio and outside it, and I am still filled with the curious optimism that sometimes partners me as I wander in the trenches of choreography.

I was to teach one week of a three-week course on creative process during the twenty-fifth anniversary of the Bates Dance Festival. Cassie Meador, a wonderful dancer and choreographer from the company, was joining me in the endeavor. We had first met her at Bates in a previous summer, so it was great to have her there symbolically as well as for her great teaching and performing abilities. Since our class of about twenty-five avid students from all different backgrounds met for only five days, we had to work intensely and quickly.

I wanted to revisit an earlier idea of making a written and moving form of a manifesto, giving each student an opportunity to reflect and then state their ideas about creation in a form that would allow for directness, anger, intensified speech, and movement of their own discovery and choice.

One of the ways we decided to approach the subject was to have the students think about, remember, and describe their relationships to books. Then we brought in a pile of used volumes, gave them each one, and asked them to destroy them. They were told to do everything to the book that they had been taught *not* to do. I thought this would aid them in finding their relationship to breaking rules, a key component of manifestos, but also of making art—and of making a life, too.

I had expected some push back and maybe some fantastic alternative to fulfilling the assignment in the way it was given. But I was not prepared for the intensity of the resistance that came hurtling toward Cassie and me from almost everyone in the room. I asked the students to turn discomfort to inquiry, but they were too angry and upset to even begin to understand what that meant. And then in one of those rare moments that happen sometimes in teaching, a flash of inspiration arose out of the dire situation.

I asked them to state their anger but to put the words "I wonder why" in front of the sentence. So instead of "I am furious that you told me tear up this book," the statement would be "I wonder why I am furious that you told me to tear up this book."

And the reason I recall the incident at all is because the round of questions that followed this simple insertion let the full group see how anger and frustration can become inquiry and that inquiry opens the door to discovery and to art.

21

The Sounds of St. Albans

....

Like most things, the act of asking questions has a shallow and a deep end, by which I mean that you can think about inquiry carefully (take small steps into the water) or you can find yourself in the middle of a muddle and realize that asking questions is the only way out (throw yourself into the deep end and learn to swim, or at least save yourself). And like so many tools, a good question can come out of a gut impulse ("I just have to ask this . . .") or can be the result of a carefully deployed technique. By now, if you have read any part of this book, you'll know that I think both ends of a spectrum like this are useful and valuable, and that it is good to have the ability to move among these possibilities with ease, skill, and an unembarrassable outlook.

The technique of asking questions depends on what you are seeking. I am reminded of Charles Darwin's injunction to "observe without reason," which is a wonderful way to consider waiting for things to happen. But since I am accustomed to hiking the horizontal, I like observing with reason too, by which I mean that I am asking and waiting for something in particular. Pushing forward, either with questions or with preconceived ideas, and waiting for the spark to occur are twin activities. This is an easily misunderstood aspect of artistic process. Taking someone else's lead does not mean I have no plan or have a completely empty space in my imagination. It is more like leaving enough space for several possibilities to unfold, including the one or more that I already have in mind. This is one part of our task as we prepare to collect personal stories that will eventually be used to convey ideas, memories, and points of view for a dance, a project, a community. The preconceived ideas may have sparked the reason people are gathered. The waiting may suggest that something better or more urgent will supplant the original thinking.

Another challenge as we look for stories is the search for fresh perspectives. It is interesting to find a way to get people to talk about things that are personal but not necessarily well known to them. What I mean is that people often come prepared with their own idea of what we are talking about or what they might be willing to share. But in working in community settings over time, we have discovered the kinds of questions that allow people to remember something that is not often called to mind. So instead of getting the story they always tell, we are able to revive something that turns the act of revealing it into a fresh experience and an opportunity for self-knowledge. This in turn brings out a positive kind of vulnerability in each individual, accompanied by a willingness to listen to others that is deeper and more authentic than that generated by the mere act of taking turns.

It is not always easy to find these questions. When we do, we practice on ourselves to make sure we are asking something that will reach to the unusual. If we are, then we tend to keep the question and bring it into another community or rehearsal. These questions actually function like repertory. We can depend on them, and like good repertory the thrill may be in the relationship formed with the audience as opposed to the internal discovery and excitement that comes from new work.

"What is something that you miss and something that you wish for?" is a question that emerged from a series of conversations we had in the early stages of a long residency sponsored by the Flynn Theater in Burlington, Vermont. The Flynn had arranged for us to spend time in several rural communities within a fifty-mile radius of the theater. One of these towns, St. Albans, proved to be a very important component of "In Praise of Constancy in the Midst of Change," the piece we ultimately made for our *Hallelujah* project in Vermont. It was at our very first visit that I met an older gentleman who clearly held a leadership position in this small town. His participation made it so much easier for us to recruit others.

I don't remember the first question we asked in order to make a little gestural dance, but whatever it was, he responded by talking about the train that used to go through town. What caught my ear was an echo to stories we had been hearing in big cities at our other *Hallelujah* sites, stories about how transportation systems tore towns in two. I listened because even in this tiny rural place you could still have the "wrong side of the tracks." And then he added, in his wonderful, wavery, ancient voice: "I miss the sound of the train whistle." Suddenly everyone was talking about sounds they missed.

Later that week I made an appearance at the Kiwanis luncheon. Encounters like this can be wonderful. The expression "lead with your heart" turns out to be alive for so many Americans when you find them having lunch at their civic clubs. Without irony they pledge allegiance to the flag, support their local young people through scholarships, wish good health upon a neighbor's family, and listen to a visiting artist.

This time they first listened to me talk about the project and then answered the new question I was practicing about wishing and missing. They each stood up and solemnly spoke, fragments of their days and nights reflected in the simplicity of the loss. We returned to the town twice a year for four years. There was always a party and always poetry.

Was Einstein a Choreographer?

All the biographies of Albert Einstein eventually tell the story of his "thought experiments." In this seemingly unusual manner of thinking, the scientist would ask himself a question, then picture intently in his mind a series of imaginary events in a cause-and-effect sequence. Given what he was asking, the pictures he created were always moving—part of a kind of physics theme park in which the rides whisked through the universe with a very curious person on board. This mental activity led Einstein to some of his discoveries.

Ask a difficult enough question, and you will need more than one discipline to answer it. And so the young Albert gaily envisioned himself in a multitude of situations and eventually arrived at his answers. Later he had to also get the math to work. That part I think he did with paper and pencil.

What interests me is that he was able to stay in his imagination long enough to visualize the story to its ending. I think that most people notice the pictures that move fleetingly through their minds, but because these images often come unbidden, they are deleted as soon as possible by the mere act of turning our attention to something else. Maybe we hear the voice of the teacher in us telling us to stop daydreaming.

Some people, artists especially, have the discipline or skill to successfully harness these unbidden ideas for what they are or can be. If heeded or observed for a moment, they can turn our projects down new paths. Sometimes you have to interview yourself to recognize something of use or importance in these slyly emerging images. But just a lingering of thought can turn the page on a new chapter for a dance itself, or maybe just for a costume or a light source or pattern of movement.

What Einstein did was something more than this because—beyond perhaps the first thought—these pictures were not just "coming to him." Once he had the initial picture in his mind, he stayed with its implications *in his mind* for a very long time, sorting out all the impracticalities, the extra problems born by taking a particular route, even backtracking and redirecting when he needed to.

That is what seems akin to choreography. I can spend hours in my head picturing the stage and then moving the dancers through a thousand steps trying out different approaches to a piece of music. Or I can sequence and then resequence sections in order to see what might be more effective. Or I might just play with what will happen when the curtain opens. This imagination of ours is the perfect computer: able to change the field of vision in a flash and able to work on no battery for a long period of time.

When I started reading about Einstein and came across these references, they made me wonder what to call my own cranial activity over all these years. "Thought experiment" seems like a good description of my mental choreography. I had actually been thinking it was some kind of cross between a lovely fantasy life and what others called imagination. What I know about it is that it is like a vast push–pull: a great volley in an excellent tennis match. The images appear, one pushes at them, one creates new ones, and one deletes them, puts several in play at once, witnesses the consequences, and tries from the start all over again. And in the midst of all that pushing comes a new thought or image that shifts all the thinking in a split second. And out of all that backing-and-forthing, painting and erasing, suddenly comes a new discovery. It doesn't have to be relativity each time; a good solution to a little choreographic problem will do.

Anyone can do it. It just takes practice, concentration, and a really good question.

Influence, Inquiry, Action

By the time we laid my father's stone in the spring of 2000, I thought I had heard every story about him. But as people came to share in their experience of his life, I was overwhelmed with the number of people and incidents that spoke to his grand mission in life. One in particular stands out. A young woman appeared on our porch, introduced herself, and began crying. She was a Latina lesbian who had sat next to my father at a human-rights conference luncheon. He had engaged her in conversation and somehow had convinced her to go back and finish school. She couldn't believe he had died, and she wanted us to know how critical that moment had been for her. I remember thinking at the time that my father never stopped. He worked in the world right up until his death. As this young woman's story demonstrated, part of my father's calling was to be an influence.

He was certainly a profound influence on me. The accumulation of all the stories I heard after he died made me think that my work was in many ways just my father's world and ideas reconstituted. He did it through politics and business; I was doing it through dance and culture: questioning authority, viewing action in the world as a sacred mission, lovingly challenging Jewish tradition, bringing people together for reasoned dialogue, making distinctions among allies, championing the regular everyday life of regular everyday people—well, actually, celebrating the brilliance of the unrecognized. This was my father's world and this had become mine.

My father had apparently always loved dance. He had gone to college with Anna Halprin and passed out flyers for her concerts. He took me to see anything that came through Milwaukee, where we had moved when I was eight. But his most important legacy to me as a choreographer was his complete lack of high-art/low-art thinking. He made me watch everything. "They are dancing on TV," he would yell up the stairs to me, and I was expected to drop anything I was doing, including homework, to come and watch. And he made me read. Like the man himself, his interests were big and broad. And so, in my youth, I read about Katherine Dunham, about ballet, about Jewish theater artists, about Native American ritual—anything that moved, I was expected to respect and appreciate.

But it wasn't just my radical father who forged my concerns for thinking large about the world. My mother, too, had impact on the direction my life would take, even though she died so young, in March of 1975. My mother was an elitist, the great opposing force to my father's populism. She didn't like people that much. She preferred her garden and music. She wasn't compassionate about the shortcomings of human beings, but rather expected honesty, integrity, intelligence. If you couldn't be direct and to the point with her, she would just as soon be alone. And she was alone a lot.

She believed in Art. She also believed in the myth of an artistic life. She told me daily how tough it would be. How I would have to learn to stand up for my own ideas. How being part of a crowd wasn't worth it. To her, exclusiveness, like everything else, meant having integrity. Seeing one's own vision was much more valuable than being accepted. That was how she was an elitist. It was about ideas and vision, not status and wealth.

Even in my earliest memories I can see how parental influence, cultural values, and the thrill of performance got tangled up in my enthusiasm for dance. I can sequester these memories, as they are bracketed by a change in climate and neighborhood that occurred when my parents moved us from Venice, California, to Falls Church, Virginia, as I was turning five years old. Otherwise, I think these old images would have all morphed together in a generalized category of baby memories. But instead, I can picture pretty clearly in my mind what it was like to sit next to my mother at the Hollywood Bowl. In this scene, I am ecstatic even before the music starts. And then, as the sky darkens, the stage lights up and the people begin to dance the story of Icarus. A man comes out with giant wings that actually move. I am sure I am on my feet, my own hands stretched far above my head, then clapping together in front of me in total congruence with the stage vision. I look up at my mother's face, expecting to see the sheer joy I am feeling. But no, she is shaking her head and muttering something like, "This is terrible, kitschy." She turns to me and says, perhaps, "I want you to see something better than this." It is the first time I disagree with my mother, although I keep that to myself. The deflation I feel is total and very confusing.

Another California night and we are at the drive-in. If I am not jumping up and down to the music, I have my nose pushed up against the windshield trying to get closer. The movie is *Annie Get Your Gun*, and I spend the next months of my life wearing a cowgirl skirt and boots and stomping around our backyard. Just before our move east, my parents take me to see fountains dancing to classical music and the La Brea Tar Pits, which give me nightmares for weeks. But I also get a promise of dance lessons after we settle.

In retrospect, I think my parents had a thing for outdoor theater, or maybe that is what they could afford. But in the few short years in which we lived in the nation's capital, I am also taken to Carter Barron Amphitheater to see one ballet company after another. On a family trip to North Carolina, we see *The Lost Colony*, which puts my imagination into overdrive for months afterwards. I am filled with the unsolved mystery of the vanished settlement that's related in this historical pageant, and amazed by what seems to my child's eyes to be hundreds of dancers against the open-air backdrop of a local history.

Another move, now to the Midwest, and finally to indoor theaters. We climb the steps of the old Pabst Theater way up to the top and see Ballet Russe de Monte Carlo. I just love saying the name over and over. My father and I go to see Rogers and Hammerstein's *Flower Drum Song*, and again I am confused by my own love for what I see in contrast to my father's annoyance with the musical's particular depiction of a Chinese American community.

Then two performances take me into a new stage. I see *Fancy Free*, the Jerome Robbins/Leonard Bernstein modern-dress ballet about sailors on shore leave, and somehow grasp the possibility of merging story, physical daring, and great music. And Birgit Cullberg brings her company from Sweden to perform her signature ballet, *Miss Julie*. Somehow, though way too young to understand the implications of Strindberg's story, I comprehend that psychological drama, darkness, and subtlety can also be mine while dancing beautifully. (Many years later I got to meet Cullberg when the Dance Exchange toured to Sweden. She was by then quite old, but I think my telling her what an impact her dance had on me made her a little bit happy.)

When it came to my education in dance, my mother, typically, saw no reason not to have the best. So when we moved to Milwaukee, she searched out the most unique and authentic dance teacher she could find. Of course, she eschewed the popular one that everyone told her about. Instead she found me Florence West, a woman whose influence on my early life would parallel that of my family, my religion, and my brothers.

Florence had studied with Ruth Page and Martha Graham. She was trying to develop her own style of dance, which would somehow combine the best of modern and ballet. At that time, in most parts of the dance world, it was impossible to study them together. You were expected to make your choice and stick to it, and never let the two cross. But Florence had other ideas, which she called the "Dance of Dimension." I took as many technique classes a week as I could. These consisted of barre work and floor work similar to what would be found in a Graham class. Then the last forty-five minutes were spent doing a dance phrase that Florence had choreographed that mixed it all up. We studied the same phrases for a year and then performed them at a recital. Every other Saturday was choreographers' workshop day. Then for two hours we would draw and paint and dance and sculpt and dance and improvise and draw some more. Anything was possible, except playing with scarves. Florence was afraid we might suffer the same fate as Isadora. I loved her.

But Florence was also impossible. She yelled (as did my mother, which, as I like to say, is why I hardly ever do). I never knew if my behavior was the cause of her hollering or whether she just needed to let off steam. But she was a brilliant teacher. I tried to arrive early to class because then I got invited into her one-room apartment/office/library that was off the main studio. She would show me books and pictures and make me touch different rocks and fabrics. She would tell me about yogis and Isadora; they all somehow blended in my mind. In her own way, she was the intersection of my parents: demanding and rigorous in detail like my mother, broad-minded and a grand mess of ideas like my father. She left Milwaukee for New York City when I was fourteen.

An Interlude on the Nature of Influence

Influence starts early and seems to persist whether we seek it or resist it. I had occasion to think about this on one of our first trips to Japan, when I met an official from the Ahi Beer Company. Our sponsors took me to see him because it was rumored that his company was interested in supporting contemporary dance in Japan, including foreign exchanges. We started to talk through our interpreters, and then all of a sudden his voice began to rise, and without allowing any interruptions he began to talk loudly and urgently. It was quite uncharacteristic of any of my experiences in Japan up to that point, as everyone had been so cordial and even-tempered.

It turned out that he was angry about American influence. He almost shouted with fury about how important it was that Asians affect Asians and that we, Americans, should not be part of the new international exchanges that were beginning to flourish. I was fascinated and, without knowing the full history, could imagine how a person might believe and feel this way. Although I didn't think my work was the particular problem, I could see how he might think that I represented a part of his country's dilemma.

Perhaps because it was all getting translated, I somehow didn't feel like I was under attack. I was able to listen carefully and began to formulate something I had been musing about with the Critical Response Process. I decided to try to hear the question inside his opinion so that when he finally stopped, and I could have a turn to speak, I might answer a question he *could* have asked me. When his diatribe had dissipated enough for me to comment, I said something like, "What an interesting question you are posing. When do we want to be influenced and when do we not? What is the nature of influence in a good sense and in a negative sense?" I proceeded to speak about my own moments of desire for influence and total rejection of it.

What is the issue with influence? Are there times in our lives (and the life of our country, I mused aloud) when we might want or need to be influenced, and were there times to seek privacy and isolation? Part of why I had come all the way around the world to meet him was *to be* influenced. I wanted it. But then I was pretty secure in what I knew and in what I wanted to change.

The Civil Rights Movement

Knowing what one wants to change is itself a capacity that is cultivated through influence. In the summer of my fourteenth year, I danced for President Kennedy at the White House as part of a group from the National Music Camp in Interlochen, Michigan. My picture was in *Life* magazine, and I supposed that all would continue to go well in my little world of dance dreams. But it did not, and I entered my time of troubles.

With my teacher Florence gone to New York, we looked all over Milwaukee for another school of dance. Not finding one, my mother hired Ann Barzell, a ballet mistress and writer from Chicago who came to Milwaukee once a week and tutored me privately, focusing on solos from the classical repertory. I had learned the Lilac Fairy's dance from *Sleeping Beauty* and was beginning to work on the Blue Bird variation from the same ballet when public history barged in the door.

It was the early 1960s. The civil rights movement was beginning to gain momentum, and my family was very active. In northern cities such as Milwaukee, there began a series of marches about equal housing. Then, as part of the protest against segregation in the public schools, Freedom Schools were set up and I was enrolled. Just going to this radical alternative school was an act of protest, and the content of what I was learning was radical too.

I would attend Freedom School in the early part of the day, then travel to my Blue Bird study in the afternoon. The trip took only a half hour on the bus, but it might as well have been centuries long. I had no way of understanding the relationship between the subject matter of my life and the subject matter of what I was dancing. I wanted so intensely to make the dance matter, but there was no way that my bleeding feet, the silly steps, the make-believe of the dance could match the power and urgency of the stories I was learning in Freedom School.

So I stopped dancing. It was a terribly difficult decision, carried out with great emotion. But at that time I didn't have the skills to understand how to synthesize my worlds, nor did anyone else see a way to help me comprehend the possible bridge between them. This would come much later. In the 1990s, dancer Jeffrey Gunshol and I would discuss the impact on me of living through the sixties as a teenager. His comment was, "You got the civil rights movement, we got the *Challenger* blowing up." It led us to a long discussion on the idea of efficacy and how the events we live through influence our perspectives on the world and our own personal sense of hopefulness or cynicism.

Two Books and a Movement

I can be influenced by a book, because when I read it ideas that have been nascent in my mind are embodied on the page. I am not sure how I discovered *The Quest for Community* by Robert Nisbet. It was written in 1953 but reissued in 1969, and that is the copy that I own. I recently decided to look at it again after a long time. I enjoyed coming across my own notes, the sections I had underlined, the ideas that spoke to me in the years predating the Dance Exchange.

Here, on the second page of the forward to the new edition, was the clarion call I needed: "It is not the revival of old communities that the book in a sense pleads for; it is the establishment of new forms: forms which are relevant to contemporary life and thought." That was precisely what I was imagining somehow for dance—that we could use our extensive skills and tools to build, or rediscover, or create a community, a sense of community, an awareness of a collective existence.

Since working between generations was to become a primary tool for me, I found in this book some thinking on the subject that was unexpected. Nesbit gets into a discussion of how the past and future play out in the present, and he makes this claim: "In genuinely creative societies . . . there is a telescoping of the generations that is not hidden by all the more manifest facts of individual revolt. Past and present have a creative relationship not because of categories in men's minds, but because of certain social bonds which themselves reach from past to future."

Finally, he gets into a wonderful description of the difference between power and authority, which has had a profound impact on the way I lead. First he explains that power is external and based upon force. Authority is rooted "in the statuses, functions, and allegiances which are the components of any association." But what really excited me was his discussion of multiple authorities. He wrote, "There must be many authorities in society, and that authority must be closely united to objectives and functions which command the response and talents of members. Freedom is to be found in the interstices of authority: it is nourished by competition among authorities." Without knowing it, I was discovering some principles for running a dance company.

Also at this time I read and reread a book called *Artculture* by Douglas Davis. The subtitle, *Essays on the Post-Modern*, both attracted and repelled me. Although now I talk about postmodernism frequently, at the time I stayed away from too much art theory. But this book was the only place I could find a synthesis of two distinct threads in my own life: serious art training and a political point of view about the world.

The opening chapter is called "Artpolitics: Thoughts Against the Prevailing Fantasies." Here he gives a history lesson that underscores one of my own primary thoughts and frustrations about who artists are and how we are supposed to behave:

> The Hollywood view of the artist as childlike naïf—a view cherished by too many curators, critics and collectors—is a particularly pernicious form of paternalism, which robs the artist, in this case Courbet, of his humanity, of his natural right to be a citizen. In his 1855 manifesto he wrote: "To know in order to be able to create, that was my idea. To be in a position to

translate the customs, the ideas, the appearance of my epoch, according to my own estimation: to be not only a painter, but a man as well; in short, to create living art—this is my goal." These words have been printed in a thousand textbooks, yet are rarely understood. Any artist now who acts on that advice is automatically considered less than serious (about his product and his image perfecting).

I remember so clearly my sense that my work in the nursing homes and senior centers in the mid-seventies was weakening my position as a rising avant-garde artist. I kept telling people that it felt as though I could be an artist if I waited tables, but if I wanted to spend time working with old people, then I was relegated to a lower caste, that of a therapist. Later still, when I compared notes with Jawole Willa Jo Zollar, founder of Urban Bush Women and a committed community artist, we laughed because she said she had been made a social worker. We guessed that white people could be therapists, black people social workers, and that there was probably a hierarchy in that as well.

Here is another quote from Davis's *Artculture* that states in one sentence a complaint that I heard again at a National Performance Network meeting: "What is wrong with acting collectively? Only the belief that in doing so the artist relinquishes the psychic individuality that is his prime value, as product, in the art market." We are still having to explain over and over that sparks of genius lie everywhere, often dormant until odd ideas and people move together. They come alive in combination with each other. I find much inspiration, pleasure, and challenge in my collaboration with company members, other artists, and members of community, just as I enjoy the moments of individual creative leaps. It would be good if we could find a language that supported the idea of artistic vision crossing back and forth between collaborative genius and individual brilliance.

It was also Davis who, in one brief sentence, set up for me the single biggest leap of my theoretical work: understanding the poverty of either/or thinking. "The error of Guerrilla Art is directly opposed to the error of elitist art," Davis wrote; "it sacrifices form for content." Recently, reading about Leonard Bernstein, I came across a quote in which he almost screams against the "dread dichotomy." Here is one of these false dichotomies laid out before me so many years ago. How many times have we in the community arts world been accused of giving up form for content? And how many times have I tried to get people to see that the form is everywhere—on the stage, in the unique designs of each residency, in the problem solving of bringing people onstage who are not professionals. On the other hand, how many late nights at artist retreats and regional gatherings could I be found talking passionately about how we "community artists" had to get better at our craft. And how many dance concerts have I left wishing the choreographers could have given me more to think about than just the beautiful bodies in space doing sometimes beautiful and interesting things? In my world, form and content, process and product, nurture and rigor, individual vision and collection creation—these all form delightful spectrums that I get to dance along. Sometimes I may spend a lot of time at one end of the spectrum, but I always check out the other to be sure I haven't left something out. And the older I get, the more interesting it is to stretch the spectrum and to live at its edges.

An Art Movement: Or How Dada Kept Me Fresh and Enthused

I really thought that I was part of what some of us jokingly called the New Avant-Garde. I felt that those of us embarking on political/access/identity/ community art-making were, in effect, taking the best of contemporary art forms and, by turning them to usefulness, inventing a new movement. I, for one, however, relied on some history to help me discover this. The bulk of that history was not in the dance world but in the world of theater and the visual arts. And mostly it had taken place during and just after World War I.

I was inspired by the Dadaists and a companion movement of that time, the Russian Avant-Garde. I found their ideas about art quite compelling. Looking back, I would say that their theories and actions affected mine in four areas: anti-art, pageants, readymades, and collage. Briefly, here is a glimpse of their impact on my thinking.

The Dadaist stance of anti-art-world-establishment suited me fine. I was among a group of artists who were interested in reframing most of the art world's mechanics and way of doing business. I was quite conscious early on of how much of my methodology grew out of rebellion and the need to make a dance world different from the one I had grown up in. For me, this project went beyond art-world politics. I was interested in creating a different mythic base for our own behavior and addressing some of the romantic perceptions of what an artist's life was supposed to be. The Dadaists did this with humor, attack, political thought, and camaraderie, all tools that I admired.

Somewhere in my history books, there's a paragraph about an incredible reenactment of a major battle that had occurred during the Russian Revolution. Apparently, theater artists were the directors of a grand show that included some five thousand participants and a gunboat in a harbor. This tantalized me. I have not been able find any reference to the event since then, but it left an indelible mark on my imagination. I think some of what has evolved in my own process of community engagement harks back to this notion: that people use their bodies to learn their history. The Russians did this in the 1920s on a huge scale, or at least I think they did.

One form of integrating my personal and professional life came from the movement of objects between my house and the studio. Material goods traveled mysteriously from home to rehearsal to stage and back again. My mother's glasses and the last nightgown she wore before her death made their way into my piece about her dying. I put them on right at the end and then jumped, yelling NOW! I loved this moment for myself, of thinking of her and becoming her. I found all kinds of inspiration in my small daily activities and tried to see my surroundings as Duchamp and others had, a world of ready-made art all around us.

I took a theoretical base for this from my understanding of Kurt Schwitters, who turned his whole house into a tower of art. His use of collage was an extension for me of the readymades, and in some ways more useful for choreographic structure. In the early years of my work with older adults, I often thought of them as a part of a collage, that their presence was like an old button, or piece of fabric, which audience members could use to connect to their own memories quickly and deeply.

Small Things with Powerful Influence

We are always aware of the straw that breaks the camel's back. We know the moment it is added that things will be undone, fall apart, be destroyed. I wonder how often we are aware of the "last straw" that does the opposite. Enough small ideas and events accumulate, and then, by noticing one final detail, we are possessed with the need to act.

In my case, at my parent's home in Madison, Wisconsin, while my mother is dying, I see a picture in the newspaper. It is of a nun, and she is in full habit, teaching an exercise class to the elderly. I look at it and think . . . Wait, if she can do it, I can do it.

And so I did.

Maybe I would have done it anyway, but I think the photograph was the last straw that pushed me past my ambivalence and fear. At some point influence leads to action.

Swan Lake (1982): Judith Jourdin, Thelma Tulane, Liz Lerman, Vee Hollenbeck, and Jess Rea. Photo: Dennis Deloria.

Who Gets to Dance?

Manifesto (in the form of a *Village Voice* help-wanted ad recruiting artists for the *Hallelujah* project, October 1999)

Performers wanted for a project from January 1, 2000, to December 15, 2002.

You will be performing often, on main concert stages, in hotels, classrooms, churches, on hillsides, beside oceans, next to and with accomplished dancers and also with rabbis, neighbors, dogs and their trainers, gardeners, history.

You will be teaching from movement ideas you already know. You will be thrown into situations that require new concepts, new vocabulary, new relationships.

You will be asked lots of questions. You will be asking more questions. You might often be bewildered.

You will do a lot of planning, for yourself and for the multitude of collaborations which will unfold.

Often you will throw out the plans, but not the thinking.

You will work very hard. You will have a living wage. You will have health insurance.

If it is important for you to have time to make a dance of your own, in your own manner, in your own voice, it will be produced along with that of your colleagues.

You will be challenged to develop movement, share it, watch it change, lose control, gain control, be acknowledged for your efforts.

You will train your body in both familiar and unorthodox ways. You will help train other bodies. You will help structure the formal and informal means by which this daily miracle happens.

You will get to engage in stories that matter to strangers, to yourself, to the people you dance and travel with. Sometimes you will hate all of this interaction and yearn for a refuge alone. The studios are yours.

You will get to help build and rebuild and build again a 23-year-old dance organization that is always in transition.

You will speak your mind. You will be delighted by your condition and exasperated by the responsibility.

Real Work, Real Reward.

The Roosevelt, Dancing

My life changed when my mother was diagnosed with cancer. Only in my mid-twenties, I was able to go home to Wisconsin and be with her. The end was swift. I was propelled into an emotional period of loss and reflection. Although still fairly new to choreography (I had at that time made one formal piece for the concert stage and many informal works for my high school students in a Maryland boarding school), I realized that I needed to make a dance about what my family and I had gone through. I was interested in finding older people to be in that dance.

This was in 1975. It was the same year that Robert Butler had written his book *Why Survive: Being Old in America*, which was the beginning of the aging consciousness movement. It was before people were jogging in the streets. It was before any broad awareness of the possibility of aging well or being physical late in life. In fact, the idea of old people dancing was quite outlandish to most people. But for me it was the only choice I had.

The problem was that I didn't know where the old people were. Returning to Washington, D.C., I began calling around and discovered a retirement residence that was within a mile and a half of my apartment. Officially titled the Roosevelt for Senior Citizens, it was known as the Roosevelt Hotel because the building had started life as a grand hotel back when the neighborhood, now a little shabby, was an elegant embassy district. I went to the Roosevelt and told the manager I wanted to teach a dance class. She actually hooted with laughter as I explained that I meant it to be for the residents of the building. But she'd lost her entertainment on Thursday nights, and she needed somebody to fill the slot. She said I could come in for five dollars a week. I accepted.

When I arrived on the first night, the residents who had gathered were all seated in chairs, facing me. I danced a little solo for them. Then I said, "It's time. We're all going to dance together. I want you to start by turning your head. We're going to warm up . . . just turn your head." Nobody moved. I thought they couldn't hear me. My own experience with older people had been so fragmentary that I immediately jumped to the stereotype and assumed I was addressing a room full of people who were partially deaf. I started yelling, "We're going to turn our heads!" Still nobody moved. Then I began to run back and forth in front of them, and finally they began to turn their heads left and right to follow me.

In that moment, I realized that I had stumbled into a weird and wondrous laboratory. Suddenly, everything I believed in was called into question—especially everything that I believed about how to train a person to become a dancer. What exercises did these folks need? How and what could I ask them to achieve? What would good technique mean on an eighty-year-old body? What made them look beautiful? In fact, I began to question accepted notions of who and what was beautiful. As the weekly classes went on, usually attended by twenty to fifty people, I found each one a struggle and an inspiration.

The residence was primarily for frail older adults, people trying to stay out of nursing homes. It was mixed-race, mixed-class, mixed-everything. Several younger retarded adults also lived at the Roosevelt because the city had no other place to assign them. Everyone was lumped together. I was astonished by the things I noticed and then began to think about as I spent time among these people. For example, some of the residents were labeled senile by the staff. This surprised me because I saw these people in dance class and they didn't seem senile to me. I began to muse about the nature of dance and its present-time usefulness. Maybe it was a way out of the symptoms of senility, depending on what definitions people were using for that illness. Of course, I thought to myself, I would be senile too if I had to live in the conditions and isolation of so many of the residents. We were at that time doing a good job of warehousing our elderly. The simplicity and cost-effectiveness of art as a natural intervention seemed all too obvious to me then. It still does, all these years later.

It was also interesting to see how people responded to touch. You can't teach dance without touching. Sometimes I would ask residents if I could touch their backs and then worked on their spines a bit as they unrolled from a forward bend. At the start of one class a woman approached me and said, "What did you do to my back?" I wondered if I had hurt her and asked what happened. She said, "I cleaned my apartment, I vacuumed, I did stuff I haven't done in years." She was so happy. I was the first person to touch her in five years.

I discovered new ideas and new processes at every moment. Slowly I realized that my own teaching was changing, and I brought these changes with me back to the academy, for I was at the same time pursuing my master's degree in dance at George Washington University.

As I began to spread the word about my work at the Roosevelt and invite friends, colleagues, and guests to visit and observe the classes, I was struck by the number of well-meaning people who would pat me on the head and say, "Isn't that good for them?" Now it certainly *was* good for many of these older people. The physical range of their bodies increased as they found the joy in moving, their imaginations became animated as they learned new mind/body connections, their trust in each other grew as they partnered in dance, and their self-esteem blossomed as they made works of art. They were strengthened as a community as well: when the residents of the building staged a rent strike against the management, it was the dance-class regulars who organized it.

But it puzzled me that while observers immediately recognized the social good of this practice, they never conceived of the possibility that my work at the Roosevelt was also good for me as a person, as a teacher, and as an artist—and ultimately not only good for me, but good for the art form of dance as well. These benefits were most observable when I brought my undergraduate dance students to the senior center. I encouraged each of them to move around the room before the class actually began, meeting the older people and learning their names. They were greeted with great smiles and often with direct, outspoken comments about their looks, such as, "You are so pretty" or "What a great body you have!" I had become used to this type of conversation, but I was unprepared for the positive impact it had on the women students. I also warned them that, because of the hearing and vision impairments that affected some of the older people, they might have to exaggerate their presence to make connections. I noticed that some of the shyer students were laughing, talking loudly in order to be heard, and in general participating at a very high level. The older people made it so easy to extend oneself, converse with strangers, and be big about it all. I wondered if I hadn't stumbled into a way of teaching dancers how to project character onstage. If dancing is primarily a mute form, perhaps we had found a way to evolve performance personality that was both authentic and larger than life.

At the Roosevelt, I taught a modified technique class. We began seated in chairs and worked our way to standing while holding onto the chairs as a kind of barre. Eventually we would gather in a circle in the middle of the room and do some kind of extended improvisation with the goal of keeping the older dancers on their feet for as long as possible.

I made sure that everyone could and did participate at the beginning of the class. But I also made sure, as the class became progressively more physically demanding, that those who had reached their limits could become encouraging observers, able to reenter the movement whenever they saw fit. I also encouraged all to keep adapting the movement so that even as many of us stood up, others could continue seated.

I realized that the participants were learning theme and variation in this way; when I posed all of this as artistic practice, the participation level soared. What became evident to me is that conventional technique classes assume that every student's body will work at the same pace as the teacher's. (For example, I've known many dancers who come to a class early to warm up so that they will be ready for the teacher's warm-up, making clear the inaccuracy of this assumption.) At the Roosevelt, I was learning a way to allow for many levels of achievement as well as capacity. And at times, this diversity contributed to something quite beautiful and unusual.

Toward the end of class we would sometimes use an improvisational structure composed of a free-form dance done in the center of the circle with each person taking a turn to solo. I found a way to "shadow" the soloist by allowing plenty of room for him or her to move while remaining available to each in case of imbalance. Sometimes, in the excitement of the music or the audience's appreciation, the older dancers would find themselves close to falling. I wanted them to stay aware and be responsible, but I also found that shadowing them was interesting form of partnering.

So often a structure like this has multiple outcomes. In this case, the undergraduates who came to class to help also had to take their turn in the middle, and this is when I noticed how the circle of older adults affected their dancing. Taking their turns, they danced more freely and more beautifully than I had ever seen in their university classes. On the way back to campus they were full of excitement: "I was never able to do triple turns before. What happened?" or "My leg has never gone that high and with so much ease." This happened so often I began to wonder why.

I decided that they were dancing so well because they were so loved. The dance environment in which most of these students had grown up was harshly judgmental. It was a liberating experience for them to perform for an audience that offered such unreserved appreciation of their dancing and admiration for their bodies. Instead of reinforcing their own feelings of self-loathing about their physical imperfections, they danced with people who were free with their appreciation. That affected the dancers' technique, so they danced better. I found myself telling my friends, "Older people are an underused natural resource, literally dying to give their love." I wondered how many people were just sitting out there waiting for some kind of interaction. That's when I began to see that not only is dancing in and of itself fantastic, but it is also a way to bring isolated people together.

I began to experiment. What happened when my students started from a place of positive feedback? What if they had a way to appreciate what they had accomplished? I observed that if they could name something particularly meaningful for themselves in what they had done, they could more easily take the next step, isolating a particular technical problem they wished to work on. It wasn't just a global "I need to be better," but rather an "I want to work on the way I swing my leg in my hip socket."

But my larger concern as a teacher of dance was how to get my students to be human as they worked on their technical deficiencies. I have heard the same thing from other teachers, not just in modern dance, but in ballet and in classical music too. Just recently I had a conversation with a ballet master who said, "We train them to be phenomenal technicians, and then we damn them because they have no passion or personality when they perform." I had tried numerous approaches in college classes, mostly various partnering schemes in which students had to accomplish difficult physical tasks while facing each other. It seemed they could handle either seeing their partners or working on their technical assignments, but not both at the same time.

So back to the Roosevelt we went. (An interesting aside is that when I brought my students from George Washington University with me to the Roosevelt, the number of older participants sometimes doubled. It was as if the residents could smell young people in the building. Perhaps many came just to socialize, but eventually they were all dancing, which led to wild events with as many as a hundred people cutting loose.) I began to push the older people more in their physical prowess by expanding the idea of shadowing. I paired everyone up early in the class, reminding my college students that they had to keep dancing while keeping an eye out for their partners' health, balance, and technique. As the exercises became more demanding, problems for the young dancers increased. If they stopped dancing in order to be sure their partners were okay, they found their partners quit too. So they had to find ways to be externally involved with someone else while maintaining their own physical work.

We had spent time both at the university and at the senior center talking about what we meant by a safe environment. I had become convinced that a safe environment meant not just a nurturing place but also a place where people were challenged to do better. The older people didn't want to be commended just because they could raise their arms at the age of eighty. They wanted to learn how to do it better, bigger, in unison, with dynamism. They wanted to improve. The older people took pride in the fact that some of them were able to do push-ups, dance for a full hour, turn, or jump. I didn't realize how important this was until I brought the younger dancers to class.

I also noticed that the older people danced harder, with more investment, if they understood the source of the movement. From this discovery, these older dancers and I began to develop what would become a methodology of text and movement encompassing talking and dancing, storytelling and research, information and feeling, and the means by which these elements could be integrated into a choreographic whole. When I also engaged my more sophisticated college students in these processes, they too discovered a new investment and curiosity in their dancing.

My young students began to develop real skills as they partnered the older dancers. They learned how to dance fully while remaining aware of someone else. They learned how to be in support roles and how to step forward into leadership roles, whether partnering or taking a solo turn. They learned how to focus outwardly even as they listened to their own inner stories. They figured out how to read a room for space, for personality, to spark new movement ideas. But above all, they learned how to be themselves, to be human as they danced. I began to talk about the work in senior centers as a training ground for professional dancers. I talked about how it was like money in the bank: the experiences we had at the senior center could serve us later in so many capacities in the dance world.

Beyond the benefits for the seniors and the students, we also discovered the power for everyone in bringing together unlikely groups. Pursuing my intention to make a piece about my mother's death, I held a gathering to explain my plan to the Roosevelt residents, and eight of them agreed to be in the dance. They were joined by local professional dancers and a couple of my students from George Washington.

We were to have a cast dinner at one of the student's homes the week before we opened. Given the social standards of 1975, the student who was hosting got nervous because she was living with her boyfriend. She was afraid that the older women would disapprove. Hardly! What happened instead was that the older women, so happy to be out of their institutional environment, spent the whole evening talking about sex, who had done what and when. It was an eye-opener for everyone.

It was then that I began to see that from an artistic point of view, we could change people's lives, and from a community point of view, we could change how people interacted. And the evidence kept coming that from a personal point of view we were changing people's physical beings. Every week I got reports from women who could once again zip the backs of their dresses or from men who could get in and out of the bathtub again.

After the premiere of the dance about my mother, *Woman of the Clear Vision*, a regular performance group emerged from among the Roosevelt residents. We made short tours with this group, and I engaged them in a project supported by a Baltimore presenter in which I explored my Eastern European roots. In my research about dances done in the Jewish ghettos, I learned about the "angry" dance. At Jewish weddings the soon-to-be mothers-in-law did an "angry" dance at each other, which would end with them making peace and embracing. What an idea for a community to think about! (It might have helped my first marriage.) Two of the older women danced this. I could not have imagined it any other way.

In this Baltimore project we also worked with young people from the inner city. This was the first of many Dance Exchange projects that I would describe as either cross-cultural, cross-racial, or cross-class. We did the wedding dances with young people and invited them to make their own celebratory pieces. So in the midst of all this Yiddish dancing, the kids came storming through in a fabulous street dance. The kids and the old people came to love each other in the few weeks we were together. Their thinking about what ghettos are and what ghettos mean created an amazing image and raised questions about culture and identity that I would keep revisiting for many years.

Postscript

Since these first ventures into dancing with older people, the Dance Exchange and I have conducted many other intergenerational projects. The presence of senior adult dancers in our core ensemble has continued to provide a particular grounding to our work as well as a distinctive look to the dances. Who is old and what old means in our society have also changed. Embedded in the perspective that "sixty is the new thirty" is an enormous amount of upheaval, a multitude of new understandings about the biology of aging, and a generation that refuses to retire, myself included. Thus, it is still surprising to me that when the company holds post-performance discussions, almost always the first comment is about seeing the generations together onstage. I wonder why it is still so new, even though it has been thirty-five years since I made *Woman of the Clear Vision* and first considered the fact that older bodies make for great storytelling, beautiful movement, and a curious form of courage.

The Shipyard, Dancing

There is a symbiotic relationship between choreographing in community settings and for the stage; in my artistic practice, the way they inform each other at the deepest levels keeps both evolving. In the beginning, I taught people in community settings a dance that I had made for them. The most successful of these dances (which we still perform) is called *Still Crossing*. The company performs the first part of that dance alone. At the end they are joined onstage by many others who have all learned the work's culminating dance. Originally choreographed for older adults as part of the centennial observances for the Statue of Liberty, the piece went on to be used in large community efforts to help diverse groups work together quickly and with satisfaction. While we always teach the dance so as to ensure that the movement has real meaning for the performers, in *Still Crossing* they are not the originators of the movement.

Over the years, however, I began to feel that I could intensify the art-making experience for all of us if I worked differently. In the early 1990s, with *Safe House: Still Looking*, a project that reflected on the history of the Underground Railroad, we began to integrate new stories into an existing work. As we toured, we invited community members onstage with us to tell stories of their own that we had curated for the performance. But after a while, this too felt formulaic.

Then around 1994 we got a call from the Music Hall in Portsmouth, New Hampshire, where a couple of years earlier we had conducted a short residency focused on senior adults. The Music Hall had a very specific concern. Their city is just across the water from the Portsmouth Naval Shipyard, a federal facility where battleships and submarines have been built and serviced for two hundred years. As a place where some local families had worked for twelve generations, the shipyard was a central part of the town and its history. Now it was on the federal government's list of military bases proposed for closure. The Music Hall wondered what a community-wide artistic project might do to address the potential impact of shutting down the shipyard.

Several things about starting this project made be a little nervous. I had awkward feelings about the military—feelings I had expressed directly in some of my earlier pieces that questioned the U.S. defense budget and foreign policy. Environmental controversies were also part of the mix: as a site where nuclear submarines are serviced, the yard was on the Superfund list as a toxic-waste dump. And the scope of the commission seemed vast. Still, I went to meet with the Music Hall staff. I was overwhelmed by what I found, and we committed to a project that would engage the community that lived in Portsmouth and that worked in the shipyard.

We decided to enter the community with no preordained idea of structure or content or even the form of the culminating event of our collaboration. Through months and months of conversation, participatory workshops, and small gatherings, including little performances, the final event took shape. This process opened up an entirely new world of choreographic exploration that would continue to unfold for several years.

In a departure from the more fixed approaches we had been taking, the community in Portsmouth was treated as a full artistic partner from the beginning. What we would do, how we would do it, who would perform, and what it would be about—all questions were resolved in the context of time spent in the community devising the dance together. As the artists leading the project, we still made many decisions, but these decisions were taken in dialogue with the participants.

Over a period of two years we made many visits, eventually carrying out a weeklong festival with events occurring both in the shipyard and in the community beyond the yard. It took constant attention to introduce the idea of a modern dance company working with the history and stories of a shipyard and the people who lived there. We continuously enlarged the circle of participants. As we entered community settings, engaged conversations, and led experiential workshops, our participants often introduced me to interesting and subtle choreographic ideas. These are ideas I would not have had alone or by staying in the studio working only with my wonderful company. For me, this is where it gets so exciting, because the more I think I understand, the more mysterious the road in front of me becomes.

Often what happens at a first encounter allows me to develop "muscles" that come in handy as a project unfolds. Our initial public meeting in Portsmouth brought out a very diverse crowd, including retired engineers, older community members who had worked with us before, several arts professionals, a relative of someone lost in a submarine accident of enormous consequence to the yard, and some folks from the staff of the Music Hall. I talked about how we might develop the project and gave people a sense of what I imagined might take place. During a question-and-answer period, one of the engineers asked if I knew how submarines worked. I didn't. As he began to explain, his hands flew up with a delicacy that belied his size. Other engineers jumped in with their own explanations, and again hands danced through the air as they made me see the physicality of the boats and the design elements that allow them to function.

One of the tools I rely on is something we call spontaneous gesture, which means watching for choreographic ideas in the natural movement of people's hands as they express themselves. I had rarely before seen gestures so graceful and lively. As I watched the engineers work to express themselves, I also gleaned a new understanding of another tool—physical metaphor—which describes the many ways in which an idea and its meanings can be translated through movement. This concept would prove to be one of the aesthetic paths we would pursue as the project unfolded. In short, I noticed at this first meeting that while I could continue to depend on a choreographic tool I knew and understood, I was also beginning to discover and utilize another one, one that had emerged from the engineers.

At another point early in the project I went to visit the Rotary Club to explain what we were doing. In previous experiences of these kinds of civic clubs, I had often encountered the most intense skepticism. I knew I would have to make my points clearly, directly, and with charm. I was delighted to find that the Portsmouth club was not a men-only affair. American women had entered these formerly all-male clubs, making the atmosphere decidedly different. I talked for a few minutes, then asked people for images of the shipyard. In a moment of swift enthusiasm, with stories told one on top of the other, they generated many images that we were to draw on for the remainder of our work together.

As the project progressed, it was suggested that we have lunch at the shipyard with the heads of all the departments. This meant a mixture of military and civilian employees, most with administrative responsibility. I was given ten minutes to talk and take questions and another few minutes for the company to perform. (They ended up doing an improvisation based on the conversation they had heard dancing around tables throughout the room.) What I remember most about this encounter was the amazing quantity of artistic ideas that poured out from the men who had gathered, beginning the moment they were invited to speak. One suggested that the berth where boats were docked for maintenance was a natural amphitheater; in fact, he had privately thought of his work as a kind of performance. Another mentioned the different uniforms connoting different services carried out at the shipyard. Everyone laughed at this, taking enormous pleasure in imagining the various colors and types of uniforms as costumes (especially those for workers in the nuclear division). Once again, I was taken into new choreographic avenues and given ideas we could take back to the studio and prepare as structures for the community to explore and that we could use in our concert work.

Eventually the expanding nature of our work onsite at the shipyard meant we needed to address the ongoing problem of getting access to what was still a semi-secret government operation. With our collaborators at the Music Hall, we decided that I should meet with the naval base commander to negotiate a little more ease in our comings and goings. I was given five minutes of his time.

I spoke very briefly about our project. The commander responded by saying he thought projects like this helpful. When I asked him to explain more, he really began to talk. He said that the shipyard was still cloaked in the secrecy of the Cold War, that the public didn't understand what they were doing, that it all seemed like a great mystery. And that he wanted to change this.

I asked him if he was talking about the shipyard or about modern dance. Except for the Cold War imagery, I said, we could have been discussing either. We both loved that connection. Access was granted, and we launched what we both thought of as a literacy project. I was able to give a new name and new slant to our work by making an analogy to the story I heard from a shipyard commander. And he got to see his work and the work of those around him in a new light. The shipyard is a place of immense creativity, collaboration, performance—much like a small modern dance company. By giving a name to our common concerns, we each discovered something new about our disciplines.

Over the course of two years, we had dozens of encounters and heard hundreds of stories, many of which found a place in the culminating performances of the project. On one occasion the women in the Dance Exchange company and I went to meet a gathering of naval officers' wives. The first thing they said to us was, "We are the most liberated women in America." While we respect the people we meet and always seek to listen with openness,

I have to confess that at that moment I did not share their perception. They went on to say, "The guys are gone. They are on a boat overseas, under the Antarctic—they're gone. We birth the babies, we change the tires." Instantly my perception shifted. At the same time, I realized the value of my own role as an artist in a moment like that. I was there to hear the poetry in a throwaway line. "We birth the babies, we change the tires" became a key theme of the Shipyard Project.

One story we heard that night came from a woman who said that when she was pregnant she used to measure her belly with string. She'd cut the string where it met, then send it to her husband through the system our government has for getting mail to the crews on submarines. He would get the string and know how big she was getting. He hung these lengths of string in a graduated row on the inside door of his locker. One day a shipmate went by, looked at the row of strings, and asked what it was. "That's my baby," the husband responded.

As we develop projects like the one in Portsmouth, we may begin to collect movements that we share as we travel from group to group. Thus the simple gesture of wrapping a string around the waist, and the story behind it, was soon something we were taking with us everywhere we went. It was part of the completed piece that we performed outside the yard before a big gathering of Portsmouth residents at the culmination of the project. Members of the Dance Exchange and town residents did the dance as the high school band played. When it was over, we all stood looking toward the yard across the water. One man came over and identified himself as a welder. He said he had known the project was going on and hadn't chosen to take part except by coming to the final performance. He said his favorite part was the string-around-the-belly story. I asked him why. "Because I've been building these boats all these years, and I never thought about the people who were on them. Now I have a way to think about them."

The next summer I received some string in the mail. It was from a member of the company, one of the dancers who had been at that first meeting with the officers' wives. She was pregnant.

This was a large project. We addressed big topics. I think the most complicated were the environmental issues, and the fact that the yard was so toxic. During the final week of performances, we did a full day called "From Crosscurrents to Common Ground." One of the events was in a church, which proved to be an effective site for both subject matter and dancing. At the beginning the audience was asked to stand in the balcony. Looking down as they heard the story of Noah, they could watch the performers sitting on the backs of the pews begin a motion of "paddling," which sent the dancers sliding sideways. It was completely beautiful and magical, and for a moment the boatbuilders of that city could feel their connection to their biblical roots as well as the portent of disaster. Later we danced in other sections of the church while the audience heard a series of statements, each starting with the phrase "Some people say . . ." All of the language was verbatim, taken from conversations with town and shipyard members, all of it about the environment. None of it was attributed. By literally moving their own positions and perspectives, the community was able to practice hearing and seeing new viewpoints on very old and contentious divisions. Because of the dancing, I believe, people could hear and see the information in ways they hadn't been able to before. It prevented them from automatically taking the sides they always take when discussion about political issues begins.

Throughout the Portsmouth experience I was continually struck by how inspirational it is to work with people who are untrained in artistic practice yet totally committed to making art together. One of my jobs was to communicate where we were at each point in the creative process—sometimes to apathetic listeners or curious but skeptical onlookers—and to help people understand why we were doing what we were doing. That communication seemed to inspire people to join us and to stay committed to a process where the outcomes were always in a process of being discovered. As a schoolteacher in Portsmouth said to me several years after we had finished our work there, "You taught me that I didn't need to know the ending before getting started at the beginning. This is a great life lesson. In fact, it has changed my life completely." I am convinced that her confidence in us came about in part through our willingness to explain the artistic process as it unfolds, to name the parts of the experience as they happen. We don't do this alone. There is ample time for reflection by the participants as they begin to discover their own ability to acknowledge to each other their personal and collective experience.

Sometimes I think this naming feels counterintuitive and frightening, especially for artists who are trained to equate inarticulateness with the mystery of art. Quite the contrary, I have found that the more I can describe and name, the more mysterious and miraculous it all becomes. Indeed, it appears that this very understanding makes it easier for me to take on risk. Comprehension leads to freedom in quick problem solving that gives me the courage to enter even more complex and challenging circumstances. It helps me to work quickly, which is good because so often there is very little time and people are busy.

But this naming process has a peculiar and, I think, useful effect on me too. The act of naming helps me understand my own choreographic methods better, to repeat them as needed in other settings, and to pass them on to my students and colleagues. It doesn't mean that I act in a rote way, but rather that I have become accustomed to communicating with my collaborators as either intuitive leaps or familiar methods lead us to our goal.

Postscript

The project at the shipyard changed many things for the Dance Exchange. More than any other, it demonstrated the power of art to shed light on dark corners of a community's history and allow the people whose story is told to emerge stronger for the telling, and for the sharing that comes from it. The translation of all this emotion, memory, and privacy made public, while engaging a shared structure over a long period of time, produces subtle and radical change that people can see, feel, talk about, and re-experience. By the end of the two years, even the ugliness of the shipyard sitting across the water from the city's main park could be seen as almost beautiful because the meaning of the yard itself had shifted. Everyone gathered on that day knew that hardships were still to come, but they also knew that their history and the individuals who had built the shipyard would strengthen their fortitude and their commitment to those present. In addition to the actual bridge that carried the workers to the yard, the movement itself was the bridge between past and present and definitely to a renewed sense of possibility for the future.

Speech and Silence: The Who Matters

After thirty-five years of dancing in communities, one way I have come to see our projects is as a precursor to reality TV. By bringing onstage people who live in the local community and who have a look about them that is far from that of a professional dancer, the possibility for truth-telling is intensified. Nothing brought that home to me more that the performance of *Small Dances About Big Ideas* at the International Festival of Arts and Ideas in New Haven.

Once I found a literal performance "voice" in *Woman of the Clear Vision*, I realized that I liked talking to the audience. In some dances it was quite formal, while in others in was a more cheeky form of storytelling. The concept evolved through many dances and then found a new power in *Small Dances About Big Ideas*. It turned out that it didn't have to be me talking, and it turned out that when the talking stops, the "who" can matter even more.

We created a new version of the dance after it had already been performed at several sites. In Vancouver, our presenter couldn't afford to bring the fully produced version with set and many dancers, so she suggested I lecture about it with excerpts. I decided to put the lecture into the dance itself. So we made a smaller and more portable version and performed it at EARTH: The World Urban Festival for UNESCO. A few months later, I met Harlon Dalton at Yale.

We first came into contact because we were on the same panel at the New Haven festival. He impressed me that afternoon because instead of talking about his own ideas, he spent his precious minutes actually responding to what everyone else said. I promised myself that I would do that the next time I was on a panel. Afterward, we all walked together to get some coffee, and Harlon and I chatted with one another most of the way. The quality of the conversation made me realize that we needed to get together again.

Harlon has a joint appointment in Yale's law and divinity schools, and I was interested in his assessment of the loss of habeas corpus and its implications for our country. So on our next trip I found him in his office with a copy of a film about Abu Ghraib on his desk. He had watched it the night before, and it saturated our conversation. Up to that point I had been considering protection prayers as a possible reference point for an upcoming full project that we would launch through our work with the Festival of Arts and Ideas. Harlon said we were "overprotected," and then I knew I had a lot more to think about.

Eventually the focus of our work together switched from the prayer piece to a new variation on *Small Dances*. Harlon suggested we work with his colleague Jim Silk, who had spent a lifetime on human-rights issues. As it turned out, Jim was a great conceptualist but couldn't be available for the performance, so he got us to Jonathan Freiman, a prominent human-rights attorney also affiliated with Yale.

We were imagining a version of the piece in which Harlon and Jonathan would be stationed at different sides of the stage with a bell or some other interruptive device. Whenever they wished, they could stop the action of the performance and talk about it however they wanted. After several meetings, we started actual rehearsals. Jonathan had acted professionally after college, so he brought with him a great ability and agility on the stage, as well as a keen understanding of brevity that he exercised through pointed intercessions into the performance. After one rehearsal, Harlon followed suit. Suddenly, instead of just being on the sidelines, they wanted to be in the dance itself. I was delighted, although it meant shortening and adjusting other parts and extra rehearsals for all. It also meant a new investment from the full cast. Flexibility allows for customization, which lets the dance be reinvented and become true to its new contexts.

With each rehearsal they brought more terse, provocative language:

Jonathan: If we look to trials of mass atrocities to establish truth, are we really ready to live by the ordinary rules of trials? Under those rules, a defendant is not convicted unless his guilt can be proven beyond measurable doubt. Is that the right standard for determining the truth of history? What do we do if a defendant is found not guilty? Do we conclude then that an atrocity has not happened?

Harlon: For the prophet Ezekiel the valley of dry bones is but a metaphor. For ancient Israel had been dismembered and its citizens scattered in exile, and the question of the day was: Would that nation ever come together again? But in our times, in Rwanda, in Cambodia during the Khmer Rouge, and in so many other places, the valley of dry bones is real.

Harlon and Jonathan looked closely at what and when and how to say things. They began to talk to the dancers, to me, to each other about where to look, who they were actually speaking to, and when to be quiet. They also wanted to be more physical.

I decided they should be in the scene that we called "Autopsy Duets," which occurs twice in the piece. The first time we see the duet, it is performed to a text taken from the story of a young forensic anthropologist describing her first day on the job in Rwanda. The second time, while three simultaneous duets take place, the audience hears a male voice speaking different definitions of truth taken from South Africa's Truth and Reconciliation Commission report. The duet itself consists of one dancer lying down on the floor as if dead. In this performance, Harlon and Jonathan assumed this role. The partner in the duet, danced by a company member, stretches and pulls at the body through a series of gentle probes and somewhat more forceful manipulations, as if studying, looking, discovering. It is not acting, but really a dance of sensation, skin to skin, limb to limb.

What Harlon Dalton and Jonathan Freiman did by agreeing to be the dead bodies in this scene was profound for their community. First they gave up their voices. By this point in the dance, the audience has grown accustomed to listening to their bright and energetic minds tackle the difficult subject matter of the piece. But as they become entwined with the story and become present with their entire bodies, something else begins to stir. We watch them become vulnerable as we begin to understand that words are not enough to describe this situation. Second, they gave up their standing, and by virtue of that surrender we truly come to see what happens in genocide: senseless death for every member of the community. Status means nothing. Profession is not a shield.

Who is doing the dancing matters. It matters so much because only with this cast was it possible for an audience of peers, neighbors, and colleagues to understand what really happened in Germany, in Rwanda, in Bosnia. No one is safe.

A Liberation in the Gallery

When I got the idea for *In the Gallery*, it came with the beginning and ending right from the start. A living nude woman would be onstage, beautiful, young, slowly shifting so that you really couldn't see the change, but when you looked again she would be in a new position. There would be a large line-drawing of a body, also without clothes but much more abstract. And then there would be a cube, ready and waiting for someone to sit on it.

That someone would be Vee Hollenbeck, then eighty-two years old, a small, slightly stooped woman with a radiant visage. At the end of the piece, after we have seen psychological solos about desire, fear, and delight, after we have seen a group of Cub Scouts come through on a field trip—after all of that, Vee would wander across the stage, take her seat, and drop her blouse so that for a split second you saw an old woman without clothes on the upper half of her body.

On opening night at the Kennedy Center, this final moment was greeted with an audible gasp, followed by the blackout, a slightly stunned silence, and then applause. In the dressing room afterward, I was approached by the Evelyn Swarthout Hayes, the wife of Patrick Hayes, founder of the Washington Performing Arts Society, our presenter. Evelyn herself was a wonderful pianist, a poised, elegant woman, at that time probably in her seventies. She said simply: "You have liberated my generation."

Being Another: One Kind of Technique

Getting the physicality right is a delightful challenge, a kind of devotional for professional dancers. People who use their bodies as both research and outcome know that nuance matters and that with effort the tiniest change can make a difference in how movement feels, looks, and is to the dancer, the audience, and to the choreographer. Consequently we build all kinds of technical systems to give ourselves the physical range that might be demanded and the perceptual capacity to manifest what is being asked by the choreographer, teacher, or by the movement itself. It is a very complicated set of tasks, and dancers are amazing in their abilities to merge the mental and the physical with immediate results.

This subject is a source of constant conversation with peers. Choreographers are always discussing how they can get the best from the dancers, while dancers talk about various ways that they work their bodies to achieve whatever the current situation demands. When the vocabulary was standardized, either by tradition as in ballet or by the unique character of a choreographer such as Martha Graham, dancers got their bodies to conform to the task through technique classes. In these constructs, bodies are taken through a series of physical actions that over time bring mastery to a set of skills.

But as the dance vocabularies began to shift and the demands of the choreographers grew, dancers were increasingly expected to have a vast range of physicality. Mastery over a single genre may give a dancer a base, but command of many styles is now the prevailing job requirement. At the Dance Exchange, this situation has been exacerbated by the intergenerational nature of the company and by the diverse physical and cultural backgrounds of the dancers. The challenge is to find a way to at once train a group of individuals who design and perform movement that celebrates uniqueness, to cultivate common ground and even common practice, and to build technique to meet the needs for any given piece.

I am fond of saying that the more one dancer is her own self, the more another dancer can be his own self. Once that's understood, all this awareness of self can be more easily partnered with the search for the common beauty of moving in synchronization with shared vocabulary. But training for this?

How? Oddly enough, I began to find solutions while teaching in a nursing home. Although one might imagine that conventional dance technique has only a small role to play in these settings, it turns out that initiating certain movement practices with the frail and old aided my ongoing investigation of broad training issues for professional dancers.

It is a worthy challenge to try to embody exactly the way someone else does a movement. We step out of our patterns of both doing and perceiving when we succeed. This exactitude is taken for granted when training in conventional technique. The opportunity to hone this precision is one very big reason that one goes to class. A dancer succeeds in part by mastering a series of techniques that have been acquired over time.

In the nursing home, the first piece of the puzzle was a focus on spontaneous movement, the kind of gesture that is very particular to a person's story. We usually found this by conducting a substantial part of the class in a storytelling framework that would lead eventually to making a dance. The trick was to get the residents to realize that questions were being asked and that they had the right to answer them. Later we worked to make sure the questions were ones the participants could answer with some relish. On a trip to Maine, I asked what jobs people had had in their youth. After a lot of support from the other residents, one very elderly woman said that she had worked in the mill, then resolutely defied our attempts to get her to say or do anything more. Eventually one of her friends said, "Show her how you sewed," and instantly her hands were dancing in air, shaping a kind of paper-thin silvery-veined filigree as she did a variation of threading her machine. She wasn't showing me about it. She was doing it. I gasped at the beauty. But when I tried to do it, I realized I didn't have the physical capacity to find the essence of her movement. Where I "pretended" to hold thread, she had her thumb and first finger in the most unusual connection. Where I made circles in the air that were generalized from my own years of training, her hands made shapes I had never quite seen before. I realized I needed a different way to see, and that by both using and selectively discarding the technique I had gained from years of training, I might eventually be able to perform her movement phrase. It wasn't physically demanding in a typically virtuosic sense, but I could tell it would require just as much from me as the most demanding concert dance variation if I wanted to do justice to her dance and maintain its originality so that it was interesting to others too.

The nature of this challenge became clearer to me as I worked with these ideas in rehearsal with the professional company. We generate movement material from a series of tasks that I set out as the choreographer, although sometimes these tasks are amended by the dancers. The material that is made is then shared through another series of tasks, then shared again, and then edited in all kinds of ways. Almost inevitably, the original maker of a phrase will teach some or all of it to someone else in the company. This is the moment when the very nuanced and extreme distinctions come to the fore. How dancers embody each other becomes a game of clever perception, physical dexterity, and movement memory that brings pleasure and excitement when done successfully and enormous frustration when the key to the puzzle is difficult to discover.

I remember one very long afternoon when the whole group tackled a phrase made initially by Ted Johnson. Ted is beautifully trained in several forms of dance, and his tall frame and natural ability make being him difficult, by which I mean learning his material is a significant challenge for the others. Ted is so self-aware that he takes great pleasure in noticing the smallest detail in order to make things clear in the body as well as in the mind. As I watched the group work, I realized that this task functioned as a technique class both in that the dancers were enlarging their physical capacities and in that there was a concrete method to embodying his phrase well.

Ted's phrase was eventually used in *Ferocious Beauty: Genome* as his exit and that of Cassie Meador. No matter how many times I have watched the dance, I always find this particular moment quite beautiful, as they find their synchronicity and I see how Cassie has subsumed herself in another's musicality and physical energy. Thus each dancer has imparted a particular quality to the physicality of their colleagues. Being Sarah Levitt makes the dancers find the swiftest and often the riskiest way to the ground. Being Ben Wegman means finding a quirky rhythm, and a staccato torso lined up with free-flying legs. Being Matt Mahaney means finding a relationship to the Earth that comes from his wrestling years in high school but that matured through his long walks in the woods. When the others find it, they are changed. Being Bea Wattenberg means finding an odd timing between the gesture of the hand and the nature of where to focus. Being Jeffrey Gunshol means expanding the chest just before the arms open wide into some way of rearranging the fingers in the hands, and suddenly nothing looks exactly like you expect. And although everyone has tried to be Martha Wittman over the years, we still have not quite found her musicality and the way her weight shifts onto a beautiful foot that makes just walking so achingly lovely and strange. For all the dancers who find their way to this company, this empathic form of discipline paves the way for physical dexterity and human attention, and for a set of beliefs that we all share: uniqueness lives in the body, and our dances are enlarged by the contributions each makes.

Moving to Hallelujah, site-specific performance at the Skirball Cultural Center in Los Angeles (1998): Thomas Dwyer. Photo: SheShooter.

What Is the Dancing About?

I Met a Physicist

Once I met a physicist who said to me, "The world exists so that I can do my math."

I thought about that for a split second and then said, "You mean the world exists so I can make my dances?"

He grinned and said, "Why not?"

Actually I think the dances exist so that I can live in the world.

Finding the Fish: On Meaning, Narrative, and Subject Matter Dancing

I had only been at the Sandy Spring Friends School for a few days. I could look out of one tiny window of the tiny bedroom they gave me as part of my first-year teacher's salary and just barely see the little pond and dock that was within several hundred yards of the science building that shared a wall with my living quarters. On that day my attention was drawn to a few of the faculty children who were on the dock, squealing. They were also shivering and then lying down shaking and then getting up and laughing and repeating the procedure. I thought the whole thing looked intriguing. I was interested in the movement they were doing with so much commitment, so odd out there in the sunlight, and so clearly performed in its theme and variations. Not that they knew they had an audience. They were entirely absorbed in their environment. So I went out to look.

I saw that the kids had caught a fish. The fish was doing what fish do out of water: shaking and flopping around on the dock. The kids were doing what human beings do when they want to understand something. They were putting the experience in their bodies.

As I walked toward the dock to get a closer look, I allowed my mind to wander to my own fishing stories, which invariably included my father, our early-morning outings at least once a summer with the Wisconsin perch flopping into the bottom of our little rental boat, both of us content to catch ideas more than fish.

I think that choreography is, in part, finding the fish: giving audiences some clues into the movement they are witnessing and even feeling in their own muscles and bones. These clues and images have their own shimmery edges that let us see what the artist sees or that give us a moment of private reverie into our own experience. I was drawn into a group of children's personal moment by movement I saw from a distance, a very curious and delightfully performed sequence of physical events on a dock. I didn't need the fish to have that encounter. But once I saw the fish, then I got the movement and their story and then my story.

That is the pleasure of dancing about something.

Subject Matter Choreography

When I first started making dances, I insisted that they be about something. But soon I discovered that I riled up the dance world unnecessarily by talking about making dances that had meaning. I say unnecessarily because I had enough issues with the dance world not to add this one. I was fine with all the dances that were about the movement itself. I understood them, although they sometimes bored me both as performer and as an audience member. But I realized I didn't want to get into that argument, first because I would lose, second because I agreed that the movement itself might be enough, especially in the hands of a master visionary like Merce Cunningham. He had—through his compelling works, his capacity to endear himself and his ideas to so many different people, and his absolute commitment—been able to bring about a real change in how we saw dance and did the dancing. I experienced this transformation in both grand and small ways and observed it first-hand in the physical forms of dance I was studying. In classes devoted to the technique of Martha Graham, I would learn how to "contract" the center of my body by being asked to curve my center as if "hit in the pit of the stomach, or screaming in pain, or in laughter." But in a Cunningham technique class we were supposed to "round the middle back" and therefore achieve something that might have looked like a contraction but felt and performed in an entirely different manner. Cunningham's essential idea here—that movement could be just movement and that meaning could emerge from the physicality itself—was an important element of modernism and a key factor in the evolution of twentieth-century concert dance. And so early on I coined the term "subject matter dances" as a way of describing narrative, story, and "aboutness" in contemporary dance. This made it possible to retain the idea of meaning for whatever kind of dance was on the stage, including those made purely of movement.

A Question with Some Personal Answers

I wonder why the subject matter of dancing mattered so much to me. Was it really the midwestern lyricism and epic poetic dances of my main teacher, Florence West, that got me so engaged in the idea of dancing about stuff? Was it my father's vast interpretive mind dominating family car rides and mealtimes? Was it my keen sense that information and feeling needed a place to exist side by side, and that dancing was one of the ways that created this place for me? Or was it my own incessant personal storytelling, the use of fantasy as a means of thinking that got me so entwined with stories? By second grade I had begun to notice my attachment to the narrative lines of the young women in the books I was reading. Historical fiction in particular caught my attention, and I read and reread accounts of young women doing good things in the world. Soon I began to twirl my own fantasies in my head as a means of going to sleep. I created epic narratives that I returned to night after night. Sometimes I would fall asleep just trying to figure out the name of a character that I might meet; other times I could carry on the actual storyline for quite a while. The tales were ridiculously heroic, and I always played a central role. Looking back, I can see that the part of me that has grandiose ideas began early, but also that I was building a muscle out of my imagination, learning how to partner with it for long hours at a time.

Later, walking to school by myself, I found that I could carry on more sophisticated thinking processes through a similar kind of internal storytelling. I would place myself inside a story in which I had to think aloud, and then I did. Much later in my life, when I began having to talk to about my work, I continued this tradition. I would find myself in the studio in front of the mirror, practicing what I was going to say that day to a funder about our goals, to a board member about our needs, or to my family as I prepared for yet another road trip. Over and over, I would try out the words and the ideas, turning them inside out and looking at them from other perspectives. This talking was an attempt to describe the dancing in different ways. I even turned that into a story. The fact that I often discovered new meaning in my endeavors fueled my interest and conviction in the overlapping uses of imagery, movement, ideas, and language.

Over the years I found comfort in narrative. I found philosophy and ideas embedded in the stories, and I found meaning and depth in the enormous effort of translating ideas into the body and back again. I also found myself in an uncomfortable place within the field of dance. For by the time I was coming of age to make dances, the Cunningham revolution was in full swing, and that meant no stories, no narrative in a formal sense, no meaning but the dance itself.

Another Dilemma

I am suspicious of the idea that dance can speak for itself. Maybe if everyone danced, we would not need the narrative, or at least not the amount of storytelling I use. When we are all moving together, without an audience, ideas, stories, and meaning flow between the bodies in an unspoken pattern of communication that comes from kinetic closeness, touch, the way weight is shared, and a history in steps that might be known or improvised that is unique, satisfying, and full of nuance. It is not the same as talking or writing, but it is absolutely a form of communicating. For me the trouble starts as soon as some are dancing and some are audience. The communication shifts. Can people long separated from their bodies find a way into the movement material as if they were still dancing? I doubt it, though I fear that many of us choreograph as if our audiences still remember how to listen to their bodies and comprehend ideas through the language of movement. If audiences could trust that they felt the rush of energy when the dancers take a fast diagonal, and that they know how to let their imagination fill with images brought about by that change, then perhaps the dance could speak for itself. If people had experienced, in their own bodies, the thrill of tension cutting through their center from one stretched arm to the foot supporting them, then maybe they would re-experience it in the performance and that displayed tension would remind them of a time in their own life when high tension was paramount. If people were used to noticing the pictures in their own mind as the performance flowed, then maybe a movement could spark a deep connection.

But most audiences need a place to park their brains, and actually, as a dancer and choreographer, I need that too.

Universal What?

So I am not convinced that dance is a universal language. It is a particularized language that allows us to share intent, purpose, and some steps with our fellow dancers around the world, but its vocabularies are quite different and may mean entirely different things to different peoples. I remember visiting a rehearsal of some wonderful young dancer–choreographers in a big city where we were on tour. They were wearing sweats and T-shirts, and their hair was all cut in relatively the same "I don't care" fashion. The steps were familiar to me as part of a new wave of release techniques that were beginning to make their way across the country. Ah, I thought, a form of folk dance. Although I understood the origins of what I was observing, I knew that many dance people from around the world would find this as strange as an evening of ethnic village dancing somewhere on the other side of the globe. Movement as meaning for itself is possible, but context is everything, and we should make no assumptions of a universal language. Why do we dance? For whom do we dance? Who loves to dance? These may be universal questions, but they have an infinite variety of answers.

The Meaning Question Again

When I want to make a dance about something, it doesn't mean that the movement is legible overtly, as in mime or charades (although both may be useful steps along the way to understanding or crafting or abstracting movement possibilities). It means that in the end something exists that allows a watcher to dream, learn, discover, understand, comprehend, notice, laugh at, or be surprised by ideas—ideas of the body, ideas of the mind, ideas of both. And it means that sometimes there is dancing that is just about movement, and sometimes there is dancing that is a descriptor of what went before or a predictor of what is about to come. Movement can be made to do so many things and to stretch meaning in so many ways. And sometimes it can even be very literal.

A Few Things I Keep Thinking About

It is a mistake to think that making a work accessible is the same thing as dumbing it down. In fact, "dumbing down" is a concept I wish we could lose for a while. Its use is a cheap shot that gets those doing the criticizing off the hook of having to explain what they mean. And it is a generalization that makes us squeamish about understanding the nuances in our subject matter. It is actually a very complicated task to give people in an audience the right amount of information or images or clues so they can be sparked and energized enough to search for their own connections to what is being expressed onstage. It is so odd that in the art world we fear being made to feel stupid if our audiences understand something of our work. And it is a disastrous joke that we shy away from bringing all of our knowledge to bear on a subject for fear of being too "obvious." So I will just say this again: *Accessibility is not the same thing as dumbing down, though some people may think so.* To me, accessibility means that I have spent enough time with my subject to understand its concrete meaning and its potential for depth through abstraction, form, style, point of view, tone, and vocabulary. I have suffered through many iterations of in idea so that I can believe that the art and the audience have a chance to be moved together toward new understandings.

A problem with this kind of art-making is that sometimes we are living in abstractions and sometimes in concrete imagery and sometimes in the many places in between. Thus our audiences must be able to constantly shift their positions along the spectrum to meet us where we are. One of my earliest understandings of this dilemma of now-it-means-something, now-it-doesn't came through my use of older people onstage. Sometimes I asked an audience to see the older dancers as old people, whereas at other times I asked them just to see moving bodies. How was an audience member supposed to know which I intended? I knew of course, but the knowledge was embedded in my hidden intentions and willfulness. What clues could I set out for an audience so that it could also follow along? The many answers to this question drove me to consider new ways to contextualize what was on stage and to seek choreographic techniques that would help make these ideas clear when necessary.

Truth and Expression

While we were making *Small Dances About Big Ideas*, I received a very interesting e-mail from Martha Minow, the Harvard Law School professor who had commissioned the work, as part of the commemoration of the sixtieth anniversary of the Nuremberg Trials. Martha explained how the Truth and Reconciliation Commission formed in South Africa at the end of apartheid had defined four different kinds of truth: objective or forensic, personal or narrative, dialogical, and healing or restorative.

These categories helped me to understand that meaning could have separate but overlapping definitions and uses. Here are some that are vital to me, though even as I write I see how porous they are.

Narrative, story, or idea-related meaning that makes it possible for a person to say, "This dance is about X." At times this type of meaning amounts to a series of explainable images. At other times it is like poetry, whereby a person might be able to string together a series of images. These can be intertwined and layered so that the energy of the dance itself ties together an accumulated sequence of pictures, of feeling, of story.

Emotional meaning is harder to describe but can be a powerful outcome of doing or watching the dance. People might cry or catch their breath or respond with a physical sensation. Often it is the music, the beauty, or the wild uniqueness of what one is seeing that reveals this meaning. Among people who have this reaction when they are participants, it may often be triggered by the smallest gesture of authenticity. It can come without the narrative, but there is no need to set it up in opposition to the idea of narrative. It can arrive when least expected.

Representational meaning seeks to make a direct translation from one thing to another. This means that. The act of translating requires sensitivity to more than self because there are requirements in being true to the original idea or story. Some of the usefulness for an accomplished artist in making representational meaning lies in paying attention to the "other" and removing self-expression as the dominant first step, leaving a space for new craft and new process.

Symbolic meaning is a specific kind of translation that allows images, movement, and things to stand in for something else and asks a viewer to find or make a connection in that extended relationship. Over the duration of a piece or of a people, these symbols use repetition to gain comprehension and acceptance.

Informational meaning is fact stripped down to essentials. Information is a way of giving knowledge. It is also a way to lie, misinform, misconstrue. It, too, can be subject of the body.

The fact that I like meaning—that I like to translate movement into meaning and back again, that I find that concrete subjects motivate me to locate movement—does not diminish the power that the movement has for me. Subject matter dancing doesn't feel less than, or like a crutch, or like some simplistic pretend game. It offers, rather, a fantastic dialogue of intellect and impulse, feeling and the matter of the mind, gathered in a weird kinesthetic wrapping paper that makes it all make sense to me and makes the struggle of art-making worth it.

False Dichotomy, Yet Again

I suppose what most drives me in the nature of my subject matter work is my conviction that the reality/abstraction dichotomy and the representational/ "dance for itself" dichotomy are ultimately lies. My own experience shows me that so-called reality and abstraction are ever-present and that most of us move frequently between these poles. I am at a loss to explain why we would want to live exclusively in one of these modes alone. Each requires the other in order to be experienced.

As a dance company, the Dance Exchange has told so many stories. We have made so many dances about so many things. I have learned so much as we tried to figure out what to say, how to say it, to whom and why: dances in communities where we told people's stories back to them, dances in communities telling our versions of their stories, dances from the company members' lives, dances from history, dances from the newspaper, dances from dreams and from images and from obscure details and from clichés, dances from statistics, dances from commissioners and partners, dances from remakes of other dances about the same subject. And we are always subjecting the story to a vast array of perspectives through visualizations, translations, metaphor, and detail.

In our best choreographic experiences, the stories forced the structure, the structure supported the investigation, and all were subject to subtle shifts, variations, and wholly new directions when things failed. And things failed all the time. We just plowed through again, sometimes never finding the right translation and sometimes learning something new, finding a fresh metaphor or letting go of a precious favorite to make room for the unexplored.

The questions may be universal, but the answers are particular, and infinite.

Back to Subject Matter

In subject matter choreography, various thinking processes are subjected to physical examination. These processes might resemble an editing tool, a lie-detector test, a recipe that needs different ingredients, or a dictionary–thesaurus that constantly illuminates possible new definitions or the need for new words to describe nuance. While all of this is being brought to bear to make the dance, the mind and the intellect get a good thrashing out. You get to see the issue, the question, the problem, the movement, the story, the character, and the act—in so many multiple forms that at least one outcome is fresh thinking. And I like that. I like that as much as the dancing. I wouldn't like one without the other.

Dancing on Both Sides of the Brain:
An Essay on Text and Movement

During a residency sponsored by the Wexner Center on the Ohio State campus in 1994, several of the dancers from my company and I went to speak to a class of general-education students. They had been required to see our concert as part of the survey course they were taking on dance and theater in the twentieth century. We arrived at the classroom and began the discussion by asking them to tell us what they had connected to during the concert: which dances, which dancers, what moments, which movements, which images? The hands flew up, and a quick series of answers portrayed an exciting, diverse, communal response to our work.

I wish the local dance critic, who had complained bitterly about our use of talking and dancing, had been there to listen, because what this audience of some sixty twenty-year-olds liked, needed, responded to, was the relationship between the language and the dancing. Over and over, they spoke of how we integrated the two mediums and how they consequently enjoyed the irony, the puns, the jokes, the spontaneity, the symbols, and the metaphoric properties of the dancing. For them, the combination was in the best sense challenging, satisfying, delightful, and new.

Having worked with text and movement since the early seventies, I am no longer surprised by the difference in the critic's reception of our work and the students'. The dance audiences I meet in senior centers, synagogues and churches, schools, prisons, concert halls, college campus dance programs, artist colonies, and conferences are relieved, excited and profoundly affected by the mix of dancing and talking. It is only among the most pure dance folks that the use of language raises suspicions. In fact, one way to define a dance purist is a person who wants to see only the movement.

I am at times myself sympathetic to this desire. In fact, my most private dance moments are almost always quiet. But at least for me, the demands of being an artist right now in history seem to require that we use every element within our power to make work that addresses our private visions and public realities. Language is one such element.

It may come as a surprise to people who have seen my work, but I did not always talk and dance. For me, beginning to study dance seriously at the age of five meant entering a quiet world of intense physical training where talking was banned and even a certain kind of thinking was discouraged. But during the years of study, questions dogged my path, questions about the nature of dance as a performing art form and the contexts in which it is experienced. Questions such as: Who are we dancing for? Why do some people watch and other people get to move? Why this movement instead of that one? I consider my attempt to answer these questions as one of the driving forces in my work. And that force took me down two sometimes distinct and sometimes overlapping paths of investigation. One path is the art of community engagement, and the other is talking and dancing.

So if I didn't always talk, what made me start? If every bit of my dance training was about silence, about pressing mysterious forms of communication into my muscles, then what started me on the dizzy path of language? What follows is a brief compilation of the little moments of experience that brought me to this place today, a place that recognizes the power of pure movement, the delight of language, and the limitless possibilities of bringing the two together.

1967. Merce Cunningham and John Cage at Brandeis University performing *How to Pass Kick Run and Fall.* Cage is sitting at the side of the stage telling stories. The dancers are moving in a fast, clipped abstract form that I had recently been studying at Bennington College but as yet had not integrated into my midwestern lyrical style characterized by a certain kind of flowy, long legato line of the body. Suddenly, or rather during the course of the dance, my whole being woke up. I became alert, almost frantic with energy, and very determined to try dancing again. At the time I didn't have a clue why. Only later, in retrospect, was I able to see that the talking gave me a way into the movement vocabulary, and the stories brought me to a total engagement with the theatrical event.

1970. Composition class at the University of Maryland with Betty Moehlencamp, doing Louis Horst's "Pre-Classic Form." I complete a little study, sit down to await the criticism. My teacher asks if everyone could hear me singing, sighing, breathing, being generally noisy under my breath? She means it as a sign of my connectedness to the movement. I am embarrassed.

1971. After teaching dance in a Quaker boarding school for a year, I decide to study theater over the summer at Washington's Arena Stage. My teacher is the actor Robert Prosky. For the first two weeks all is fine. We are improvising with movement, and my only task is to try to not look like a dancer (something I am still struggling with). But one night we are asked to do an improvised scene with language. It is hot and it feels like camp. After my meager attempt—perhaps I say two or three words—I sit down, shaking and sweating. Why am I so terrified to open my mouth? I repeat to myself that this is why I am a dancer, so that I don't have to talk. It is a mantra I hear repeated every time I teach voice and movement to dancers today. But even as I utter those words to myself, I know that something more powerful is at stake. I just don't know what.

1971–72. I study for two summers with Twyla Tharp at American University. During the first summer, there are only about ten of us. We take a barre each morning, and each of us must take turns teaching it. We are in a huge cavern of a gymnasium. I notice how differently I perform the movement when it is my turn to teach and I am bellowing the counts.

1973. I am teaching adults who are new to dance. I notice how much fun they have if I make them sing or count aloud or make sounds while they do simple combinations of difficult technical ideas such as pliés. I also notice that they perform the movement better and that their countenances shine when they are being vocal as well as physical. This bears more watching and experimentation.

1974. I am a go-go dancer in New York trying to earn a living and continue my study. I am in the ugly bathroom of some bar getting ready for my turn on the "stage," and I see myself in the mirror and think about Martha Graham in her filmed manifesto, *A Dancer's World,* as she talks about the nature of art and what it means to be a performer. I laugh at the thought, at myself, and at my condition. I think, How can I use this odd moment of connection with my history in a dance piece? I decide that I could "tell" it straight: a monologue in the middle of some dancing number. And I do. *New York City Winter* is the first dance I make as a conscious adult choreographer, and I find it thrilling as a performer to be that direct with an audience. I tell them exactly what it is like to be a go-go dancer, and I dance about other aspects of the experience. I dance about things I don't want to tell.

1975. My mother dies of cancer. I make my second dance as an adult, *Woman of the Clear Vision.* It is about my mother's death. My friend Toby Tate composes the music. He says after watching the first version, "Very nice, very powerful, but no one will know it is about your mother." He is right. I decide to begin the piece with a brief monologue, except that this time I am dancing and talking at the same time. I like how they feel together.

1978. Ever my father's daughter and my brothers' sister, I decide to do a piece about sports and art. I read and read about sports fans, sports icons, about the guys. In the end I create ten movement phrases and a three-page script. I put them together randomly. *Who's on First?* is a hit. I begin to notice others are talking and dancing too, and I wonder how many of us have taken the dictum that Cunningham and Cage handed down to us about separating the music and the movement. How many of us are using this method to explore the possibility of text?

1980. I make a piece to Peter Handke's play *Self-Accusation.* Titled *Journey,* it alters my whole relationship to movement. In it, I take each word and make myself find a movement for it. Finally I have found a personal way to break the lyrical line. I am thrilled and live off the discovery for five years. I call this kind of choreographing with words "equivalents." I use it heavily in senior centers as a way to get people to make up interesting movement quickly that they can "understand."

1980–83. The knowledge I gain from the Handke piece makes it possible for me to do a series of dances I call *Docudances.* Here, I begin to use text that is information-based. It is not about a story or about me or about the people dancing. It is facts, figures, government dialect. And clearly the dancing and the words team up for a new effect. I claim that it gives me a way to combine information and feeling, and cite the news and most art experiences as examples of how our culture continues to separate these phenomena.

1983–85. I work on a piece about Russian history. Here I discover the limits of nonfiction dancing and find my way back to art through personal story. The first version of the dance is really an animated textbook covering the most general of ideas and portraits. It is only after I begin weaving my Russian Jewish grandfather's history into the bigger picture that I see why I am a choreographer and not just a very bad historian. It is when I tell his story and mine in the context of Ronald Reagan's "evil empire" declaration against Communism that the work begins to be fresh. In this full-length piece, I return to the idea of simply sitting and telling a story without always having to "dance" to the words. And I discover the fun of taking visual images from photographs and posters and describing the images in words while finding a movement subtext.

1985–89. I am teaching many workshops about words and movement. I see the strengths of different methods, and I see the ensuing debates. The question of being literal comes up a lot. I argue that being literal is not the problem. Pretending and redundancy are the problems. Pretense gives interpretive movement a bad reputation, and I press my students to be direct in communicating an idea. Often words help students find a specific movement, even if the language is dropped from their final version. And often we discuss the problem of being redundant. I patiently explain that the words and the movement can do different things at the same time, and that one does not have to detract from the mystery of the other. This whole discussion begins to lead to other internal debates about context, about program notes, about how much you tell. There is an art to everything, I keep saying.

1990. I am tired of movement equivalents. I am tired of random selection of movement phrases with scripts. I begin to take notice of what is going on with my work in senior centers in particular, the relationship of gesture to memory. I begin to see the most beautiful, unique, idiosyncratic movement coming out of these ancient people, if I ask the right questions. I translate this to company work along with some new approaches to emotional subtext. I am renewed in the search for meaningful movement.

I make a new dance, *Anatomy of an Inside Story*, in collaboration with the then associate artistic director of the Dance Exchange, Kimberli Boyd. We use many different methods to find the movement for intense family stories about growing up black and female in this country. Finally I view the movement as not illustrative of the language at all, but rather as a motor that keeps the dancer going. There is no way that Kim could tell the stories without the dancing, and probably no way the audience could hear them, either. The dancing is a kind of ever-present witness, soul, or just an in-the-present experience for the dancer and the audience as she recounts a painful, sometimes glorious, funny past.

1991. I take a workshop at the annual Alternate ROOTS gathering, where my colleague Celeste Miller introduces me to the idea of details inside a story, giving me a way to be quite literal without being redundant. It feels like information that will feed me for a very long time.

As we're working on *The Good Jew?* our composer, Andy Teirstein, gets us to chant, as in my own Hebrew tradition (although I myself grew up hardly ever singing). It is a revelation and takes the language to a new level of poetry.

1993. Ysaye Barnwell of Sweet Honey and the Rock composes the music for our new work *Safe House: Still Looking.* Just like Andy, she asks the dancers to sing. Again the sense that there is a whole new and clearly ancient way to work with the dancers. "Take the words out of my mouth," she says to us in rehearsal, and that is a very physical act.

1995. We are in one of those busy years when several intersecting projects allow me to work across a wide variety of ideas and formats. The use of text and movement, storytelling and dancing, is stretched a lot.

With *Flying Into the Middle*, I decide to take a piece of music that I love (Tchaikovsky's *Trio in A*, first movement) and make a dance about being in the middle, using only trios of dancers till the last few moments. Moving among them, I deliver bits of a monologue, and as I develop the piece I attempt to talk and tell stories in relation to the music, not just the dancing. I try to score the talking as if it is a lyric to a song but spoken and happening while the dancing is going on. I like the discipline of it.

Faith and Science on the Midway, partly set at the 1904 St. Louis World's Fair, is a multilayered piece that demands much text. For the first time, I draw some of the these words directly from primary sources and find that absorbing. It helps that we have a performer in the company with a great voice who can match the language of President Teddy Roosevelt. The quirky use of equivalents to help an audience hear the history is interesting, as is the use of a bench that requires Jeffrey Gunshol to take vocal and physical risks.

This is also the first time I make an obvious use of different texts, matching them to the very same movement, even to the character. The audience sees Andy Torres as a carnival barker doing a medicine-show shill. Later he repeats the exact same gestures in telling the tragic tale of Ota Benga, a Congolese pygmy put on display at the fair. I find this captivating and useful, and although an audience member may not recognize the reuse of the movement on first viewing, I suspect that its unconscious familiarity might cause the discomfort to feel personal, in the best possible way.

It is also in this dance that I experiment with real dialogue. I had steered away from this over the years because I think it demands that the dancers be actors, which we are not. In fact the dialogue is actually a paired monologue in which each dancer tells a story about a bath house: an older woman describes her immigrant grandparents sharing communal showers with their urban neighbors, and a young gay man describes his visits to a Los Angeles sex club. As they casually exchange observations, neither seems the least bit conscious of the overlapping imagery or the connections being made. That is left to the audience, and their raucous response makes me think we are working well within our artistic capacities.

Also that year, *Room for Many More* at the Chicago Historical Society is a fulfillment of three years' work with various communities in the area, including a summer workshop with local mothers receiving state aid. In the piece, we place them in the historical rooms of the museum, where they stand, sit, dance, and tell stories about their family histories. I am particularly fond of the juxtaposition of some of the family stories with the luxury of the rooms. It brings poignancy to what they are saying, as well as a certain dark kind of humor reflecting on days of slavery: "My great grandfather used to spit in the water bucket before he brought it into the big house."

1996. I set *Nocturnes* to songs sung by Willie Nelson, and it is the first time I have made a dance using song lyrics to set the story. I think all the work we have done up till now on text and movement makes the piece something more than merely a retelling of the songs.

1998. On commission from Arizona State University, I make *Fifty Modest Reflections on Turning Fifty*, a solo for me about my turning fifty and Israel's fiftieth anniversary. It is all about text and movement. There are new aesthetic demands because in two of the sections I just sit and talk. In one of these, I repeat a single gesture while remaining otherwise motionless, touching my cheek as my mother did when I was little. A stagehand tells me that the gesture moved him to tears, which makes me ponder the nature of economy in movement.

One section stands out in this dance; it has something to do with the way the piece tells its story. It plays with dual images of valves in the heart and gates into Jerusalem. It earns praise from some tough critics. It is short, essential, and it seems to represent a finish for me, as I have made no solos since.

2000. In Praise of Fertile Fields is performed at Jacob's Pillow in Massachusetts and built from primary sources in the center's archives. Among them is a diary by the Pillow's first cook, filled with specific images and stories that were danced and spoken by the radiant Martha Wittman. But Norton Owen, the chief archivist there, also finds for me the most wonderful two pages of old writing. Ted Shawn had choreographed a piece to the spiritual "We Are Climbing Jacob's Ladder," and he annotated the words of the song with the movement instructions he had given the dancers: "Bend forward from waist until hands touch floor. Ready to start climbing twelve rungs of the ladder." I hand these to the dancers in small amounts and let them use the words as a movement script. Everyone does exactly as the words say, but of course they are all different from each other and different from the original. Two of the older dancers in the company share the text, Martha Wittman reading the words of the song and Thomas Dwyer reading the instructions in a directive manner: "Lifting right foot at same time and put in down in place." Martha says "ladder" and Thomas says, "Move up from about hip height to overhead gradually, raising up body as you climb but keeping head down until twelfth rung. Then lift head." Meanwhile, each dancer in turn comes forth and performs his or her interpretation of the movement notation. Coming toward the end of the piece, this section gave multiple interpretations to simple texts, afforded the dancers full range in their physicality, honored Ted Shawn, and placed a current generation of dancers side by side with their historic forebears.

2001. We find ourselves in residence at Grantmakers in the Arts just a few weeks after the events of September 11. The plan was for folks to work with us every day, and we would close the session with a shared experience. One of the first people I talked to said, "If I could only laugh," which sent me to the Internet to find out what it takes biologically for human beings to laugh. I learned a lot in that search, including a story about a laughing epidemic.

Over the next few months we develop these ideas into a stage piece called *Uneasy Dances*. I find a wonderful track from the comedy band leader Spike Jones in which the musicians "take solos" featuring loud sneezing and raucous, cartoonish laughter. Though I normally avoid a strict "music visualization" approach to choreography, I ask the dancers to develop phrases that are explicitly in sync with this score. It is a great redundancy, and although not strictly a text and movement idea, it is definitely a sound and movement idea.

2006. *Ferocious Beauty: Genome* moves our concepts of text and movement forward because of the wonderful hand of Darron L West, a sound designer of enormous soul and skill. He advances our tools in a section where videotaped scientists direct the dancers to embody the mechanics of gene function. Darron turned the spoken words into a rhythmic score that the dancers express with total commitment to the scientists' exact instructions.

Ferocious Beauty: Genome also incorporates a folktale essentially told in three modes at the same time: a folksy voiceover, dancing, and video that transports the audience through time and place. I think the effect is a great blend of worlds and lets the audience have a most unusual time at a dance concert.

The work features an enormous number of ways in which the scientists—all video projections—talk: directly to the audience, to each other, to the characters on the stage, in fragments, in full paragraphs. Through video and sound technology we are able to give scope, movement, and visual integration to all this material, which ultimately makes the whole experience work as choreography.

. . . .

On another occasion during the residency at Ohio State where the education students responded to our performance, I was asked to review and respond to student choreography. The issue of talking and dancing came up again. There were comments that implied that if I could really dance or choreograph, I wouldn't need to use the voice. I tried not to feel bad. Later, a very talented young man approached me and said, "You mean there are methods for how to put talking and dancing together? You mean you can teach it?" I smiled.

This scene would be repeated many times over the years, and my answer is always similar: Yes, there are lots of approaches I can show you, and lots more you will discover. And maybe you will be of a generation in which those who write about dance will grasp the importance of this form. They will grapple with you about the abundant aesthetic questions this work raises, and they will delight in the opportunity to address the subject matter that you so ardently care to think and dance about. They will be glad to participate with you in exploring the juiciness and messiness and loveliness of tearing down artificial walls in order to see what's behind and what's in front of the walls and the people.

Justice and Genetics: Two Program Notes

Preparing a program note is a particular kind of challenge. It is an art to design ideas and data in a way that satisfies people's curiosity and increases their appreciation without being redundant to the actual experience. It's not just that some audience members crave more information than others; it's also that different people like to get the knowledge at different times. Some get to performances early to read everything they can in the program, whereas others might just check it out when they get home or days later before they throw the playbill away. In addition to their job supporting the audience member's experience, program notes serve as a kind of documentation beyond the realm of performance, because in the long run they may be all that remains of these works.

The following notes appeared in the inaugural programs for two large projects. The first, for *Small Dances About Big Ideas*, was read by an audience gathered for an international conference on human rights convened at Harvard Law School. We decided to include some of the correspondence between the commissioner, Martha Minow, and myself to give people insight into the research process. Later, when we were asked to bring this work to the U.N.-sponsored EARTH: The World Urban Festival in Vancouver, I decided to include this dialogue in the piece itself. I think that using the program note to highlight my exchange with Martha made me more aware of its significance.

Avenues of Inspiration: A Program Note for *Small Dances About Big Ideas*

Commissions are magical business. Someone points you in the direction of an idea and gives you some resources. Suddenly you are challenged to make an abrupt turn in your life to discover something new. If you are lucky, you may start this process because someone asked, but you bring it to completion because you have become passionate and absorbed by the subject. So it has been with *Small Dances About Big Ideas*, commissioned by the Seevak Fund for the Harvard Law School/ Facing History and Ourselves conference Pursuing Human Dignity: The Legacies of Nuremberg for International Law, Human Rights, and Education which took place in November, 2005. I am grateful to the individual behind the commission,

Harvard Law Professor Martha Minow, for her wisdom in seeing that art in general, and dance specifically, could bring something unique to this gathering. Her commission charged us not to draw solely on the history of the Nuremberg Trials, but to observe the evolution of international law and the traditions of both western courts and the tribunals of other cultures. I thank Martha for putting her trust in me and my colleagues, and I deeply appreciate her probing and incisive mind; she is indeed a visionary partner.

One of the pleasures of beginning a piece is the opportunity to be porous to many avenues of inspiration. A conversation with Martha Minow would suggest a structure to pursue in rehearsal. A report on an International Criminal Court investigation in Uganda might supply an image. But a major source of ideas came from a relatively small list of books. These provided the strongest source for the characters that appear in the piece.

Reading Samantha Power's book *A Problem From Hell: America in the Age of Genocide*, I was moved to learn about Raphael Lemkin. This Polish-born lawyer and activist worked ceaselessly for international legislation to oppose genocide (a term that he, in fact, coined). Power's appraisal of such "mavericks" brought to mind the annoying persistence of certain artists and provided ample inspiration for building a character that never stops moving.

I had already listened, with fascination, to an interview with Clea Koff when another conversation with Martha Minow convinced me to read her book, *The Bone Woman*. Koff's language of dreams and her great capacity to describe the Rwandan landscape gave us many avenues of entry to create the role of the forensic anthropologist. And as an example of the power of detail, a passing mention in the book about the slashing of Achilles tendons in Rwanda provided the point of departure for the scene in the dance using crutches.

For much of my life, I have pushed at the boundaries of the definition of a professional artist, and I have sometimes questioned the assumptions that dictate the codes of that profession. Thus, I found the role of journalists covering genocide to be stimulating as they made the choice to move beyond neutrality. Reading Philip Gourevitch's narrative of the Rwandan genocide, *We Wish to Inform You That Tomorrow We Will Be Killed with Our Families*, I was moved at how they didn't let the discipline of their professions impede a larger calling. To read Gourevitch or Power is to understand events through the account of a disciplined reporter, but to also hear from an individual voice trying to understand, trying to convey the impossible. That journey, which in the end demands involvement and not professional distance, stood as an inspiration to us as we developed *Small Dances About Big Ideas*.

CHOREOGRAPHER TO COMMISSIONER

From Liz Lerman:

Can you tell me once more, why you think a dance, or a theatrical moment will help at your conference? What will bring the people who attend to a different place in their own process or journey? That will help me as I prepare for our first serious rehearsal period.

. . . I myself continue to be moved, in part, by my own incredulousness; that I have lived on the same planet with this going on and done nothing. So [the] idea of becoming an upstander is very vivid for me. But that does not exactly address the needs of the professional, i.e., the person who thinks about [these issues] all the time.

From Martha Minow:

These are my hopes: that a dance would reach people who seldom think about mass atrocities—students, lawyers—with the chance to be drawn in emotionally and intellectually, with the pacing that can allow people to absorb or begin to absorb the incomprehensible scales of atrocity, the limits of legal responses but also the dignity in the effort to frame and respond to atrocities through law. For those who think about these matters often . . . the chance to imagine images and voices about these things, and to have a shared experience with others who seldom attend to these issues, would be a gift. The central problematics rather than more information would be a valuable focus. And rather than the typical academic discussion that implies the capacity of logic, empiricism, and argument to contain, resolve or manage an issue, the dance might give people experience dwelling with the problematics. What are the problematics?

1) How could a trial be the right response to mass violence? How can the scale of the Holocaust fit within a courtroom, how can a few individuals be responsible, how can soldiers be to blame for what generals and politicians demanded and how can big guys be responsible for mass murders and rapes requiring the willing participation or passivity of hundreds, thousands of others?

BUT Also

2) How could a trial NOT be the right response—if the alternative is doing nothing, holding no one responsible, repeating the passivity during the atrocity with passivity afterward, leaving silence as the rejoinder?

From Liz Lerman:

I wonder . . . how Nuremberg was honored at each decade . . . and then when we get to 60, [if] that might be the way to see our country . . . through anniversaries . . . I was at an official ceremony in Warsaw during the 50th anniversary of the Warsaw ghetto [uprising]. The ceremony was both awesome and disgusting to me.

From Martha Minow:

At the time of the 50th anniversary of the Nuremberg trials, the U.S. commemorations understandably focused on the emerging use of trials in response to situations in Bosnia and Rwanda. The U.S. was not imagined as the source of aggression or violations of human rights. Now we cannot avoid that image even as people divide politically over whether the analogy to Nuremberg has any purchase after 9–11, the Afghanistan and Iraq wars, Guantanamo and Abu Ghraib . . . and whether we should be treated like other nations (this [George W. Bush] White House thinks not because we stand for freedom? We are the only superpower and thus unfairly judged?)

Since [the Nuremberg trials], finding rape a war crime is an accomplishment of the Rwanda and Bosnia tribunals. [Subsequent events] also revived the Nuremberg model so that it is taken for granted that trials should occur to [Saddam] Hussein, and in Cambodia, and elsewhere, with truth commissions and reparations as potential alternatives or additions. But preventing atrocities: that we don't know how to do. But we hope that teaching, talking, remembering, provoking will make a difference.

Some program notes need to make audiences aware of the behind-the-scenes work that went into making an event possible. This was certainly the case when we premiered *Ferocious Beauty: Genome* at Wesleyan University because the Center for Fine Arts was essential in the success of this very complicated piece.

Pamela Tatge, director of the center, brought the piece to the campus as part of meeting the university's goal to connect art and science. Pam is an exemplar of her kind, a visionary deeply committed to artists and to the generation of new work. She linked departments, people, and ideas from opposite ends of the campus, bringing tremendous benefits to the project. We rehearsed in beautiful studios where the dance department's Susan Lourie made us welcome, and we foraged in the sciences with some brilliant minds. Foremost was Laura Grabel, former dean of natural sciences and mathematics. A scientist with a dance background, Laura afforded us an elegant and generous entrée into the lives and the labs of scientists on campus. She and her co-teacher, Lori Gruen, brought us into their classes where we could test and advance ideas about the value of linking these fields. In addition, Laurel Appel and I spent many nights e-mailing each other, swapping unorthodox ways of thinking about science and art. Michael Weir went on to develop a new program devoted to teaching science using creative principles and embodied learning for middle and high schoolers. That work continues.

Nonfiction Dancing: A Program Note for *Ferocious Beauty: Genome*

When we started to create *Ferocious Beauty: Genome* almost four years ago, I realized that we had set ourselves a curious challenge: to take a subject, genetics, and a form, modern dance, both of which can be difficult to understand, then to combine them into something that *would* be understandable. This paradox became a standing joke at the Dance Exchange as we researched and rehearsed the piece. It was with us as we generated ideas, talked to scientists and mediated all the information we gathered through our bodies. Along the way we came to understand a lot, not just about genetics, but about dance, not just about scientific method, but about artistic process. We learned how ideas come into being when scientists ask questions, and we also saw how structure, characters, and meaning can come to artists when they rattle around in someone else's universe.

After over a year of performing this work in cities around the country, I am confident that at least some of the understanding we gained is communicating across the footlights. But I also hope that your experience will be about more than just understanding. In any case, here are a few things you might want to know: First, we didn't do it all. Once we entered the very large realm of genetics, genomics, and developmental biology, we realized we had tumbled into a place far deeper and stranger than Alice in her fall down the rabbit hole. I soon realized that this project could be about capitalism, or religion, or nutrition, or population control. It could be about race and identity, or about ethics, policy and professionalism. It could be strictly about the mechanics of the genome, using dance to describe biological processes for those of us who cannot stomach dry lectures or thick textbooks. It could be about the future and what the conflation of genomics, robotics, and nanotechnology might mean for the human race. While *Ferocious Beauty* touches on a few of those topics, the piece is ultimately about some particular sparks of interest we discovered in our explorations and in the minds of people we encountered. It poses some small and large questions, but it doesn't attempt to seek answers to all of questions currently being generated by scientific research. No single work of art ever could.

In choosing the subjects and sections that you see gathered in this work tonight, we employed an idea that I have come to call nonfiction dancing. This is a way of developing and presenting content for a dance that parallels how one might read nonfiction (or at least how *I* read nonfiction): it allows for deep, absorbed comprehension, but also for skimming, and for what I call the *I Ching* method: randomly opening to a page and picking up the thread wherever the eye falls. Through this process we arrived at the same things a reader can gain from nonfiction: amazing stories, details, specificity, and the benefits of research that someone else has done for us.

This material was filtered through the Dance Exchange's unique method for making dances, a process in which the company members engage as full collaborators. These brilliant artists pursued research of their own, proposed particular content, and responded to assignments that I designed in order to generate movement, images and structures. In addition, we took some new approaches for this project. We spent many hours with scientists, on their turf and on ours. We used movement to form a language, making a direct translation of what we were hearing and reading. We asked the scientists to watch us for a while and do their own translating back to us. Ultimately we were doing what we always do to understand the incomprehensible: putting the questions in our bodies and sorting through the answers. Out of the mass of material generated, we began a process of sifting, and the work assumed a shape in which selection and omission are critical. Just as the author of a nonfiction book decides on what to include, how to sequence, and how to interpret, we reached beyond the facts—central though they are—to present what is actually a very subjective journey.

Being aware of the complexity of the subject we were tackling, I determined early on that *Ferocious Beauty: Genome* would incorporate some additional elements, designed to help convey information, carry feeling, and to shape the stage pictures and the structure of the acts. So the production you are seeing incorporates projected video and still imagery, a complex soundscape, and richly textured lighting. We were very lucky to be able to work with masters of these media: John Boesche, Logan Kibens, Darron L. West and Michael Mazzola. All were true partners in shaping the form and content of *Ferocious Beauty* and made an incalculable contribution to the piece.

In the end, I hope the performance is like a great nonfiction read. Although the structure of concert work means that you can't exactly skim, I do think you can allow your attention to dive in and out and to meditate or rest in between. We have designed the piece to let the scientists speak for themselves, though subject to our editing. We chose the ideas to highlight through long conversations among ourselves, with the scientists and with the public.

So what, ultimately, will you experience in this essay in nonfiction dancing?

Act One takes us into the laboratories of scientists, and offers a fantasia on some genetically related themes from history and folklore. For Act Two, I selected three ideas I was interested in exploring away from the science laboratory: long life, selection and perfection, and the nature of ancestry.

It could well have been many other stories; after all, genomics touches everything. But I chose these three and perhaps that is where nonfiction, curiosity, subjectivity and fiction finally merge.

The Problem of Abstraction

Last year I visited the large Edward Hopper exhibition that was touring the country. I saw all the old paintings that I loved, the ones I used as the basis of scenes and images in an early piece, and the ones I had rejected for that work but still found curious and magnetic. Just before turning the corner to exit the exhibit, I saw one last picture by itself: a window and light. Perhaps there was the suggestion of a breeze, or perhaps just a feeling in me that there should be a breeze. Then I noticed that the image showed just light and not really a window. I stood there absorbing the picture, the idea, the feeling, and the color.

It was an "abstract" picture, and my absorption was intense. If one takes the amount of time that I stood there as a measurement of greatness, one might assume that abstraction trumps narrative, story, or concrete literal images. But I don't think so. I think what this picture did in that exhibit was to give the viewer, or at least me, a way of marking the journey through the exhibit. It represented the completion of a very long evolution of ideas and images. By the end of Hopper's life, and by the end of this exhibit, artist and viewer had come to an essential place. It was essence, small and true and clear.

But I get the feeling as I reflect on my own dance training and meet the next generation of artists on college campuses, that abstraction is treated not as a process of expressing essence gleaned painstakingly from experience over time, but rather as the first (and sometimes only) step in visual expression. In other words, abstraction is now the only expression permissible, and it comes not from toil but from fear of making legible any idea of image.

I don't mean too overstate here. Let's hold two ideas in our head at the same time. Sometimes I, too, start with abstraction—or at least with a translation from idea to something that looks abstract. And let's also acknowledge the beauty of non-narrative, the wonder of making line and shape and color and energy and dynamics all real without including a tint of reality or literal connectedness.

But often abstraction can only emerge after a long and sometimes torturous route involving many attempts at specificity and much grappling with idea, subject matter, meaning, and legibility. Abstraction is a hard-won skill.

Two Ways to Be an Angel

I learned over a long period of time that meaning is wonderful but sometimes it isn't. We danced the piece about my mother's death for several years. We would be asked to come to small conferences for hospice workers or gatherings of people concerned about the elderly, and we would do the dance. That way it stayed available well beyond the amount of time that a choreographer of my relative young age might have expected.

The old people in the dance had several moments onstage. They made their first entrance in a kind of improvised social-dance-y way, singing "California, Here I Come" after the piece referenced my mother's upbringing in San Francisco. Later they had a more lyrical section in unison, which was interrupted by my saying "Now!" as the lights blacked out. In that final scene, I was being my mother, and they were being angels welcoming her, or at least that was my image.

After we had been doing this dance for perhaps five years, Betty Harris, the youngest of the older dancers, who was at that point about sixty-five, said to me, "Well, Liz, today I finally was an angel welcoming your mother to the beyond."

I smiled and said, "Great, but what were you doing with this scene the rest of the time we have been performing?"

"Counting," she said.

Moving from the physical to the image and back again. This is another example of hiking the horizontal. For five years Betty entered her role by counting, waiting perhaps for the right time in her life to address the meaning of that particular image. It didn't make her less of a performer, as she committed herself totally to the moment by the physical and mental means most available to her. But as she grew as a performer and matured as an artist, she was able to enter the material in more than one way, giving her and perhaps those of us watching her, multiple perspectives in the moment.

Rehearsing *Woman of the Clear Vision* (1975): Betty Harris, third from left; also pictured are Ms. Mary, Thelma Tulane, Vee Hollenbeck, Helen Rea, and Marty Belin. Photo: Liz Lerman Dance Exchange Archive, Michelle Smith Performing Arts Library, University of Maryland.

Portfolio of Site-Specific Dances

Moving to Hallelujah, site-specific performance at the Skirball Cultural Center in Los Angeles (1998): Chris Morgan, Gesel Mason, Reginald Ellis Crump, and Judith Jourdin. The dancers are borrowing movement from then-current repertory, a normal practice for some parts of a site-specific performance. Photo: SheShooter.

Moving to Hallelujah (1998): Thomas Dwyer. For its point of departure, the performance used Larry Rivers's painting *The History of Matzah: The Story of the Jews*, which was on display at the Skirball Cultural Center. Thomas is a wanderer who reappeared at various locations as the audience moved around the galleries. Photo: SheShooter.

Moving to Hallelujah (1998): In site work the audience is sometimes on the move and at other times invited to settle at a particular point of focus. Here I perform a section of my solo *Fifty Modest Reflections on Turning Fifty*, which includes a direct reference to the Larry Rivers painting, seen at left. Photo: SheShooter.

Pollution Dances at McPherson Square, Washington, D.C. (1979). The pollution index had been running chronically high during the summer when we gave this performance in one of D.C.'s small urban parks. When a local television station interviewed me for an eyewitness segment, I just coughed in response to their final question. Above, Vee Hollenbeck leans over Judy Grodowitz. Photo: Liz Lerman Dance Exchange Archive, Michelle Smith Performing Arts Library, University of Maryland.

Pollution Dances drew its audience from people working in the lobbying and legal firms along Washington's K Street corridor. The cast included students from Dance Exchange classes and our Dancers of the Third Age senior adult troupe. Photo: Liz Lerman Dance Exchange Archive, Michelle Smith Performing Arts Library, University of Maryland.

EL CAMINO COLLEGE
LIBRARY

Fanfare, performed to Aaron Copland's *Fanfare for the Common Man*, was premiered at the City Dance Festival on the National Mall in 1980, where it included more than 800 performers from dozens of local dance companies and schools. Photo: Tim Dillon, courtesy of the D.C. Public Library, Star Collection © *Washington Post* (top).

In the decade following its premier, we included *Fanfare* in a variety of community projects, like that at Philadelphia's Meredith Elementary School in 1990. Photo: Ed Seiz.

The Portsmouth Naval Shipyard Project (1994–96) focused on the relationship between the town of Portsmouth, New Hampshire, and its historic and controversial shipyard. As part of the project we created a series of dance-and-story videos designed to be shown in public places around the town. Here is company member Jeffrey Gunshol with the shipyard's Ken Lanzillo. Photo: Still from video by Hank Madden.

Hallelujah: First Light, on the dock in Eastport, Maine (2000). We launched our multiyear, fifteen-city *Hallelujah* project on January 1, 2000, greeting the sunrise of the new millennium from the easternmost city in the United States. Photo: Edward French.

Pas de Dirt, featuring this duet for mini-bulldozers, started as part of *White Gloves/Hard Hats* at the Garde Arts Center, New London, Connecticut, then under renovation (1998). *Pas de Dirt* remains in the Dance Exchange repertory and has been used to celebrate the opening of an art center in Charlottesville, Virginia; post-hurricane reconstruction in Del Ray Beach, Florida; and family day at the National Building Museum in Washington, D.C. Photo: Liz Lerman Dance Exchange Archive, Michelle Smith Performing Arts Library, University of Maryland.

With CHAMMP Dance at Meridian Hill Park, Washington, D.C. (1994). A site-specific performance that incorporated various elements in this formal park—statuary, gardens, a life-size chess board, and this cascading fountain—and marked the culmination of a project engaging residents of three adjacent D.C. neighborhoods and offering hands-on experience to dance practitioners enrolled in our Community Crossover institute. Company members Jeffrey Gunshol, Peter DiMuro, and Michelle Pearson and are joined by institute participants. Photo: Jeffrey P. Kessler.

The dance of worship. In the sanctuary of Washington, D.C.'s Temple Micah, congregation members Alex Shilo and Mike Feldman participate in a movement workshop. Photo: Judy Hurvitz.

Travelon Gamelan, where bicycles are outfitted to become musical instruments, is the brainchild of my brother, composer Richard Lerman. He invited Dance Exchange to join the act when New Music America brought it to the Old Post Office Pavilion, Washington, D.C., home of the National Endowment for the Arts. Richard is seen standing on the platform at far right. Photo: Dennis Deloria.

As part of *Hallelujah*, I choreographed the stage piece *In Praise of Animals and Their People*, which included a pair of border collies that leapt and caught Frisbees to the accompaniment of Tchaikovsky's *1812 Overture*. Concurrently, a pair of Dance Exchange interns developed a community-based dance for people and their dogs. We brought the two together during a residency at Jacob's Pillow in 2000, where the community piece, seen here, was part of the annual Berkshire Day festivities. Photo: Mike van Sleen.

Man/Chair Dances with the Omaha Symphony Orchestra, Holland Performing Arts Center (2005): Adam Scher, Peter DiMuro, Ben Wegman, Matt Mahaney, Robbie Cook, and Teresa Chapman. The dancers move through the orchestra during this piece, seen here in rehearsal. The score was John Adams's *The Chairman Dances*. Photo: John Kubat.

Darwin's Wife, a solo for Shula Strassfeld, found a perfect setting in one of the formal rooms of the Corcoran Gallery of Art in Washington, D.C. It was part of a site-specific event titled *Tour Starts Here* (2009). Photo © 2009 Paul Gillis Photography.

Judith Jourdin in *Home Is Where the Art Is* (1999), site-specific performance in Takoma Park, Maryland. Photo: Hector Emanuel.

Where Is the Dance Happening?

Scene at a Bedside

I was in Milwaukee, where I had grown up, because I was to be the keynote speaker for the Theater Communications Group's annual meeting. I decided to stay with my stepmother, whose own mother, Kathryn, was in the last stages of her life. We went to her bedside and spent the last night of her life with her. Somewhere around two in the morning, I heard my stepmother announce: "Well, it's over." It was true, her mother had stopped breathing. We began to cry a little, and then Kathryn started to breathe again. "Oh," I said, "she is rehearsing."

Maybe she was, maybe we were. I know that my stepmother got an extra hour of life with her mother, as well as a glimpse of what the world would be like without her. This is a precious thing, and this is one of the powerful aspects of rehearsing. When everyone is committed fully to the project, the room is filled with small and great opportunities for gaining insight into life's mysteries.

As a choreographer, I have learned to take great pleasure in the demands of unconventional space. I mean "unconventional" both in terms of where dance usually happens and in terms of the space itself: the steps of the Lincoln Memorial, the bathrooms and loading dock of the Kennedy Center for the Performing Arts, the central four-story concrete spiral staircase at Intelsat headquarters in D.C., the bowling alley at the Portsmouth Naval Shipyard, the landings that give onto the airy atrium of the Hult Center in Eugene, Oregon, the storied churches and open spaces of the historic New Haven Green. I have witnessed so many meaningful, delightful transformations of both space and dancing in such places that now it is almost second nature for me to enter a building or a plaza or a park and immediately imagine the place filled with movement.

It began for me by chance. I was asked to curate a major presentation in a big downtown theater, designed to feature representatives of the Washington, D.C., dance community. I was flattered by the invitation but felt a little hesitant about my skills to both choose the participants and navigate the political landscape that forms the base of any small arts community, which Washington was in 1980. So I suggested a trade. I would choose the performers for the formal concert if this same presenter, the Washington Performing Arts Society, would also allow me to offer a totally open call for the dance community to participate in a large-scale event. They agreed and asked where we might stage the second event. Not having considered this question, I named the thing that leapt to mind. "How about somewhere on the Mall?" I asked, meaning the stretch of green between the Capitol Building and the Lincoln Memorial. They liked the idea. Soon we had permission to perform on the steps of the Lincoln Memorial and the spaces on either side of its reflecting pool.

An imposing eight hundred dancers agreed to participate in the event, representing jazz, ballet, and modern companies as well as period and folk ensembles from many traditions. The concept was that I would choreograph a simple dance that a representative from each company would learn at one of several centralized rehearsal/workshops. These dancers would go back and teach it to the rest of their group or school. The participants would then gather for only one rehearsal on the Lincoln Memorial steps, and an hour or two later do the public performance, accompanied by Aaron Copland's *Fanfare for the Common Man*.

In addition to giving each company an opportunity to participate in a show of communal solidarity expressed through a large ensemble dance, I wanted to provide each an opportunity to perform its own work. This piece of the project required a slightly more complicated structure. After the *Fanfare* dance, they would fan out around the reflecting pool and perform simultaneously, each company to its own music. (I was very into Charles Ives at the time and relished what it would be like to watch a jazzy number while a cacophony of sounds from several neighbors wafted through the air.)

This plan proved unfeasible, however, because the groups couldn't all fit at one time around the pool. So I had to develop a system for taking turns. Each set included twenty companies that would dance for approximately eight minutes and then switch. Being totally new to site-specific activity, I had no idea how complicated such a simple procedure would become. The distance was too great for the groups to hear a sound signal or for an announcer to tell them to change. I was stymied, until I remembered a flag-tossing, flame-throwing juggler who had tried out for the adjudicated downtown performance. Though he hadn't seemed right for the formal concert, he was perfect to play the focal role of signalman. Positioned in front of the memorial, he was visible from any spot alongside the reflecting pool, and his brightly colored, fiery batons lit up the sky above the water, triggering two hundred dancers at a time to change places.

The bigger challenge, and an issue with which I continue to struggle at each new site, was the question of scale. I was unprepared for the interaction between large spaces and small bodies—even eight hundred small bodies.

The rehearsals to teach the dance had been held in dance studios or community centers all around town. Even with only one dancer from each group, the rooms were packed. It was an amazing sight to see this little dance, set to Copland's brass–and-percussion scoring, performed by the fifty or so people that gathered at each rehearsal. After standing quietly through the opening drumbeats, everyone raised their arms majestically on the melody. It was incredible. I couldn't wait for all eight hundred people to do the movement together, something I would see only twice: at the back-to-back dress rehearsal and performance.

On the day of the event, I arrived at the Lincoln Memorial full of anticipation. My mental picture of the dance had featured bodies very close together, filling the steps immediately in front of the memorial's portico, arms sweeping skyward. What a shock to discover that eight hundred people barely covered three steps on the imposing staircase. I was crushed. It looked like nothing. Arms raised barely registered against all that marble.

Desperately I looked around for a solution. Finally, I moved them all away from the iconic sculpture of President Lincoln and closer to the reflecting pool. A plaza area separates the steps leading up to the statue and a much smaller set of steps leading down to the reflecting pool. These smaller steps worked much better. We filled the stairs, especially when we put enough space between the dancers to accommodate the various costumes, such as kimonos, tutus, and Renaissance skirts.

In the end, it was a fine day. Gorgeous blue sky, shifting clouds, fabulous and ridiculous dances, great American music, and President Lincoln sitting above it all, far enough away to appear human in scale, his countenance both amused and serious as he watched the dancing.

In reality, this was not the first time I had done site-specific work. I had experimented with the form almost a decade earlier when I taught dance to high school students at a Quaker boarding school. My students were nervous about their first performance, so to make them more comfortable I decided to stage it in the dark. We presented it outdoors, at night, under the light of the first full moon. It was all appropriately shadowy and mysterious, and no one could see them very well. The evening was a great success, and as long as I taught there students inaugurated their performance careers under the light of the first full moon.

At the time I didn't have the consciousness to think about these outdoor recitals as a choreographic statement or to consider them site-specific. Perhaps I didn't perceive their unique qualities because I was so focused on my student's needs. I was certainly aware of the awe and beauty of the hillsides under the soft light of the night sky, but it took time for me to see the merits of conceiving of the performance with the site as a central element.

In the spring following one of these fall events, I gave my now-savvy performers a choreographic assignment to find a way to dance in a natural setting. The school was situated in what was then countryside beyond Washington, D.C. (it is now solidly suburban). It was easy to find lovely, quiet, intimate places in nature to dance. My students made beautiful little movement essays, dancing duets with trees, with ivy, with the small hills and ravines that surrounded the campus buildings, and with the walkways. Several danced in the creek itself, making fine use of the sound of the water and the stones and boulders alongside it.

I liked their work so much that I promptly invited the rest of the school to see it and quickly learned a very important lesson about site-specific work: audiences often ruin it. I don't mean that they aren't appreciative or that they don't enjoy the good humor or unexpected beauty of it all. But from an aesthetic point of view, the audience is often in the way. When I watched the dances alone, I had a perfect view of each performer. But when several hundred parents, students, friends, and faculty tramped into the woods, each view also included twenty to fifty people doing nothing but watching. What I had seen as an intimate portrait of a young woman in the water, others saw as a sixteen-year-old moving exotically in a creek in front of fifty voyeurs. In site-specific choreography, the audience is not just observing the dance, they are the dance.

So I began choreographing for spaces other than the theater for several reasons. I wanted to celebrate a community of dancers and needed a site appropriate for such an event. I wanted to nourish a group of young dancers who needed a safe place to begin their journeys unencumbered by the weighty history and conventions of a traditional theater space. I hoped that audiences would delight in new opportunities to see bodies in relationship to familiar and unfamiliar landscapes. Since those early years, I have made many more dances in many other places, motivated by curiosity about performance, site, audience, vocabulary. Practically any question that has arisen for me as a choreographer has received a new treatment outside the theater.

Sometimes the building itself attracts me, such as the Old Post Office Pavilion in downtown D.C. Finished in 1899, this structure on Pennsylvania Avenue was saved from demolition by historic preservationists and revived in the 1980s as a retail/office complex. It houses both the National Endowment for the Arts and the National Endowment for the Humanities. I was most attracted to its balcony structure, where ten levels of open walkways surround a large central atrium on three sides, their beautiful columns pointing up to a soaring ceiling. When you watch the office workers coming and going along these walkways, the whole thing suggests a piazza surrounded by a stacked village.

I always wanted to hang out the laundry, set up potted plants, or pipe in some birdcalls. (When I was actually able to do a piece in this building as part of a New Music America festival, we put dancers around the balconies, where they did indeed hang out their towels. But that old nightmare of scale reappeared, and the laundry appeared to be about the size of postage stamps. This was not terrible for, after all, the building was the Old Post Office, but it was unintentional on my part.)

Sometimes we are drawn not to a site as an attraction, but to a site for what it means to us. We were asked by the program director of the Kennedy Center for the Performing Arts to make a dance for the building that would take place not in the traditional performance spaces but in the hallways, bathrooms, and the cavernous understage of the opera house. For many of us in Washington, the Kennedy Center is an imposing, distant edifice, and not always the most approachable venue for a performing arts experience. Our plan was to make people feel and experience the building in a completely different way by virtue of how the dancing happened and how they happened upon the dancing.

Sometimes we have been asked to make a dance for an occasion and the ideas that the occasion implies. An example is the centennial of the Statue of Liberty, which was celebrated on the Fourth of July in 1986. We were told that the dance would take place on a platform erected in Battery Park at the edge of Manhattan, where the monument would be part of the vista forming a background to the stage. In this case, from the very first phone call, the site, its history, its beauty, and its inherent problems were all a part of the process of making the dance.

And sometimes we have made dances for people in their home environments. Often these are dances to observe and celebrate an institution. The occasion may be a special anniversary, or a desire to rethink how the current inhabitants understand the history of a school, monument, or other setting. A two-week residency at Meredith Elementary School in south Philadelphia was one such project. The culminating event was a tour of the building with some students dancing for other students in the hallways, library, and cafeteria. In the finale, the entire student body, and some faculty, clustered in a giant group on the playground and performed in unison. This final dance was a recreation of the dance we had done on the National Mall to Copland's *Fanfare for the Common Man*. In this particular version, the dancers had to stand still for the opening drum roll, which took about thirty seconds. We taught the dance to seventh and eighth graders, who in turn were to teach it to the rest of the students. As rehearsals progressed, I was sure I had made a serious mistake by not choosing more popular music and by leaving this beginning in quiet. But when the whole school assembled on the playground and those loud deep bass sounds began *and* no one moved, it was completely magical. Later I overheard one parent saying to another that she thought that was the first time her son had been still in his whole life. This began my long musings on the role of outsiders and the possibility that breaking patterns within a community might sometimes be a good thing. Sometimes.

Despite the myriad reasons for making dances in new and unconventional spaces, projects like these have some common elements. A fresh choreographic challenge always presents itself because of scale, sight lines, intimacy, and perspective.

In most theaters, because of the architecture of the stage area and its position relative to the seating, a choreographer manages essentially the same perspective from each viewer to stage. The feel of this perspective can be altered by a set or the use of lights and multimedia. But in site-specific work, the problem of perspective is a constant. It is affected by the placement of the audience in relation to any given moment in the dance and whether that audience is massed or dispersed, at rest or in motion.

For a project at the Chicago Historical Society Museum, we played with perspective in many different ways. At one point I placed twenty college-age female dancers on a wide staircase. I asked the women to pose themselves along a central banister that divided the steps and to use its solidity to find precarious positions of balance that they could hold for five to ten minutes, the amount of time it would take the audience to pass by them. So the audience was in very close proximity to the women. They were able to see detail such as the tension in a hand as a dancer grasped the banister to maintain her position, the tight fit of a costume, or the strained expression on a face. Too close to take in the whole picture, they saw one woman at a time.

But later, the audience walked along a mezzanine above the same staircase. Still at their stations, the women could now be viewed from above and at a distance. The difference was quite startling. Now all the women were visible at once; the lines of their bodies in relation to each other and to the staircase became the dominant aesthetic. This scene of women straining to maintain their places made a provocative image that caused a great deal of murmuring at each performance. For me, this is one of the opportunities in site-specific work: as one's viewpoint and awareness of the space changes, one notices something new about the people dancing, the dancing itself, and the architecture, all of which enhance or telescope an audience member's point of view.

Another example of shifting perspective at the Historical Society performance occurred during a segment featuring the stories of several young boys. A long, narrow, dim room displayed small, intricate dioramas depicting the history of Chicago, including the Great Chicago Fire. Three sixth-grade boys, working with two members of the company, choreographed a short dance that moved from one end of the hall toward the audience standing in the doorway. It began with delicate gestures that made the boys seem like part of their own diorama. But as they got closer to the audience, they began to fall rather violently to the floor. As this was performed, an older member of the company sang an African American spiritual. The placement of the dance in this room made the boys clearly a part of Chicago's history and gave the audience an opportunity to compare our various versions of disasters, old fires, and new dilemmas.

Site-specific work often inspires a shift in attitude among people who live or work in the space in which the event is happening, accompanied by new perspectives on the place and new understandings about art and dance. In Chicago, several of the guards got so involved that one day, just before the opening and when the entire cast of seventy-five was resting, two of the guards suddenly appeared, one lifting the other in a kind of giant dance moment. Then they strutted out of the room to great applause by the tired dancers.

During a performance at the Kennedy Center, several of the technical stagehands suddenly appeared in a hallway dressed in their backstage gear with wide belts hung with tools, wrenches, and flashlights. They quickly pushed a button on a small tape deck, and sounds of Tchaikovsky's *Swan Lake* filled the space. The men began a rendition of the little swans, tools flapping around their waists, and then they promptly disappeared.

Site-specific work offers a choreographer the chance to affect audiences' ideas about art and architecture through the impact of dancing in a space. I think we are at our most successful when we make it possible for people to undergo a fresh understanding of their surroundings, of an idea, or of their own relationship to artistic experience. Often all three happen at once. Here are some examples:

A site can make it possible to connect idea, imagery, and expression in a direct way, removing representation to allow things to be what they are. We developed a project about the Underground Railroad, its history and its contemporary significance, featuring a key performance at the Quaker Meeting House in Wilmington, Delaware. This old building was an actual safe house that gave shelter to slaves traveling along the escape route from the south, a site where abolitionists Thomas Garrett and Harriet Tubman did much of their work together. As a member of the Wilmington Meeting, Garrett is buried in the courtyard. At the conclusion of the performance inside the building, we taught the audience a simple dance made up of some of the gestures they had just seen. We addressed Garrett and Tubman's strength of character, and asked people to think of ancestors or admired historical figures they wished to walk with. Then we invited everyone outside to perform the dance, encircling the large courtyard and in close proximity to Garrett's grave. Suddenly, the first movement of the dance, reaching down and touching the earth, really was just that. It was no longer just symbol. And the part of the dance where one reached behind and made a beckoning circle of the lower arm had new meaning, as if we were each calling forth Garrett and Tubman to join us in the present.

Unexpected occurrences inside site work are common because so much is uncontrollable. Such was the case with *Still Crossing*, our dance commissioned for the Statue of Liberty centennial celebration. In the final four minutes the stage is slowly filled by many people who join the company in a simple dance with very strong gestural imagery. In the premiere at Battery Park, the folks entering were all older adults, many of them recent immigrants. Just as our piece began, a ship appeared in the river behind the stage. It took most of the dance for it to cross, a kind of living backdrop. I could not have planned for it better. Its slow, stately progress mirrored the movement of the older people at the end of the dance.

Site-specific work can cause the audience to see everything differently. This is particularly true when some of the performers are not trained dancers. If you enter a space and see a bunch of older people sitting on a bench, and a little later these older folks begin to dance, it changes your ideas about who else might dance during the performance. One part of the Kennedy Center tour brought people down a hallway of offices. After the show, someone from the audience spoke to me about how fun it was to see the dancing in the offices. In truth, we hadn't choreographed anything in the offices, though some Kennedy Center employees had been at their desks that night. I later realized that this audience member had made an aesthetic leap and decided that the regular activity of the office now looked like art. If she could carry this framework forward into her life after the performance, she would be equipped with a new way of seeing the beautiful in the ordinary.

Intelsat: A Detailed Look at One Event

I'd like to examine a particular event and describe the process and impact of choreography in the space. In the fall of 1996, the Dance Exchange celebrated its twentieth anniversary by creating a site-specific performance at Intelsat, a space-age, glass-and-angles edifice near downtown Washington, D.C.

We expected a rather large audience, and because the event was also a fundraiser, we had to structure several parts to the evening: a celebration of the history of the organization, a dinner and awards ceremony, a participatory opportunity for everyone involved, a chance to highlight the company itself, and a section where the company would be augmented by performers of differing backgrounds and physical ability as an ongoing exploration of the Dance Exchange's commitment to community participation.

The Site

The Intelsat building is distinctive, especially for architecturally staid Washington. It sits on a very busy corner of Connecticut Avenue, about halfway between Downtown and the Maryland border, and is passed by thousands on their daily commute. Because of the odd shapes of its glass and metal exterior, it really catches people's attention, but few Washingtonians have had an opportunity to go inside.

While choosing a site can be a very creative and time-consuming process, in this case the selection and purpose of the site were synchronistic with the opportunity. Intelsat became an option for us through a Dance Exchange board member who was employed there. After she cleared the path with the corporation for us to use the building, we initiated a series of preliminary site visits. Some of these were geared to artistic and event feasibility, focused on determining whether the building could meet all the demands of the event. What would the sight lines be for a large crowd? Where could we highlight the company's concert work and where could we really play in the space? Would we need a theme to pull it all together, or was the building itself the theme? Some of the visits had a more practical focus. Which rooms could we use, which areas were off limits? What about food service, parking, security? Could we move the lobby furniture? Was there enough electricity to power the sound system? Would we need extra lighting? These meetings occasionally turned comical as people from vastly different backgrounds attempted to discuss an event that was completely unique to all concerned. I am particularly fond of trying to explain things to security people, who basically have to rethink most of their conventions in order to accommodate such an activity. We learn a lot in the explaining.

On an initial site tour I see the dance possibilities everywhere. Not every idea is equally good, but at the outset I will consider everything. Doing so might mean pushing the staff of the site to see their building and their space in a new way. For example, the Intelsat lobby is a large circular space from which you can look up to a second-floor glass-encased hallway providing passage between offices. I immediately asked if we could use it. "For what?" they wanted to know. I said that if we could light it, it would be a fine dancing space. I could tell they didn't understand what I meant because they couldn't picture what kind of dancing could take place in such an oddly long and narrow space. I do not take offense at the security team's inability to imagine dancing on the second-floor balcony of their building. I know few people have the experience that allows them to envision what dance is capable of being.

Each visit to the building brought more possibilities. Some ideas are content-driven: What can we do under these amazing hanging satellites? Some ideas are driven by necessity: Since we must have valet parking, how can we incorporate that into the audience's experience? Most ideas are driven by the space. Intelsat headquarters offered us many choices.

THE LOBBY AND ADJOINING ROOMS

The design of the lobby space included two rooms on opposite sides that were like secrets because the doors looked exactly like the metal walls they were a part of. One of these rooms was uninspiring, so we commandeered it as the performers' private green room. The other was one of the most magical places at Intelsat, a mezzanine overlooking an open office area. There, rows of desks faced a huge world map where hundreds of red lights indicated the positions of satellites.

The security people initially designated this map-room mezzanine as off limits to us, not because it was an issue for our guests to see the map, but because they didn't want dancing to distract the people who were working beneath us. But after much discussion, we convinced them to allow a small performance with the audience facing the map and the performers keeping their backs to the workers. Somehow that assuaged any fears.

A small screening room off the lobby served for showing old videos of the Dance Exchange, while the lavatories immediately beyond the lobby served for one of our bathroom dances. People always get a kick out of watching dances in the men's room or women's room. In this case we performed a silly version of *Swan Lake* as well as a rhythmic series of steps using rolls of toilet paper.

The lobby itself is large, flat-walled, and open. These factors made the space uninviting for unique dances. It wasn't until we broke the lobby down into smaller parts that ideas emerged. The revolving entrance door allowed us to play inside and out. Adding period costumes, we introduced an incongruous juxtaposition with the modernist space and created a little dance with an odd sense of history. Watching the cleaning crew one night at the end of one of our rehearsals inspired a strange vacuum dance performed against one wall. But the lobby primarily served to let us collect the audience, talk to them as a group, and seize our one opportunity to show the company in a full-scale performance of concert material.

THE ATRIUM SPACES

Beyond the lobby was the Intelsat atrium, a large, wonderful space. Several stories tall, its upper reaches were broken up by a series of catwalks. It is a classic site-specific space in that its beauty, lines, and spirit call for a crafted human presence, but the opportunity it offers doesn't come without a price. In the center of the atrium is a large concrete column containing an elevator wrapped by a circular staircase. The gardens of the atrium are placed in the four corners. There is no place where one can stand and see the entire ground area. Everything is blocked by something. I actually like this from the point of view of framing the bodies of the dancers. It helps reduce the problem of scale. It makes the room proportionally small, so I knew that while we would need a lot of bodies to make a statement, we wouldn't need hundreds.

The most stunning aspect of the atrium spaces were the catwalks themselves. They intersected the main circular column at each of the three stories and at different angles. Recessed ceiling lights positioned every few feet along each catwalk provided automatic playing spaces. But it was tiring to stand on the bottom floor and look up all of the time. There was no place except the ground level on which our entire audience could fit at the same time to watch the dancing.

The Rehearsal Phase

After touring the space a few times, we knew what our questions were. We had a feeling for the event, the needs of the sponsoring security staff, and our own needs for a successful evening. What took place over the next months was a process both fun and ridiculous, filled with moments of sublime conceptualization and moments of nerve-racking and difficult collaboration.

Let's jump ahead to the final rehearsal week because this is where planning and reality collide, where real time takes over from imagination time, where dilemmas posed by planning become solvable, but where unforeseen issues arise with every solution.

A space like Intelsat is pretty but barren. The size, expansiveness, and materials from which the building is made create a sharp, clean, and slightly cold space. We could have made an edgy, cold, clean dance that reflected the character of that space. But sometimes in site-specific choreography, reflecting back the exact nature of the environment makes a redundant statement. And because we were celebrating Dance Exchange and who we are, we decided instead to fill the space with human activity and to see the beauty of individuals and groups dancing together in this environment.

We amassed about fifty people to join us in this endeavor. Some were professional dancers, some were kids with their parents, and some were older adults who had danced with us before. Others we had met through community partnerships, like staff and clients from Whitman Walker Clinic, which serves primarily the HIV-positive and AIDS community. Put this many people in a building after business hours, rehearse them in small groups simultaneously, and the place takes on the busy feel of an old market or a beehive or a strange convention for fitness buffs gone a little wacky.

Of course, many problems had to be solved throughout the rehearsal period, and many new connections were made between the building and the dancing. For instance, we knew that we wanted to welcome the audience early in the evening, which on a feeling level meant "warming" the space up. Several of the members of my company are African American and have deep roots in the tradition of African dance. So one suggested he teach a simple harvest dance that is performed with scarves. He thought the audience could either learn the movements or sing the simple song that accompanies the dance. At first I rejected the idea as antithetical to the space. But once I watched all of these bodies and scarves in rehearsal and heard the stomping and the singing, I decided it was perfect. It was a kind of marriage of future high-tech with our tribal beginnings, suggesting roots embedded in the earth far below all the concrete, marble, and glass.

The Actual Performance

As the first guests drove up to the front entrance, they were treated not to valet parking but to our "ballet parking" service. A small group of ballerinas danced a rendition of the little swans from *Swan Lake*. Flourishes and high kicks abounded as car doors were opened and guests escorted into the building.

After a buffet and speeches in the atrium, our premium-ticket dinner guests watched overhead dancing on several levels of the catwalks. The performance included segments from our recently completed Portsmouth Naval Shipyard Project. The multilevel space allowed us to simulate the actual work of the shipyard, but to transform it in a very funny and paradoxical way because of our surroundings. Then the crowd was led on a brief aerobic tour up the stairs and into the lobby where they joined the bigger audience that had arrived during dinner. Dessert was served while people milled about until the starting time for part two of the evening.

At a cue, the audience was gathered and welcomed by our harvest dance. The company then performed the most traditional work of the night, showing two sections from a new dance done as if the room were a theater. We danced, and people watched from a "front" view. After that, people were encouraged to wander around the various spaces in and beyond the lobby (but not yet the atrium). For the next thirty minutes, dances happened simultaneously in the bathrooms, under the satellites, in the movie room, in the glass mezzanine above, by the escalator, in the map room and in the revolving entrance door. We call this structure a scavenger hunt because viewers are on their own to find the dances. They may then watch each one for as long as they like before moving away to find another. Scavenger hunts are useful for site-specific events because they teach each person to use a certain independent spirit in selecting what to see during the evening. Everyone's experience will be different and no one sees everything. This provides useful practice for what will happen later, when it might be the architecture or sight lines that make it difficult for people to see it all.

At the conclusion of the scavenger hunt we gathered the crowd together again and slowly led it along one of the catwalks to the center column, then down the spiral staircase to chairs that had just been put in place. As the audience members entered the space, they watched a slow, hypnotic dance on the floor below: two groups of performers doing the same dance, each to its own timing. As the crowd walked to the center column, the view ahead was obscured by the architecture. But as it rounded the column to start down the stairs, the audience was met by more dancers on the ground floor at the back of the atrium, creating a moment of surprise and satisfaction.

Once seated, the audience enjoyed a wild and ridiculous fashion show on the catwalks featuring the company dancers in costumes from throughout our twenty-year history. Narrating the runway show with stories from our history offered an opportunity to be self-deprecating and to celebrate our survival.

Then we prepared for the final dance. To very haunting music by Wayne Horvitz, the company began to appear slowly in solos and duets. They were dressed in white coverall safety suits made of Tyvek. As the company performed a more complex dance, some of our younger community dancers began to slowly crawl up the circular staircase wrapped around the center column. One played a violin as the rest slowly emerged. After the children disappeared behind the column (to enter the elevator, unseen by the audience) the guest adult performers also appeared around its edges, entering from several levels at once. It was beautiful in the natural light of the evening.

Other company members appeared high above the catwalks. Finally, the children reappeared and began to chase strings of Christmas lights that were swinging from above. It was a strong final image, one that combined the high-tech of the building with a human element to suggest a complex view of the future.

. . . .

For me, choreography is ultimately about investigation, learning, discovery. When I place this activity consciously inside a particular space, I know I am changed. We look at a body and we see the person, the shape, the line, the personality. If we know the person or we know how to look deeper, we see their history as well. The same happens to us in a building or a park or our homes. We see the place, the shape, the line, the personality. If we look deeper, we can perceive their history, too. When we allow ourselves to witness and respond to both things at once, we can learn much about ourselves, about the spaces and places around us.

My Favorite Night at Temple Micah

I never expected it to happen. When I first began to take my work as a choreographer into religious institutions, I imagined many possibilities for connected dance and congregational life: dance thriving in religious-school workshops, study retreats, or women's gatherings. And indeed, all these events did come to pass. But in the last decade I have seen a renaissance of activity through various denominations that has allowed dance and movement to happen, and even to be accepted, as part of the actual worship experience.

It's been a long journey. I was raised in the classical Reform tradition. My childhood synagogue in Milwaukee was a huge, hushed, but welcoming room. I loved its oddly painted ceiling and plain white walls. At that time in Reform Jewish practice (it was the late 1950s and early 1960s), most of the prayer "work" was being handled by others. The choir sang for us, the rabbi spoke to God for us, and, except for occasional responsive readings, there wasn't much for congregants to do during worship. So I kept myself in an intimate relationship to the service by looking around this distinctive environment and musing on what I saw. One day during my adolescence, I returned from summer break for the High Holy Days to find new velvet seats and my beloved paintings covered with repetitive gold pattern. The loss was acute. It would be a long time before I reengaged with Jewish institutions.

It happened through a combination of community practice and performance. Around 1991, I was choreographing the performance work *The Good Jew?* which examined the challenges of Jewish identity and the possibilities of living in both the secular and religious worlds. As part of its development, we did a small tour of synagogues presenting a work-in-progress version followed by conversation. During one of these, a congregant suggested adding a scene in which one of the characters, the Sabbath Bride, would be lifted on a chair as the group danced around her, a tradition at Jewish weddings. The temple's rabbi suddenly rose and said, "No. No more Eastern European images." He turned to me and said, "We are looking to you, the artists, to show us new images to take us into the next century." The congregation was Washington, D.C.'s Temple Micah, the rabbi was Dan Zemel, and the incident sparked a collaboration that has made Temple Micah the laboratory for over a decade's work exploring the role that dance could play in worship and the community life of a faith institution.

In this laboratory, the aesthetic rigor of concert work and the social value of participatory engagement have become united in the act of prayer, danced by the whole congregation, sitting or standing, committed to using their bodies in connection with their minds and the ancient texts in order to reach what I think each individual calls a spiritual place. It turned out that the tools I had amassed in order to use text in performance were the most useful pathway into the prayer life of the congregants. And, specific to Jewish settings, the evolution of a rigorous methodology regarding text-based movement forms probably helped my work gain recognition in a culture where so much respect is accorded to scriptural study, spoken discourse, and the written word.

In the long traditions of liturgical dance, some people typically dance while others watch. But being a person who is restless with prayer and who needs an active connection to the service, I decided early on that if I was going to involve dance in worship, the dancing would have to be for everyone in the room. And I was interested in developing a means by which even those who thought they couldn't or wouldn't dance might somehow be convinced to join in, or at least feel a part of it by watching.

The work at Temple Micah has taken on many different forms over the years. Here is the story of one service. I call it my favorite night at Temple Micah, but actually, I usually feel that the one I just completed is my favorite.

We met in the lobby as usual for an early spring Friday-night service. A congregant lit the candles, and our rabbi, Dan Zemel, began the ritual of pouring and sharing the wine. He handed the small cups personally to anyone who was there for the first time, including Kevin Malone, a member of the Dance Exchange who had come with me to help because my arm was still in a sling from a recent surgery.

After the blessings, Danny introduced the theme for the night. He said that some of rabbis over our history had come to think of Shabbat as being like paradise. And then he told the story of an unhappy and restless man who goes looking for paradise, which he knows is a two-day journey from his home. The first night, he has to sleep in the woods, and he carefully arranges his shoes so that they point in the direction of his travels. But during the night someone or something turns them 180 degrees. The next day, he goes toward paradise, which looks strangely like his own town, except that everything is just a little bit nicer. The streets are a little cleaner, and the sun overhead is just a little bit sweeter. He heads toward a house that reminds him of his own, and the woman on the front porch looks like his wife but is just a little bit softer. She says, "Get to work," and he thinks to himself, "Ah, even in paradise you have to have some tasks to do."

When I am part of a service at Temple Micah, I always begin as if it were my first time there, even though some congregants have been coming for years. I assume that there are people who may not understand or want to try what we will do with our bodies and minds in the next hour. So I find ways to introduce the essential ideas. On this night I began my usual bit of introduction, but started each sentence with "Paradise is . . ." Information almost always sounds better when rendered with some kind of poetic litany, something we learned long ago during the Portsmouth Shipyard Project. I end with: "Paradise is changing plans because it is so beautiful outside," and just as in the rabbi's story, the congregants went outside, took a little loop in front of our building, and returned to the synagogue. And just as in the story, this subtle change in perspective made everything almost as wonderful as paradise.

Over the previous few months, the rabbi had been reading an Abraham Heschel book one paragraph at a time on Friday nights as a way of studying. So when the congregants reentered the synagogue, the chairs were arranged in twos and threes, and they were asked to read and study this week's paragraph. It is important to me and the synagogue that many things in a "dance" service are left unchanged. After, all, we do not want to innovate everything. Many parts of the service are perfect already, and part of their perfection is our knowledge and anticipation of their presence. In this case we studied the text by making a dance based on the comments of participants and then engaged in that lovely exchange of meaning as movement and words intermingled.

What followed was something new to the congregation and to me as we roused folks out of their chairs and into the space. The rabbi read a dense but beautiful piece from the Talmud. I find it much easier to listen while moving and assume others may as well. So I asked a series of questions interspersed with the Rabbi's text. After each of the questions, the congregants could ponder the text, pray silently, or meditate in whatever form they wished. And after each of these questions, they had time to move, settle, think, or rest.

Where in the room do you feel safe? Go there. Where in the room do you feel most prayerful? Go there. Where in the room do you feel holy? Or what part of this space do you think is most holy? Go there. Where do you think paradise is? Go there.

At some point, I mentioned quietly that often at Micah we make dances just with our arms, but that tonight the dance was also about geography, about relationships, about how close or far we are from each other. It is an odd kind of side coaching: letting people in on the choreographic challenge. Giving them a way of seeing that they have taken on a more difficult artistic task actually helps them to settle more deeply into the experience. Information can be a form of permission, encouragement, and rigor.

It was fascinating to see where the congregants moved to and what they wanted to do when they got there. When asked about a holy spot, they moved closer to each other. When I asked about paradise, they went to find their mates and family members, and there was a lot of kissing and holding of one another. It was a sweet expression of Shabbat and a little unusual for a prayer service. Fixed seating in houses of worship preclude the rearrangement of bodies, who you sit next to when, and how closely you can connect. By moving around the space, people found their own forms of physical connection, which I suspect brought them closer to what they call "spiritual."

It takes a lot of planning to do these services. I enjoy the process because I get to have such intense conversations, not just with Dan, but also with Meryl Weiner, the incredible cantor at Temple Micah, and sometimes with other members of the congregation. During these sessions we often ask ourselves what of the traditional service needs to remain and what we can leave out. On this night our Rabbi decided to maintain the Kaddish but encouraged us to take even this sacred prayer into our bodies.

One of the challenges of participatory art-making is that you frequently have to teach people the skills they need to make the dance while they are doing the dance. At Temple Micah, it can't feel like a classroom because we are actually in synagogue. And even though the participants may be new to dancing, they are old and wise and accomplished in their relationship to a prayer service and to intellectual enterprise, so it is difficult to ask them to try something so new that they feel like children. It is very easy for people to feel that dancing is childish; it is really more like a sophisticated but illusory university.

With this in mind, I asked people to get in small groups, think about someone they would want with them in Paradise, and then describe their choice to each other. Up to this point in the service, all of the dancing and movement choices had come from me. I literally showed them, and people copied. But now I was about to ask them to choreograph a movement for the person they were describing. Many could do this with ease, making all kinds of choices from their own intuitive base or from what they had come to learn from other movement services we had done. But this time I also gave them new information with a quick demonstration in which I told them a fragment of a story of my mother and used a movement from earlier in the evening to underscore it. It is favorite postmodern activity, allowing the same movement to have multiple meanings. What makes it so interesting is that I then have the opportunity to consider why both uses of the same movement might "talk back to me," giving me new insight into my mother.

So now the congregants had new stories and some old and new movements they had shown each other. We gathered into a much tighter group of concentric circles and recited the Kaddish. People had the freedom to dance, pray, chant, do all three, or just watch. And then, just before the final song, I said one more thing: "You might have trouble describing what happened to you tonight. Just because you can't describe it doesn't mean it didn't happen."

Postscript

From the beginning, dance has been a way for human beings to grasp what they otherwise could not comprehend. This function of dance has always been a motivating force for me as I've made dances out of my own struggle to understand things in the world that challenged or perplexed me. So I am taking my restlessness about prayer and faith to people with different perspectives and making a suite of dances. At the same time, I continue to make dances with the congregation at Temple Micah and with the other congregations who invite me to join them—Christian, Jewish, Buddhist, and spiritualist. I continue to look for the links between the mind and the body, knowing that when they combine, people experience something that transcends both, whether it happens onstage, in a studio, or in a place of worship. I am convinced that it is the human connection to the body, and the body's connection to the mind, that provides a ladder, a safety net, or a trampoline, enabling people to experience the spiritual.

The Stage and Why It Matters

The auditorium was dark, the dancers were onstage, the tech crew was at work. Everyone was working, but there were still a few moments to go until we would be all together. The lighting designer was testing yet again a look for a particular moment; I was sitting back observing some small detail as the dancers rehearsed. The sound designer was listening carefully to one piece of music over and over. My daughter, Anna, then about four years old, turned to me and whispered, "Mom, are you causing all of this to happen?"

In a way I was. But the much larger frame she was experiencing was the enticing magnitude of the theater. I love the exhilaration of dancing in a ship-yard, the warmth of moving in a worship service, the healing comfort of a hospital corridor filled with laughter and swaying bodies. As much as those unconventional places for dancing speak to me and to my art form, the theater also compels with its intensity of purpose, its capacity to demand a unique standard of excellence, and its ability to bring so many disparate people to work together under enormous odds, with low pay and no guarantee of success. The theater is a wonder.

I am not sure that the challenge it poses to us as artists is due to the space itself or to its other contextualizing aspects: the fact that people pay to see you, that money has been spent on production, that a critic may appear and praise or damn months of work. I don't know if we have simply internalized thousands of years of festivals, happenings, stories, and mystery. But I know that when I am part of an audience that has gathered in a theater—whether it is for my own piece or someone else's—as the lights come down, the curtain goes up, the music begins or some signal starts the action, I feel it in my bones, my muscle, my brain.

It is this amazing confluence of time, focus, people, and the creativity they have chosen to share for a few hours that makes me nervous about the virtual world. I love the dexterity of the computer, the speed of the Internet, the fantastic unleashing of innovation we now experience as commonplace. But I for one cannot imagine a world without the profound and at times inexpressible experience of being onstage in front of a group of people who have given up minutes of their life to see what you have to say, people who have decided to throw themselves into another world that we have created in order to bring themselves to some new understanding. It is amazing to me that they are willing to submit to discomfort, tears, and the risk of laughing out loud in a dark room at what no one else thinks it is funny. It doesn't matter if they are teachers, stay-at-home parents, farmers, politicians, or soldiers. They come and sit to join in creating a mutually defined space for the sheer sake of having an experience.

. . . .

The theaters themselves give us an impression. We walk into an empty auditorium, and right away feel a sense of the place. It might be grand and pretentious or modern and curious. It might be cold and new with sight lines that looked promising in an architect's picture but not in a performing artist's body. Or maybe the place is warm-old and pretty or warm-old and shabby. The crews that come with the theater are just as varied. When they are good, it is a stupendous thing. When they are bad—and it has nothing to do with the distinctions between professional and amateur—the obstacle can be insurmountable. I like it best when the crews are problem solvers. The show improves, the backstage chatter and work ethic go into high gear. The extreme endeavor visible in the behind-the-scenes choreography is an awesome sight to see.

. . . .

A few winters ago I was asked to speak at the Abbey Theatre in Dublin. My host put me up in a hotel not far away, and although I had a few days of other work in the city before the night of my talk, I wandered by the theater every day. I went inside and sat in the lobby and just stared. When my time came to go backstage, I breathed the air as fully as I could. I was in love with the whole idea of being in such a historic theater and willed into my imagination the faces of the greats who had been there before me.

Ancestors. They come to me at different times and in different forms. Sometimes they are called forth by the theater itself, which may hold the physical marks and palpable vibrations of performers who were there before us. Lots of theaters have signed posters along the hallways in the back where the dressing rooms are laid out. Sometimes we follow the footsteps of other dance companies that seem to have undertaken similar tours. The recognition of this usually generates stories from our own ranks of earlier tours when the company had different personnel.

Ancestors. They come in the form of the building itself. The Kimo in Albuquerque where the lights in the house are made to look like skulls with red eyes glowing. The big theater at Jacob's Pillow with the paintings of dance pioneers Ruth St. Denis and Ted Shawn that flank the proscenium. The Sadler's Wells in London with the marquee that brings my childhood back so fast as I round the corner and come upon it for the first time, just because the name was once synonymous with the pinnacle of ballet art.

If ever there were a challenge to excellence, it is in knowing in whose path you are walking and in which space you will get to show or make or describe or teach your life's work.

. . . .

Time. Sometimes I envy museum directors. Their audience comes and goes at its own choosing. But I am also sure that the museum director envies me, for at least I have the public in their seats for a certain amount of time, probably more time than they would give me if I let them wander. We both struggle with the issue of information. In fact, you can watch at museums who reads the interpretive materials and who doesn't, who reads them first and then looks, and who sees what they want first and then collects the biographical and contextual materials on the way out. This is such a personal phenomenon.

But time behaves very differently for those participating in a performance. The dancers want the most time. They almost want real-life time, to give them the space they need to feel what they are doing. I think the audience needs the least amount of time. They comprehend what's happening and are ready to move to the next idea. As the choreographer, I need an amount of time somewhere in the middle. Mediating dancers, story, audience, babysitter, current events, emergency at home, constantly mediating.

. . . .

Experience. Performers have our experience in making a dance for the stage, and we have another kind of experience each night it is performed. The audience has its experience too. These, though tied together in time and space, are not the same thing. As a maker I had to learn to fix my own sense of the performance before I met with people after the show. I would come off the stage after the bow and perform a quick review of my emotional state and my technical observations. Then, I would literally give a nod to myself, take a deep breath, and let myself slip into the next moments of conversation, dialogue, smiles, hugs, and enthusiasms brought into the space by others. Taking that moment allowed me to be more gracious. And to not apologize too much and to let it rest, whatever it was that was pricking my brain, perhaps some small mistake that only I felt.

But what I can't quite figure out is why on some nights I am fine if there are lots of little mistakes and miscues, while on other nights the very same problems leave me a mess. I can't always know whether I am reacting to the stakes at hand, to my own feelings about the piece we are doing and where it is in the arc of its life, or to a quiet inside me that sometimes takes hold and sometimes eludes me.

. . . .

Video. When video first became easily available, I thought it would be a good idea to tape everything in rehearsal. I would go home at night, look at it, and prepare revisions for the next day based on the video.

It worked well, until we got into the theater. Then I realized I had fixed for the television screen, not for the stage. The scale was wrong, the space between dancers was wrong, the relationship to the edge of the stage was wrong, and the movement itself didn't make sense. So I stopped that practice. Video makes better video, not better stage work.

. . . .

Critique. What is it about seeing the flaws in our own work? What makes that so hard? I think it is about artistic will. We need "artistic will" to give us the courage to actually make anything at all. We will into existence the very idea of making art—countering the practical advice or our families, the accepted norms of our society. It takes will to think of an idea, to think it is a good enough idea to get others to be involved with you. It takes will to raise the money. It takes will to go into rehearsal stupid and hope that things will evolve over time. It takes will not to repeat oneself and wait for the good stuff. It takes will to help everyone over the inevitable mess-ups and flare-ups and goof-ups.

But when you look at what you have made, it is hard to distinguish between what you have willed in your imagination and what is actually in front of you. Sometimes I cannot discern the difference. My imagination has morphed with reality and I simply cannot see the problems.

So someone wanders in—my husband, a friend, a colleague—and they say "Look at this" or "Why that?" and right away, I can see it. I am sometimes grateful, often defensive, but almost always ready to fix by the next day.

Sometimes I don't need the friend. I need the theater. What I willed into existence in the studio doesn't translate to the theater with as much grace as I had hoped. And so the fixing begins.

. . . .

Brevity. One of our tools is called "ruthless editing." The dancers will have made a movement phrase based on some assignment from me, and then after showing them, they pair up in various groupings and edit each other's material. The result is not always better, but it is certainly shorter. It is frequently much more difficult to perform since what is typically removed in this editing process is the more generalized comfortable movement material that proves useful in construction but unnecessary in concept. If we have time, I ask the editors to explain why they made the choices we got to see. These answers usually add up to a good guidebook for what to watch for while editing. Because of course, we can all be editors, but one has to ask for what purpose and to what end we are making the cuts. I might edit because a particular moment in a piece needs speed, or invention, or strangeness, or a sense of shape, or because the story needs a particular kind of underpinning that some movement provides better than another. But if we don't know yet how the material will be used, we often edit to remove the conventional patterns that dancers bring as part of their makeup.

The theater space becomes the master editor, as even small problems loom large under the lights.

. . . .

Shape. The theater also brings a mysterious structure to the act of sequencing. I often make dances in parts, and then slowly put them together in differing orders as I begin to understand the material. Even with a strong conceptual component to a dance, which is clarity about the shape and direction of the piece, there isn't an automatic formula for what to put first and what to put second, or even how to make the ending. Sometimes these ideas are in focus early, but often not.

And then we get to the theater with a few days until opening night, and the theater-as-sequencer kicks in and the way becomes evident. Almost. Sometimes it takes the actual presence of the audience to make clear what needs to be shortened, what needs to be moved, and what is missing altogether.

In the case of *Nocturnes*, the dance we set to songs sung by Willie Nelson, I thought I had a great sequence. It was definitely crowd-pleasing. But that was part of the problem. For me the piece, although goofy and high-energy like some country-western songs, had an undercurrent of melancholy, and by ending it upbeat I felt I was misleading the audience. If they thought about it later, they might miss the emotions that mattered to me the most. I didn't figure this out until after several performances, in the theater, with the audience. Finally I switched the order, making Thomas Dwyer's heart-wrenching solo to "Blue Skies" end the dance. Then and only then was I able to see how to bring the rest of the dancers in from the sides, moving simply like Thomas, slowly walking backward, head looking up, parched palm out, waiting for a soft rain.

This was a much more satisfying conclusion, and one I would never have found without the audience and the generosity of the theater with its opportunity to perform again the next night and the next, each time new, each time reflecting the hours of work it took to bring us there.

· · · ·

Laboratory space. Going to the theater as a child, and then years of being in the theater working, have made of my imagination a space that resembles the stage. I do a lot of thinking in a black-box environment complete with marley flooring and light stands, waiting for the cue to help me see better. It has made me curious to know whether the next generations will have in their mind's eye the computer screen and a keypad instead. But in my case, the theater space, whether concrete or imagined, is the space where ideas are put to the test, or rather, to many tests.

· · · ·

Transformation. A tiny dread creeps into my body as we enter a work week in the theater with a new piece. I know that what I have made has possibilities, but I also know that the theater is harsh and that all the little things that have gone unfixed will become vivid under this microscope. I also might be a little excited and overly hopeful, because I am willing myself to believe that I have solved all the problems of a new work. Of course I discover immediately that I haven't. The problems show up quickly when I have better sight lines or someone else sitting in the house. I see that the dancers don't have it in their bones yet or that I haven't given them quite the right image or that we haven't taken enough time to sort out discrepancies in the way a movement is performed.

And of course once we are in the theater, the time is not entirely mine. I have to share it with the tech people, with my collaborating designers, with the union crew. I keep my head down during breaks and my brain as open as possible while we are working.

I have to compromise and pick what is fixable. There is nothing worse than getting the solution in my head and realizing that the dancers can't incorporate the changes in the limited time we have.

In college and graduate school, they tried to teach us that it was unprofessional to change things at the last moment. You were supposed to have it done and done early. At first I thought I was just slow because I was never done, even after a premiere. Then I realized that this notion of finishing by opening night is a total farce, forced upon us by someone with a wristwatch and an over-inflated commitment to time management.

I think this because I continue to change things until the piece is put away. And I'm usually ready to put it away as soon as I have no more changes to make.

The opening and closing curtains bracket a moment in time; they are a pair of parentheses within the long, ongoing project of making sense of the world. The theater calls our attention, brings us together, makes us focus, asks us questions, makes us wonder, and then releases us out again into the chaos.

Three Places, Three Stories

....

Luckily for me, the Dance Exchange made regular visits to a part of Arizona near my uncle's home, enabling me to stay in touch with him. As it turned out, I was in the state when he went into a coma as he neared the end of his life. I went to visit him and to see my aunt, who was sitting by his bedside as I entered the room.

It was impossible not to notice the way my uncle's arms were moving through the air, even though he was lying down and otherwise quite still. This restless motion was disturbing to my aunt, and the medical people said that they could give him more drugs to quiet him down. I asked my aunt if I could just hold his hands for a moment.

I wanted to touch him and to be close, but I asked especially because I was curious about the movement. What was he doing? Why was he doing it? I couldn't answer this by watching. I had to feel the movement myself.

My aunt consented, and I took both his hands in mine. I just followed wherever his arms took me. It didn't feel as jerky as it looked. It didn't seem to be about nervousness at all, more a kind of gliding through the air. Then I felt a tap on my shoulder. It was my aunt. She said, "Can I try that?"

We switched places, and she took his hands. The last image I have of my uncle alive is seeing my aunt dancing with him, which apparently they did for the next two days, the last they would have together.

It would be easy to teach people the dance skills necessary to be able to do this. It would take much more to get this culture of ours to be less suspicious of movement, so that rather than drugging someone out of the need for it, they could rather wonder about its meaning, test its need by copying it with an empathic unison moment, and then discover its beauty.

. . . .

During the five years I was in residence at Children's Hospital in Washington, D.C., we did only one major performance. On that day they brought all the kids, families, and available staff down to the atrium, where we danced several pieces from our repertory. Except for the lack of a conventional stage, it was very much a full-fledged performance. One of the dances, called *Bonsai*, was a quiet piece that told the story of how the caretaking of these long-lived trees passes on to a new generation.

I noticed as we were performing this dance that a youngster in the front row had fallen asleep. I had met this child earlier in the week and had liked her. So I was sad to see her miss so much. As I was leaving the hospital, slightly dejected, one of the nurses ran after me and said in a very enthusiastic voice, "Thank you, thank you, we have been trying to get that kid to go to sleep for three days."

Up to that point, I had thought one of the most important functions of art was to wake people up. Here I was confronted with information teaching me the opposite. I was grateful. I would never have learned this if I had stayed in the studio making my dances. If we are lucky and paying attention, we can discover over and over again that the intersection of art and real life affects the art form as much as it affects the community and the people involved.

. . . .

For the finale of the Shipyard Project in Portsmouth, we designed a full-day event that included parades from two different sides of town that met where a ribbon was tied, bringing shipyard and town together. Also on that day, we did site-specific performances all over a harbor-side park, and a final series of dances on an outdoor stage that pulled all the participants together. The last piece was the final version of a dance we had been creating since the first visit almost two years earlier. It was a gestural phrase in which each movement was annotated by a story from someone in the community. Over a thousand people in the park took part in this dance, making it a fitting end to a huge project that had captured our lives for eighteen months.

A few weeks later we received a letter from a man who had wandered into the park by accident that day. He and his wife had been on a day trip to Portsmouth to see the shipyard, as he had worked for GE at a different shipyard in Rhode Island. In his letter he described stumbling onto a scene in the park in which a group of men were dancing about all the jobs they had had in the yard. I had choreographed this dance in an area set apart from much of the park by a hedge. It made for an intimate space that I felt we needed not only to hear what they were saying but also to do justice to what they were talking and dancing about. The man from Rhode Island wrote:

We got up and stepped over to the garden to find "dancers" telling us about their "first job at the shipyard." I found myself staring at these people. . . . People in dance and word celebrating what their jobs were. Real people who worked real jobs just like me. Even as I remember that moment I can feel myself fill up with emotion . . . I have never truly appreciated the arts before . . . Yes I have seen great works onstage, but never have I been lifted up and made to feel as I did that day in the park.

Who gets to dance, what is it about, where does it happen, and why does it matter? These questions form the heart of our practice, and this letter gives us notice that the answers mattered one day to a man in a park by a shipyard.

Reginald Ellis Crump in a Dance Exchange photo from 1998. Photo:
Rhoda Baer.

Structures and Underpinnings

A Brief Conversation with a Friend

Holly: How are you, Liz?
Liz: Oh, I am fine.
Holly: How is the Dance Exchange?
Liz: Oh, well, we are in this transition . . .
Holly: You and the Dance Exchange are *always* in transition.

Yes we are. Always. Twisting a bit here or there, being opportunistic at times, stubborn at others. Shape-shifting and reinvention are daily activities. They grow from the improvisational structuring that informs choreography. Make enough architecture or "local rules" as the scientists would say, and then create the prototype, then fix and improve, then test, then perform, then fix, then restructure, then make new rules, then test, then let some fall away, then make space for the new, then test. In our case, the petri dish also contains ingredients from art-world practice, community investment and need, national agendas, the ever-present specter of economic turmoil, and good friends like Holly Sidford, a humble genius of organizational matters who somehow could tell from a distance when we needed strong opinions or gentle guidance or both.

What Happens on a Residency?

In my particular part of the performing arts and art-making world, "residency" is a word we use with some frequency. Occasionally I'll get a look of incomprehension or the outright question "What's a residency?" which reminds me that the term might need some explaining. Here I answer that question and several others that flow from it.

What's a residency?

A residency allows you to spend a certain amount of time in a particular place doing a set of activities that have been arranged with someone of that place who wants you there.

A residency is what you do when asked to work with a selected group of people to make something that gets shown at the end of your time together.

A residency accompanies a concert piece and contains a lot of events that usually have something to do with the subject matter of that concert, but not always.

A residency is a time to make something new, and because there is never enough time, the new thing is often a sketch or a single step in a bigger project.

A residency is an opportunity to consider new projects, new topics, new phases, or to formulate the next good question about a particular idea that is brewing.

A residency is a chance to share methods through training. This can mean training the local community or a local arts team that is helping to implement a project. It can be about training new company members. It can be about training young dancers or other students interested in certain practices.

A residency is a gathering time for a community to come to itself differently because of the guests it has imported and because of what these outsiders are asking, doing, catalyzing.

How does a residency get started?
It depends.

Sometimes we get invited. Someone in the community has an issue, or an idea, or a need, so they call and we visit to find out we are a good match. The Portsmouth Naval Shipyard Project began this way, partly spurred by the prospect of the shipyard being closed by the federal government. *Safe House: Still Looking*, a project in Wilmington, Delaware, began with just the notion that the community needed to "come together" somehow and the hope that the Dance Exchange would help community members discover a reason to meet and to make something in common.

Sometimes we go to a place because we have suggested a residency to someone we've met. They follow up and invite us, and then we see if we have a good match. In some ways, our entire *Hallelujah* project, which occupied us in fifteen cities from 1998 to 2002, began with us making the suggestion. Once we have made one contact, we may encourage collaboration among a variety of groups, even before we arrive. I mention that here because the beginnings can be so different, depending on who is in the room, their assumptions about each other, and what kind of mediating will take place over the course of the whole event.

Some residencies begin because there are people in this world who have dedicated their lives to bringing artists into communities and making things happen. These folks, called presenters, are usually mostly consumed by the demands of mounting a performance. But more and more, they have also come to recognize the powerful opportunities that are waiting for them outside the concert hall, and they have begun to use the artists and the art form as a connecting network for all kinds of reasons. They may contact an artist at the Dance Exchange because of the subject matter of that artist's new work, because of an issue in their own community, or because they are interested in expanding impact or exploring experimental forms of art-making.

I try to tell younger artists to be patient because these very important relationships can take years to build (though they take very little time to unravel). In some cases I have been in discussion with presenters for over a decade before we finally set foot in their community.

Some residencies begin with the artist asking questions and needing to pursue research, which can lead to a great set of relationships that unfold over time. Our experience at Wesleyan University is a good example. I was curious about genetics and scientific process and discovery. Pam Tatge, who leads performing arts at Wesleyan, heard about my interest. The school, whose dean of science at that time was a former dancer, was looking for ways to forge a relationship between departments at two geographic ends of campus, where the arts and sciences were separated by a large, beautiful field. I was invited to come to talk to people and now, five years later, I am still visiting the campus, still researching, and still "residing" for a week or two a year.

So what happens after you establish the relationship with a presenter?

It depends.

A residency that involves interacting with partners means there will be lots of listening, and different kinds of listening. One kind is listening for the theme, a theme that might emerge from issues that repeatedly come up for people in the same city, such as the loss of control over land or the question of who the real leaders are. A theme might reveal itself in how an individual puts his or her troubles into language so unusual that it that makes us listen harder. We may hear it one place and then ask about it over and over as we travel around. Early in our *Hallelujah* project in Minneapolis, I was teaching a workshop as a way of getting to know people and possible partners. Partway through, completely out of turn, an old man stood up and started talking, almost barking, in a strange, loud voice. His tone was aggressive and directed entirely at me, even though others had been involved in our co-teaching. I wondered if dementia was in play, if he wasn't sure where he was. But what he was saying was fascinating. It went something like this: "Do you believe in order? Do you think disorder is beautiful? What do you think is beautiful? What about disorder? I like disorder! Do you? And what about beauty?"

I had never thought about beauty and disorder together. I wasn't sure what it would yield, but I liked the juxtaposition. In that moment I just listened. At the next opportunity, we designed a workshop around his question, and what we discovered was amazing. If we asked people for a time in their lives when they had experienced beauty and disorder at the same moment, we stumbled into very intense stories, often about life and birth and death situations. And so our piece for Minneapolis was titled *Hallelujah: In Praise of Beauty and Disorder.*

Listening is a full-time job. The conversations that matter are everywhere. The local staffer or volunteer who is chauffeuring us around and coming along to meetings may provide an interesting running commentary between the meetings. Some of it might be corrective, as in, "That person always talks like that so, you can disregard what he just said," or maybe, "They are going to tell you this, but actually they should talk about that." I always love hearing the commentary, although I don't always use it or depend on it. It is a kind of mini-Greek chorus. A restatement of what we just heard in a meeting can often help me figure out what is important to our partners or help me see pitfalls that lie ahead. One of my favorite examples happened while preparing the *Hallelujah* in Stonington/Deer Isle, Maine. It helped that the person taking me to meet everyone, Stu Kestenbaum, was (and is) beloved by all and is a wonderful poet. To hear him rephrase or make sure I had heard or seen a nuance was to witness an act of verbal poetic theater over the few days in which we met everyone on the island. No wonder one of the groups we met was the small breakfast club of old men who met at a diner one morning a week and then went to a small inlet where they "saluted the place of indescribable beauty."

Being an outsider is one of the best things about community residencies. We just see and hear differently because we don't have the knowledge or the history of the place we're visiting. It is like being a two-year-old, before you quite comprehend cause and effect. We aren't triggered by hurts or reputation or status.

How does being an outsider affect the work?

It depends.

Being an effective outsider requires that you know how to partner. Part of partnering is true, authentic dependence. We are dependent on many of the people who have brought us in. This is mostly fine. Sometimes it is a disaster. Sometimes, the people who have brought us have their own issues in the community, their own agenda that you are expected to uphold. Such collaborative landscapes are complicated to navigate and often change over time as the issues that may have catalyzed an invitation shift in the light of creative enterprise.

Say more about listening.

Even the way you ask the question is interesting. Once someone said to me, "You get work because you are a good talker," and I said, "Well actually, no; I get work because I am a good listener."

There are so many ways to listen. I listen for interesting language that might suggest a title or an unusual way to see things. I listen for images that might give us ideas for dances, costumes, or stage pictures. I watch the hands to see what makes their gestures move from idiosyncratic to expressive. I listen for common ground between people's actions and the possibilities of dance, or between how they talk and how I think. I listen for things I have never heard before. I listen for things I may have heard in a previous conversation. I listen for a moment when I can make a connection, sometimes framing smaller and sometimes framing larger.

What do you mean by framing smaller and larger? Why is this important?

I think that framing smaller and larger is a regular task for an artist. It includes the possibility of moving from the personal to the larger narrative. Or, in reverse, moving from a big idea to find the tiny stories that make it emotional and meaningful. If you can find a way to connect the small, intimate, detailed stories we hear from people individually to a bigger idea, inevitably that helps people feel that they and their experiences matter.

I still don't get exactly how it works. What do you do on a residency?

It depends.

It depends on where you are in the arc of the project. We often talk about a big funnel. For a while everything is possible. We talk, we listen, we generate, we gather, we teach, we make stuff, and it is all okay. Of course we say that everything is still possible, but we are also listening and noticing carefully for the most forceful and imagistic ideas. Then at some point we flip the funnel, and suddenly things don't fit. I actually imagine the funnel as a cone, now heading toward its narrow top. As we aim for the finale, we begin to exclude possibilities. These exclusions may have to do with scheduling, with commitment, with concept, with venue. But the reality is that not all things move forward. And as we aim for the conclusion, we move from creative process to art-making. Now we have to mediate competing loyalties, do lots of editing, and make difficult decisions. In the Portsmouth Shipyard Project, where we had a large advisory group made up of all kinds of folks from various parts of the community, every meeting was punctuated by the question "Have we flipped the funnel yet?"

Some decisions are excruciating, but some are simple because of the many non-artistic factors in play, such as space and resources.

Oh right, resources. How do you find resources?

It depends on what you mean by resources.

Of course we need the money to underwrite all the time residencies take. But within communities there are so many different ways that people present their willingness to help. This was particularly true in Eastport, Maine, a community devastated by the loss of its fishing and canning industries. To start the year 2000, we were going to meet the first light of the new millennium in this easternmost city of the country. Much of the population in the town was willing to get up in the middle of the night to rehearse one more time the event on the dock.

Some people were interested, but certainly not interested in dancing. I mentioned somewhere along the way the need to be up high to oversee it all. And the next thing I knew, I had a brand-new pine box to stand on and the use of a huge cherry picker. I was overwhelmed with the kindness, the usefulness, the willingness.

It was also in Eastport that the local shipbuilding school decided to make lanterns designed so people could write on them. These lanterns were placed all over town, and citizens wrote whatever they wished regarding this momentous change in the calendar. Then at midnight on the turn of the century, after the governor spoke and after some fireworks, the boats took all the lanterns out to sea. It was beautiful.

Okay, so you listen, talk, teach, rehearse . . . do you perform?

It depends on what you think of when you think of performance. I would posit that if performance is "being on" and "aware" and trying to make connections between art and audience, then you could argue that there's never a time when we're not performing. Just taking a few minutes to set up why we are visiting a class is a kind of performance. You are facing a roomful of college students sprawled on their chairs, listening to iPods, plugged into computers or last night's dorm chatter, and you are given maybe 120 seconds to make a case for their attention or their participation. It is a performance.

But we also do plenty of performing in the traditional sense. These performances might take the form of a demonstration in a class. They might take the form of a section of a dance shown out of context but nonetheless danced beautifully. They might take the form of a short pre-Kiwanis lunch show or a partial performance in a school gymnasium. Sometimes such performances are work-in-progress events that include material from the local community as a project begins to take shape. If we are researching a stage piece, we might hold a discussion with a person who has helped our thinking and follow it with an improvisation that responds to the conversation at hand.

And usually somewhere along the way there is a formal concert. When we do our jobs right, it takes place before a sold-out house because we have come to know so many people. Usually there is great enthusiasm and spirit.

Residency. Artist-in-residence. It's an interesting concept.

Once at Wesleyan University, one of my residency activities was to meet with a committee set up to look at spiritual issues on the campus. The college was going to be hiring another chaplain and was trying to see what was needed before it began a formal search. We had a lively discussion, and somewhere along the way, for some reason, I suggested the committee think of the chaplain as if he or she were an artist-in-residence. This idea was greeted enthusiastically. Somehow it liberated the people sitting around the table to think differently. I'm not sure if it was the artist part, the residency part, or the short-term implication that caught their attention. That was one of those moments when I realized how lucky I am to be able to wander through life the way I do.

Dilemmas of Practice in Art and Healing:
Response to an E-mail

···

Subject: Questions from Lucia
Dear Liz,

Do you remember the question that I asked when I met you two weeks ago? I have worked for four years using dance and movement with women suffering domestic violence, and for one year with persons in addiction rehabilitation. In both experiences I felt that I was on the thin line between therapy and community-based work. Sometimes I really don't know how to react, because I do not think that everything in this process needs to operate on the level of therapy. So I have questions about how I control my role, and how can I know and strongly name my role as facilitator and not as therapist.

Or does this mean I need to study for a master's degree in therapy? My thesis advisor asked me, "How can you help people in this kind of work if you don't have the skills of a therapist? Are you putting them in danger with activities that bring forward their emotions?"

But I don't think about it that way. I have watched the beauty in the process with those great women, really connecting the body with the soul, without the rigid requirements of "therapeutic" progress.

Thanks again.

Lucia Serra Estudillo
USF, exchange student from UIA Leon, Mexico

Subject: RE: Questions from Lucia
Dear Lucia,

First, thank you for your response to the *Small Dances About Big Ideas*, and for your large and important question about the relationship between therapy and community-based dance practices. Before I try to answer the question, let me say that Martha Minow, the woman who commissioned the piece you saw, also wrote a book called *Between Vengeance and Forgiveness*. Interestingly enough, she too addresses issues of therapy, in this case in relation to the courts and the legal ramifications of human rights law. So you might find the book and look into the way she characterizes the evolution of the law in a therapeutic sense. It perhaps suggests that we tend to categorize any healing process as therapy when in fact the therapeutic piece of it might be quite small. There are, I think, many other things going on for a person and for a community of people who choose to confront difficult experiences. I think we do a bit of a disservice by labeling all of this as therapy. There is a lot of territory between noticing our feelings, trying to change our experiences and behavior, reliving, celebrating, sharing our histories and even taking some kind of action.

PART ONE

In the beginning I used to say that all artists do art as a way to feel better. From the very start, I am sure I turned to dance as a way to improve my own condition. Even as a small child I saw that twirling made me laugh, that jumping made me enthusiastic, that holding hands and swinging someone else made me feel connected. These are good things, I thought, and though I might have only stumbled into these realizations, I did everything in my power to repeat the experiences that caused the feelings.

When I actually started to take dance classes, I found a few other things very quickly. First, that I had efficacy in my own existence because I could see that by applying myself I got "better" at what I was doing. My capacity to achieve whatever my teachers were asking me to do it was strengthened the more I worked on my skills. And once, when I was about eight years old and just standing at the barre with the other little girls, I had an amazing revelation: I sensed that I could be completely myself and alone in that moment, if I wanted to, or I could think of myself as part of a group, this line of young women. It made me happy to notice that I could control the way in which I identified myself at that moment and that a sense of belonging was in part mine to bestow upon myself.

I think you can see that I am building a case for the therapeutic underpinnings of artistic discipline. But I don't think we notice these things quite this way as we grow and build our artistic palette. I don't think that people in the field address these skills as therapeutic either. They only become therapeutic when we use them with populations deemed bruised or hurt by circumstance or by society.

This is a significant omission in our thinking about art, and it is why you are having part of this dialogue with yourself. That is, we have failed to understand and notate the amazing skills that artistic action brings to serious practitioners. Of course we get better at making whatever our chosen art is, if we are fortunate enough to have good teachers and a healthy amount of self-drive. But we are also gaining other skills too, and an ability to see them, understand how they arise within our artistic domain, and eventually harness them for their multiple uses. Well, that is a big learning curve.

And later still, having accomplished some of that, we might find ourselves in situations where we are teaching art-making and drawing on these other skills too. In my case I realized that holding together an ensemble of dancers, none of whom were asking or expecting therapy, nonetheless required that I use many skills that went beyond my dance training or my choreographic curiosity. I used many tools borrowed from other aspects of my life to keep the collaboration alive and vibrant. We didn't call it therapy because these folks weren't in "typical" troubles. But in many ways the emotions that arise in our art-making sessions resemble those that might come up in any community-based practice, and I believe our ability to meet them head-on makes for a better work environment, and perhaps better art, though for sure others might say otherwise.

PART TWO

After about a decade of working in senior centers, prisons, schools, and hospitals, I found another answer to the question you have posed.

I said that a therapist has a contract to make a person feel better. I have a contract to make art. And by the way, when you make art you do feel better. The feeling better is a byproduct, not the goal. And later still I would sometimes amend this statement with a controversial notion that the more I challenged people to make better art, the better they would feel as the project came to a close. This latter idea has actually been born out in the research of Dr. Gerald Cohen, who has been studying the effects of art-making on older adults. According to his metrics (all health-related, such as number of trips to the doctor, how much medication, etc.) older adults involved in art do feel better. But what really works, he says, is when they are challenged. It cannot be just some little condescending creativity session. People have to work hard.

Over the years I have come to see how my methods of art-making have evolved as I have worked with folks who are new to it or with those who might be characterized as needing some kind of therapeutic help. If you go to our toolbox online, I think you can find some of these thoughts. But here is one just to give you a taste of what I mean: when we have done a process together and I want to get feedback from the group, I will ask, "What did you notice, what did you experience, what did you observe." I never ask, "What did you feel?"

Why? Because if I ask them how they feel, I often think I get what they used to know about themselves. They say what they have felt in past situations similar to this. They cannot get themselves into the current moment. And secondly, if I ask how they feel, then they think—and I agree—that I must listen to the whole story. In art-making I can cut them off. In fact, in art-making, learning to cut oneself off is a tool of great importance. You begin to see that you don't need the full story and that learning to discover the "fragment of worth" is very powerful.

The inquiries of art-making and therapy overlap. On occasion I have moved to the therapeutic solution rather than the best one for art. When this happens, I usually have to check on my own personal goals and on the invitation that brought me to this point. For example, in my work at Children's Hospital I found that some of my own measurements for success had to be rethought. And in that rethinking, some of the ways I taught or what I was looking for changed significantly. It turned out that trying to unlock the most interesting movement, a goal that persists for my choreographic self, was not the best approach if a child could only move one hand. In that case, simply getting participation was success in itself, and I had to change my notion of what made it good. In fact, what made it excellent even was keeping the young woman engaged long enough so that her "audience" of parents and other patients could see her hand, and thus see her in a new way and applaud her accomplishment for the day.

One reason I have organized my life the way I have, with one foot in the art world and one foot in the community, is my realization that each of these shifts in my goals taught me something useful to take into the other realms of my work. Although I might "compromise," I was not going to have to give up on my journey of discovering interesting movement. I could take that aspiration elsewhere. There would be other communities and other dancers with whom I could partner to help me pursue that one. Meanwhile, working in the hospital, I could quietly go about my business of making dances with children whose bodies were in desperate need of release from pain, frustration, and lack of ownership. When she danced with her hand to our music, a young hospital patient was liberated in ways as profound as any professional dancer at her technical best under the lights in a big theater.

PART THREE

But your question has another side. Which skills do we need to be able to handle the emotions and needs of the people we work with, and how do we get them? Some of those skills we learn on the job and some we acquire in more structured ways. You, of course, will be the ultimate synthesizer of all that you already know and that which you take from others. And I am sure, there are some very good programs out there that could give you skills that you need.

Sometimes I have gained entry into difficult situations by partnering with folks who do have those skills already. Thus, while at Children's Hospital I always had with me a person the hospital called a "child life worker." People in this job always had a lot of expertise in medical areas but were not medical workers themselves. They made sure I did nothing dangerous and nothing that might have brought harm to one of the children. Over the years this has become a very important part of my understanding of this work. *Know how to partner.* This means that I don't have to have the same knowledge as other experts in the room, in the field, in the world. I do have to know how to work with them, and together we have to make up a way of working so that we can serve these people in front of us. This has proved true whether we are talking science, religion, health, almost any field.

I think you already have a lot of those skills. I think of them as listening, watching, knowing when to act and when to step back, how to check in with someone and what to ask when checking in. A big one for me is also making sure to check in on what my partner's imagination is doing. Sometimes we are each making up stuff in our head that is affecting what we are doing. Failing to realize this is what gets us into trouble.

PART FOUR

When I first started all of this, I did have a few therapeutic skills under my belt. They grew out of a several years of practice in something called Reevaluation

Counseling, or RC. I had found this practice quite by chance in my early twenties and had kept it up formally for almost ten years.

I raise it here because it, like many systems, has within it some basic ideas that have served me well in my various capacities as teacher, leader, facilitator, choreographer, and mother. I don't know if it is better than others, but I do know that it has made me aware of what emotions can do to a group, and I have felt that it gave me some skills in decoding various moments that might otherwise sabotage a teacher.

What are these? One idea in this form of counseling, is that crying, laughing, shaking, and sweating are good. And that by doing these things we are actually paving the way to changing our patterns. (This is not the time to go into the whole deal with RC, you can find that elsewhere. But I do want to take a little time explaining how I managed to "borrow" from it and show you at least one way we can take trainings from one place into another.)

Within RC you do a lot of practicing of being around people who are crying. In fact, you try to make it happen. This turned out to be of great use to me in workshops, because very often people cry about some of the subject matter we attend to, or because of the connections they are making, or for a variety of reasons I couldn't begin to fathom. But I didn't have to worry about the tears. In fact, what I worried more about is that when someone cries the whole group wants to stop and comfort them, which leads to two things: it makes the person stop crying and it makes the group stop working. I hated both of these outcomes.

So I just developed a way of explaining the moment. It went something like this: "Crying and having feelings is a natural partner to making art. It is going to happen. This is a good thing. Human beings need to do this. But let's just keep working now. You can keep crying, but also keep dancing." The response is a little miracle every time. The group realizes that I have noticed. The person is taken care of. And we can continue. Usually, at some point I see if the person who was crying needs anything, or I ask someone else in the group to see if anything more is needed. This too is an outcome from my experiences with RC, where the idea of peer counseling is very strong. It doesn't have to be the person in charge who handles the moment. Someone else from the group can do it.

PART FIVE

At the beginning of every workshop at the Dance Exchange, we will say, "You are in charge of your body." I really mean it. And I think if you say it enough, continue to treat people as if they are in charge of their bodies, and give them the skills they need to actually experience that, well, then I don't have to be therapist. I know that not everyone agrees with me, and that sometimes folks are so damaged that even if they want to be in charge of themselves they can't be. But this is my goal.

And if I find that this idea is too far away for success, then before I turn to therapy I turn to bringing in more artists. Sometimes I find that if I have enough dancers with me, and we can pair everyone up, then we can accomplish so much more. And of course, the learning does not move in only one direction. What finally makes this work, and makes it not therapy, is that everyone is doing the learning; everyone is having a chance to grow and change. It is a two-way street.

Before I finish I want to say that some situations require the presence of trained therapists. Some situations place art-making in a secondary role to the needs of the group. And in some settings it would be dangerous to everyone present to not have the right partners in the room. I don't know the particulars of your situation. This may be one of those times. If so, perhaps before embarking on another degree program, it makes sense to partner with someone who has the skills you are looking for and see if that changes things, or if that liberates you to do more of what you envision.

I hope this helps. Keep in touch. I am eager to know how your own work evolves and how your understanding of these ideas changes over time.

Liz Lerman

Structure: The Container That Holds the Dance

At one time, when I thought I was clever and knew a lot, I would say with a slightly knowing attitude: "The structure might be in the content." It was a good idea, and sometimes in small sections of dances it would even be true. But a lot of times it wasn't. Here are some examples:

I worked for a very long time in *Nine Short Dances About the Defense Budget* to get the last section of the piece to be a race about the arms race. No deal. I couldn't get the idea to go beyond a one-second joke. Eventually I dropped the whole section.

In an early solo called *Goodbye Wisconsin*, I tried to say goodbye to the state and its simple beauty by dancing at my mother's grave. I had read a fantastic story about a woman dancing on the grave of her dead children, and I walked incessantly around a square plot I had marked out in the studio, trying to make it work. Nothing doing. I could in no way merge the imagery of the story with the sentiment of my state in relation to my adopted state. I gave up.

While working on a piece about composer Charles Ives, I desperately tried to get a dance to work by spelling the letters I-V-E-S on the floor. No way. That proved neither effective as a way to create structure nor as a floor plan for the movement phrases.

So I soon realized that I might structure parts of dances by looking carefully at the content, but more than likely these explorations would not yield the overarching link I needed. Of course, having decided that, a dance did come along where I found a full-evening structure in which the content suggested the form. In *The Good Jew?*—where I was on trial for whether I was "Jewish enough"—I decided to set the piece in a mythic courtroom. This established the stage, sequence, and style for the whole piece. I can't say that knowing the structure in advance made it easier. In some ways it was more difficult because I was compelled to follow the script of a trial, albeit a kind of dreamlike version. This script forced me to be very concrete for much of the duration of the dance. It was a lesson in what I might describe as narrative discipline. It is no surprise that the next company work, *This Is Who We Are*, was comparatively quite abstract.

So how do I structure work, and why do I consider structure my lifelong companion? Structure is for me the heart of dialogue and dialogue is a source of inspiration. It begins as internal conversation between me and the subject matter. It is a way of testing conceptual frameworks of large and small moments in the dance. It is a way of determining sequence. It is a way of making decisions of what is in and what is out. And all of this can happen with just myself, immersed in the ongoing nature of discovery. Structure is the edge against which everything pushes, the wall which allows for a full body press between ideas and the word "no."

When I am working on a piece, I begin to imagine its presence onstage almost immediately. It's not the steps I see, but bodies and the square of the space and the lights. I can get an immediate feel for the sense of the movement. I mean I can see if it is clean and sharp and austere, or cluttered and sweeping, or full or small, or technically fine or more raw, as it might be with lots of people, probably from the community. I do this kind of imagining while I am walking or driving or in the shower. Anna could always tell if it was happening while we were in the car. She'd say, "So, Mom, are you choreographing right now?" She knew because I would get quiet and stop hearing anything she was talking about.

But when I am chasing a structure, I think about it most in bed, after I turn out the light. I close my eyes and picture the dance happening, and then go over and over what I know and how it can be. At the beginning there is a lot of trial and error. If I am midway in the process, I use actual sections of the dance and simply play them back to myself, often in shorthand while I examine the sequence. Sometimes I get real flashes of insight, ideas, small details, and large comprehensions.

Perhaps structure is such an early friend because most dances start with little else. We are working from nothing except a sliver of an idea. I get to look ahead to how we will structure each moment, each section, the full dance, the full evening. It is all under negotiation. If we make this decision, it means that something else has to happen, which will then affect another decision. It is very chaotic, fun, scary, and frequently—like negotiation—full of compromise and revelation.

One of the unusual evolutions of structure occurred for me as I moved from being performer to choreographer. Although this transition is common in the contemporary dance world, I have not encountered much discussion or literature on the strange and mysterious voyage that requires leaving the body as a principal tool of negotiating and taking up sight, mind, and giving direction. It isn't that we stop dancing in rehearsals; we continue, and many continue for much longer than I have. But it took me at least half a decade to learn how to tell the difference between how things feel and are understood by *doing* the movement and how things look and what they mean when one is *outside* the movement.

In my earliest dances I often worked by making a solo first, then developed the idea for a group later. Next, as I moved from making solos to ensemble dances, came a period when I would perform alone as an introductory experience before the group took over. In some dances I return again and again to set the tone, the narrative, and to tell jokes, acting as a kind of intermediary between the stage and the audience. Gradually, I began assigning this key role in the structure of a work to other performers, until in *In Praise of Animals and Their People*, Peter DiMuro portrayed me, complete with a wig and lip-synching to my voice on a recorded track. As the piece progressed, he slowly became himself. A period ensued during which this kind of interlocutor role was shared among several performers, became more submerged into the fabric of the dance, or disappeared entirely. It is only since we have been doing the animated keynotes—public talks and dialogues illustrated by dance excerpts—that I have resumed my role as narrator.

Another way I set my ideas up inside a structure was by using prologues. Many of the earlier dances worked in just this way. *Woman of the Clear Vision* began with a little solo by me to set the context. *Elevator Operators and Other Strangers* had a long prologue that had no direct relationship with the subject of the piece. In that dance I played with the idea of how far we had come as human beings, from our primal beginning to our office personas. Looking back, I see that the prologue was almost a first act. Calling it a prologue set it apart from the rest of the dance and gave the audience a chance to think in a nonlinear fashion.

One way to arrive at a structure is to wait, which is completely different from the hunt for structure that haunted the process of making some of my dances. *Russia: Footnotes to a History* was a particularly long wait. When we did it the first time, it was structured chronologically. Then I edited out almost forty-five minutes and started over. I incorporated a little family history to set against the large Russian tapestry I was creating, and I inserted material to crack open the chronology. I still wasn't happy, but the piece began to tour. At that time my father used to try to catch us on the road, so he even made it out to California for the opening. He saw it and then promptly told me I had it wrong. The story I was using about my grandfather was incorrect. And then he said, "You know he walked across Russia to escape the army and to save his life"—this because he had been an early revolutionary, even before 1905.

It took my father seeing a flawed version of the dance for him to tell me stories about my family that I had never heard. I was intrigued with how we learn history and how history makes itself evident in the world, so I found the whole experience with my father to be not just personally relevant, but a curious form of research. I realized we could add these odd pieces of information to the dance both as transitions and as interrupters of the action—footnotes, in fact, that I signaled by ringing a bell.

It was an invigorating experience to play with the structure this way. We had the joy of making the piece work by choosing where in the dances we would stop so I could deliver the stories. Arriving at a structure like this is a delightful moment in the dance-making because the questing is over and the process gets down to craft and being open to the serendipity of improvisation. Everyone can feel that the structure will work. In this case, it just took me three years to find it.

It was soon after the complexities of the Russia piece that I began to work more carefully on what I called "the M*A*S*H structure," based on the TV show where several stories are usually carried forward at one time with rough, haphazard-seeming transitions that somehow suggested that the stories continued even when we weren't seeing them, and that things could halt or begin abruptly. While watching the show I often felt that I was in a master class on composition.

Incidents in the Life of an Ohio Youth, a piece I made in 1993 for BalletMet in Columbus, is a good example of the M*A*S*H structure, where it lent a variation to the ballet storytelling model. I think my postmodern view of the usefulness of fragmentation helped me see the concepts more as through-lines than actual stories with full beginnings, middles, and endings. They emerge and reemerge in the dance, using different amounts of time and different strategies for revealing what is important. These concepts took form as characters, repeating physical images, and movement phrases that accumulated dimension and emotion over time.

Incidents featured narratives told in several iterations as well as movement themes that served as through-line, transition, and emotional reflection on what had just taken place or was about to be told. We listened to two men from different periods of history interrupt or take us into the story of the dances. One read letters and diaries from the Ohio soldiers of Sherman's army. The other, a sort of standup comic who claimed to hate history, talked about the Ohio of the present and his own life in the city. A third through-line was the actual story of Sherman's march to the sea. Once each of these arcs was set up, the fun was in sequencing so that they could impart some information or reflect some feeling through the juxtaposition of ideas. What follows what makes a difference. This is just one of many times when, as calculating as I might be, mystery can take over and the delight of new discoveries carries rehearsals forward as we find our way to the end. Who knows why we try one thing before another? All of a sudden the layering, the information, the sense of it all begins to bloom.

Probably the most complex example of this style of working is *Faith and Science on the Midway*, made in 1995 as the first act of the three-year *Shehechianu* project. I have a deep fondness for this piece and for what it accomplishes. Oddly enough, I found that my very tight M*A*S*H structure and my attempts to hide its seams made it difficult for some (mostly critics, not audiences) to enter the work. The stories and characters returned and piled up one upon another until the tiny tragedies of our personal histories and the larger tragedies of some of our best intentions as a society merge in an image composed of two old men, one black and one white, crying in each other's arms. It only works because of what you have come to know, and you only know it because of the interweaving of historical facts, unlikely conversations, and the spirit of prayer that is M*A*S*H-ed together throughout the work.

The arc of making a dance has its own conceptual periods, each with a significant kind of inquest at its core. The potential for multiple through-lines carried forth in sequence or in layers turns out to be a profound way to advance with research and rehearsal. At the time of this writing, you will often find choreographers at the Dance Exchange managing several kinds of inquiry in a certain period, convinced that the dance will have a M*A*S*H structure or will be a suite or might eventually be reduced (in the best sense of that word) to a dance with conceptual bookends. This is a clear case of the structure forming the pathways or walls of the journey forward.

As I build a dance I am asking a whole host of questions that I might loosely categorize as literacy issues. The answers most definitely affect structure. What do audience members need to know, and when do they need to know it? Stated differently, what do they need to learn or discover? Or how do I want them to see, and how fast can they attain mastery of the tools we are amassing for and with them? How we answer those questions affects what we lay out in front of the audience, when, and why. For example, in our *Hallelujah* project for Minneapolis in 2001, we had a particular challenge. We needed structure for teaching the audience how to look at a site-specific piece where they would have their attention directed at some points but would be on their own to make discoveries across a landscape of multiple dances at others. So first, we gathered them in one group to listen and watch the company perform. They heard some of the themes, and saw some images that would be repeating, including water, a Buddha creation story, brides and grooms, and the breaking of glass.

Then the attendees split into two groups to watch two very different works to begin their exploration of the sculpture garden. One was charming and strange as dancers all in red moved under an installation of stone benches while Martha Wittman danced a duet with a tuba player. Here, the audience was being shown a range of images and ways of being in the garden that would inform the experiences ahead. The other piece featured men in white dancing against a stark, dark sculpture to a Chopin etude. This was more like a traditional dance done in an untraditional way (men dancing softly, almost prettily, inside a perimeter lined with white tea cups), raising all kinds of questions about conventional ideas of beauty, since the theme of the event was *In Praise of Beauty in Disorder*.

Once the audience left those two "rooms," people were on their own for a while to discover what else existed in the garden that day. They were prepared for stories, lyrical dances, brides and grooms of all kinds, dishes, strange duets, live and recorded sound, and different kinds of people dancing.

There are many ways to accomplish this task of preparing an audience to watch the dance. For me it matters, although I think it is also possible to start with the overload and slowly strip away the parts so the audience sees that it has learned to see by the conclusion.

Journey, which started as solo in 1980 and employed a series of direct text-movement equivalents, was the first dance to give me the tools to build literacy through the course of a dance. After I completed the solo, I was thrilled with what I had learned choreographically and how I had discovered a way to break out of my conventional movement language. But I also realized I had stumbled into a way to teach an audience what movement meant. By the time I got to *Journey*'s fourth iteration, I understood what could be accomplished. In that version, which we did at our Kennedy Center debut, company member Don Zuckerman made a score of the words, and the company talked and sang as they danced. I made movement phrases based on the original material. The audience saw the solo first. The group piece followed and allowed the audience to move from knowing exactly what things meant to sensing, feeling, and discovering what the movement might be saying.

We have continued to evolve this idea. In *Faith and Science on the Midway*, Andy Torres performed a solo while barking a medicine-show pitch, then repeated the same movement as he told the history of the Mbuti pygmy Ota Benga, who was put on display at the 1904 St. Louis World's Fair. In the repetition, the jokes in the first iteration became the tragic consequences of our prejudices. A more recent formulation of this technique occurred in *Uneasy Dances* in 2002. Martha Wittman's solo, first done to a soundtrack of a single man laughing, is carried out and varied by the full company in the concluding chair section, transformed by the dark and poignant music of Alan Hovhaness. The result was immensely satisfying to me, and both moving and comprehensible to our audiences. Sometimes this device was the entire structure of the work. In these later two examples, it was part of the choreography and didn't determine the overarching structure. Other components of the work served that function.

This commitment to giving an audience a way to enter and stay with a dance is a clue to the various forms of sequencing I have evolved over time and thus to the question of structure as well. In the case of *Ferocious Beauty: Genome*, a work in which live movement and a variety of projected video content are combined in a choreographic synthesis, I paid strict attention to broadening the audience's capacity to view multiple layers and multiple forms of media. First the audience sees just dance, then just media, then just talking, then some talking and media, and then some dancing and media, and finally—twenty-five minutes into the first act—everything at once. After that, the audience can expect many forms of storytelling to bring the content forward. I like to think that the measured introduction of the various forms made it possible for an audience to ascertain the final lushness of image, music, dance, and ideas—then finally to let go and just enjoy the ride.

So far I have been addressing conceptual frames that convey structure and theme. But many types of structure emerge from the movement forms we use. In the case of the 1990 solo for Boris Willis called *A Life in the Nation's Capital*, I used space as the essential maker of the dance. Boris started by moving in a large square, using the whole stage, and was by the end of the ten minutes encased in a tiny rectangle in the middle of the stage, hemmed in by the space with nowhere to go. He and I were totally informed by this early geographic decision. All else followed.

Sometimes a dance has a movement-vocabulary theme. *Flying Into the Middle* is a dance from 1996 in which I set myself in a word and movement monologue against a landscape of nine moving dancers. I knew the piece would be configured entirely in trios until its final moments. But even within that construct I was looking for a thread. It turned out to be the image of stepping on bodies. We introduced this into the vocabulary of the trios early in the piece and in small ways, and then came back to it at the end with a grouping of the full cast, who supported me as I climbed up the ramp of bodies that they formed, making complete the idea of middle. I loved discovering such a satisfying culmination. I can't always know it will be there in advance. It just shows up one day if I wait long enough.

The task of sequencing *Flying Into the Middle*, and to some extent *Nocturnes* as well, was made much easier because we were working with already existing music. The music helps define the narrative, and what comes next. *Flying Into the Middle* used a Tchaikovsky string trio as its score; *Nocturnes* was set to a selection of Willie Nelson recordings, though with the latter it took some time before I really discovered the order of the individual dances. I was thrilled once I knew it, and I was unshakable in my commitment to it, despite the confusion caused by not ending it where the audience expected.

Structure, as I have said, accompanies me from the moment I first begin thinking about a dance. Early in developing *Ferocious Beauty: Genome*, structure was on my mind as I questioned how the piece might overcome the problems that the subject matter of genetics posed. Here is my first writing on that subject, done even before I went into rehearsal with the dancers or knew much of what the content research would reveal:

I am aware that this subject matter can be both awesome and terrifying. That is why I am interested in this subject in the first place. But I wonder where I want to leave the audience? I don't know enough yet. But I have the power to end the dance with something so scary that people might not be able to stand to hold it in their minds. Or I can end the dance with a gentle push toward getting more knowledge, or I can end it with a sense that human beings will be masters of our fate. What choice we make here will color all the rest of our decisions.

And here is my first notion about how to convey the subject matter, describing what would eventually become a single character:

I am thinking about two characters who might be an everyman and everywoman. I need to understand them early enough in the process, because how they behave may affect so much else in the dance. So in some ways the overall structure has to wait as we solve this.

As it turned out, I composed a piece that included a series of smaller units that we called "scientific delivery systems." I delighted in the dilemma posed by this substructure and was amazed to see how we resolved so much of it with technology, a new collaborator in our search for communication.

That kind of challenge and discovery is what makes structure so satisfying as a constant companion. Sometimes it might be the very reason for a dance, as in *Variations on a Window*, which was about the things you see or hear though windows. Sometimes it doesn't fall into place until almost the last minute, as it did in *Nocturnes* when I finally found the proper sequence for the songs.

But—amid all the collaborative dimensions of what I do—structure is my domain, my business. I can wait or I can hunt. I can impose or I can meander. I can greet it as my guide, my muse, or my torturer.

What Is the Toolbox?

Many of us catch on early to the fact that teaching is a great way to discover what you don't know and what aspect of what you do know is worth passing on. The dance field is fortunate in its unique awareness that we have to keep learning, studying, and thinking throughout our professional lives. We see our great dancers in class most days, and it is common practice for touring artists to give master classes in technique, choreography, or management, then to be seen the following day in workshops and training sessions led by others. I recently met an aspiring ballroom dancer who had her sights set on competitive performing *and* teaching because she knew that one fed the other.

The discipline of dance takes a lifetime to attain and sustain. The economics of the profession demand that teaching be a central part of our work both at home and on the road. Because of these factors and because I have been sincerely motivated to share information, I have had a lot of practice developing different ways of teaching people some of the Dance Exchange's practices.

This work has always been challenging because we want to share our information without imposing an aesthetic or feel that would make other people's efforts look exactly like ours. We have sought to identify what is fundamental about our work and tried to pass that on, imparting the essence of actions we have taken and experiences we have had without imposing stylistic or genre sensibilities on the people we are working with.

I was working on this idea sometime in the late 1990s when I went to Arizona for a long residency that had multiple goals and various funding sources. We were picked up at the airport by Michael Reed who was and is still very involved in the most interesting performing arts. In some ways he and I have grown up together as we have experimented over time with the methods, designs, and outcomes of intense work by professional artists onstage and in community, supported by individuals within a presenting arm of a university.

In this first encounter and part of our first project together, he told me that I was to substitute for an artist who was going to do a workshop for teachers about using artistic activities in the classroom. This was fine with me. I loved these encounters and always enjoyed the give and take that inevitably emerged from people who were so dedicated to their students that they would take time to study with artists. There was just one problem. The funding agency for this event had a set of requirements for the artist doing the leading. One of these was that the teachers were to be given an outline in advance of the workshop, so Michael immediately asked me for one. I was my cheery self and said something like, "Oh, we can do that at the end of the workshop. I prefer to have them write down what they did because the act of remembering, writing, and sharing the sequence of events together usually helped to cement the day for them." I suppose I had a satisfied look on my face as I recited this, I being such a believer in my own practice. Michael said that although he thought that was a good plan, it wouldn't fly in this case. We had to have the outline to the teachers on that very day.

I burst into tears of frustration. Michael looked terrible, as if he felt he was responsible for this diva-esque reaction. And then, in all that ridiculous tension, I had a vision. I saw a wall filled with little cubbyholes. Each one was labeled and had a stack of papers inside. The labels were simple statements that described one idea, part of a plan, or tool, which is what I came to call these activities. I saw myself pulling from the cubbies the most likely activities we would do in a plan for teachers. And then, when the workshop was over, actually giving them handouts on the ones we did (because of course, plans change, and once you are in the session, there has to be room for what these particular teachers really need, and for a response to the questions only they can raise).

I turned to Michael and said, "I don't have this now, but I wish I did. I think I can break down what we know into the smallest possible pieces of information. And then when people get their hands on these, and comprehend the basic insights, they can add them up in their own ways to meet their own needs."

This was the beginning of the Dance Exchange Toolbox.

With the help of all of the dancers and administrators at the Dance Exchange, and under the guiding hand of John Borstel, our humanities director, the concept has grown. It lives online and is free. We are adding to this body of knowledge all the time to make it more functional and to document our own expanding ideas.

Just by having the Toolbox and what I call the Toolbox Process, I have come to learn many things. Here are just a few:

It is exhilarating to discover the bit of information. There is something about detaching an idea from other concepts that gives it more power to be useful.

As we submit the tool to multiple uses, we begin to see its various implications. It's as if it is a small gem with many facets. When we practice an idea in different contexts and allow those participating with us to tell us what they notice, it almost always yields new information.

It has been curious to calculate the inception of the tools and then to watch the evolution of practice. These changes compound the dilemma of awarding recognition to a tool's beginning while ensuring that other practitioners have the freedom to develop it further.

We know that these ideas work for artists. But because we have taken them with us into religious, scientific, and educational settings, we see how they can be helpful in those contexts too. It has sometimes been a challenge to get practitioners from other fields to see how this might be so. And as we formulate ways to demonstrate this value, we are again brought up close to the power of the activity.

We try to understand when we have a basic tool, and when we have a sequence of events that leads to something useful as well. The two aren't the same thing.

We are investigating how to use different media to help make the case for the value of these tools.

How do I know the tools work? One way I know is because I rely on older ones when I am tired, blocked, or stymied by the subject. I make variations when possible and discover the nuances by the force of confrontations with real situations. But mostly I know because I see them in use by others, and the outcomes are almost always curious, powerful, and unique to the moment.

It isn't always the tool that is in use that makes the encounter work, but rather the artist who has developed a command of these methods and gained the confidence to be demanding in difficult and exhilarating settings. I see this clearly when I observe the artists who have built their skills while at the Dance Exchange. Elizabeth Johnson got five hundred freshmen at Wesleyan University to make a dance about how their personal lives intersect with environmental concerns and then have their photo taken in a special eco-grid. Vincent Thomas brought a huge ballroom full of restless union organizers to a place of absolute quiet at a Service Employees International Union convention as the crowd was waiting for the Democratic candidates during the 2008 presidential campaign. Peter DiMuro employs the tools with humor and charisma that can surprise participants by guiding them to what they know but can't quite access. Margot Greenlee puts the tools at the service of arts integration for K–12 curriculum development, combining her extensive kinetic background with her knowledge of multiple intelligences and how people learn. Michelle Pearson moves with ease from pre-teen dance classes to support groups for combat veterans to community-leadership development workshops using tools she learned while at the Dance Exchange, but also expanding them with her voracious curiosity and ability to synthesize observation and practice.

Then there is Bea Wattenberg, whom we first encountered as a sixty-something widow when she showed up for a workshop one day expecting social dance. Although she wanted to escape the class, she got stuck—unfortunately for her, and fortunately for us—in a corner far from the door and was too polite to walk through the crowd. She stayed for ten years. Bea found her own path with the tools because she committed herself to bring dance back into her life as a Jewish woman. Midrash, a traditional form of reinterpretation of text within Jewish study, became in Bea's hands a way of reworking the tools and reworking her relationship to her prayer experience.

Sometimes it was through resistance that I came to see that a tool actually existed. In my early work at the Roosevelt, I learned that a personal interaction with each student before class helped me to understand the present moment for each of them. This led to the habit of moving around the room to shake hands or otherwise greet the participants before anything else happened. From the outside it might just look like a nice way to begin things, and it is, but more importantly it is a way to truly gauge the temperament and awareness of the people who have come. We can often discover the kinds of adaptation we will have to make through these early encounters. When we toured, I always asked the dancers to follow this practice, which helped us to meet the particular needs of each person and each group. We were at a state prison for men in western Massachusetts when Bea approached me and asked if I really expected her to go around the room and say hello to each person. I looked at her and saw that she was a little frightened. I said, "Yes, of course," and Bea dutifully went off shaking hands with what turned out to be mostly young Hispanic men. Later in the performance, Bea danced a short solo that told the story of compelling and mundane moments in her life. I noticed that when she got to the part where her husband died, several of the men in the audience were crying. The idea that we make contact in different ways became very clear to me that day, as did the notion that we sometimes reach the universal by being completely personal.

The diversity with which artists deploy these tools brings us to the problem of codification. I once heard someone say about a dancer at the Dance Exchange, "But they don't do it like Liz." To which I say, "Yippee!" or "Damn right, they don't!" It is only by artists making these methods their own that our ways of working will move on in the world.

Codification poses problems that the Toolbox Process seeks to combat. It is an attempt to document and teach process rather than dictating proscriptive practice. This is a paradox for sure, because even as we come to understand and name the process we bear the responsibility for not setting it in stone. In the end then, how it will work is up to the individuals who step into leadership and use the tools.

What makes all of this both rigorous and open-ended is our capacity to be present with what is happening in this moment. Each time there are new people in front of me, I begin that process as the person I have become. Each and every time I am informed by why I am there, why the participants are there, what we are doing, and where we think we are going. Of course I will use the dependable tools that have served me before. When I use what I already know, I can concentrate more in the moment and on the specifics of the situation at hand. The process may look as it did the last time or the time before that, but actually the moment is new and so am I. (This is why I am somewhat resistant to the idea that we could offer certification for people to teach our methods, even as I realize that people need recognition for the effort, time, and resources they have applied to develop their own experience.)

If I follow the newness of the moment and veer off the plan, I then have some choices to make. I can stay on the fresh path, which despite my enthusiastic curiosity can still be frightening. I might lose track of the goals we started with but hope that I am making sense in the newfound situation. Certainly I will have learned something and might even bring about a new understanding of the tool or the process I am engaging.

Two things in history help me think about this challenge: the Talmud and the Constitution. These are two living, breathing documents. They exist with their stories and their principles and their beliefs. But they each exist with commentary from all kinds of people. And the commentaries argue, disagree, and thrive in paradox. It's true that both documents suffered in their origin and early practice because of restrictions on who in society was allowed to comment. But other than that, they are brilliant and alive and challenging.

So as we write our guidebooks or compile our Toolbox or set down our principles, go ahead and say that this is what Liz said or did. But then welcome lots of commentary and opinions and arguments. That way, anytime anyone tries this stuff, they will know they have to see with their own brain, think with their own eyes, listen with their own hands, touch with their own decisions.

Rehearsal, Defined and Redefined

They have it partly right on *So You Think You Can Dance*—the part about laughing and hugging and falling down while trying difficult physical feats. And the worry. But rehearsing is so much more: a weird mash-up of sacred time with shared rituals, emotional dynamics that race forward with undercurrents barely expressed, and strict assignments involving repetition and innovation. On some days these elements combine with breathless speed to produce new ideas and fresh solutions. On other days, they yield absolutely nothing.

Like so many other aspects of art-making, rehearsing is a phenomenon with a clear set of expectations and outcomes, while also being a unique process each time one begins. Different artistic disciplines call for distinct practices, and different directors and choreographers set up very particular environments. So much depends, as well, on where a work of art is in its development. In the early stages, when the ideas are just starting, the emphasis is often on exploration, with all of that word's connotations of adventure, discovery, and danger, accompanied by the need to pay attention to environmental changes and to choose the right crafts and tools to accompany the mission. This stage yields eventually to a phase of shaping, structuring, and editing, calling for a different form of rehearsing. Then comes the detailed "cleaning," to assure that all is understood, performable, right. As performance nears, emotional expectations accumulate, tempered by fear and a realization that so much is still not understood. After a premiere, for some, the restaging and even the rethinking begin. Performers bring their own new knowledge to the room in a more confident way, having made their discoveries with the audience. They are ready to say what moments are working and what moments aren't. We fix.

Rehearsal is a time when theory and practice live side by side in an instant. It is a place for making mistakes publicly and for deep private considerations too. To bring together a group of people willing to struggle to make something and to commit minute by minute to half-baked concepts, however absurd or beautiful or strange, is to be in a most unusual situation. Rehearsals are incredibly demanding. During the making of a piece, a lot of things change, including the people in the room. Most days I am ecstatic to be exactly where

I am, though the feeling of being stupid, frustrated, ambivalent, or wrong occasionally overtakes even the best of my intentions.

When I first began making dances, I led rehearsals in the manner in which I was trained. I gave people steps to do and rearranged them according to some kind of aesthetic taste I had in my head. This worked for a bit, but I was unprepared for how long it took for people to "get" the steps and how often the steps didn't appear to look or feel as I thought they should. In those days I also taught many technique classes, so I tried to figure out how to teach the movement that dancers would need later in rehearsal. But this also seemed a little unfair, as many in the class weren't in the dance, and as someone once said to me, "I wish teachers would teach dance not teach their rehearsals."

I am not sure exactly what caused me to begin to experiment with giving people improvisational ideas and collecting their best efforts. It just crept into the process. But I quickly observed that dancers committed more fully to work they helped build, that they often had better movement ideas than I did, and that my own role changed if the process changed. It got more interesting.

Some Rehearsals Are Expeditions, and That Means Effort of All Sorts

I pack for the day thinking that I have all I need: the right food, the right music, the right research, the right dancing partners, the right space, the right idea to work with. I get to the studio and start in. Then the weather changes and nothing is quite right. As the collaboration strives to move forward on the outside, inside I'm in a small private hell of self-doubt, worry over whether any of this will ever work and concern for the morale of the dancers. I can carry on all kinds of activities to try to figure out what we are doing, but meanwhile my thinking/reflecting/generating processes are firing all at once, and not always in sync with each other or with what is happening in front of me. Eventually it all works out, or at least some of it does.

Once someone came to rehearsal, watched us in this stage, and left pronouncing that he had just observed "happy chaos." I agree with the chaos part . . . and I am mostly happy in its midst, especially when I think we have landed on the right course of action. I am less sure when I fear that our work will be for naught because I haven't quite got the best way to move ahead. But to find that, we need to rehearse more. Eventually insight emerges.

Practice Is Not the Same as Rehearsing, But It Is a Kind of Rehearsal

Not all rehearsals are expeditions. Some are only about repetition. Tedium is a lovely aspect of life if you get to choose when and where and with what you are being tedious, and if you know that by doing the repetitions you get some nutrition. I feel that way about rehearsal days when we are in the stage of getting the phrase right, the unison together, the facing correct. When I am directing, we only get to this repetition stage when we know that the body of work we are practicing will actually be used in the dance. I love to watch the way the dancers attack the nuances of the movement and how their questions emerge because of the repetition. A movement phrase becomes second nature, and the body finds the action on its own. If it is movement that has come to mean something, what was once a challenge is now a way of being in space that brings joy to the dancer. Then repetition is not tedious but rather a glorious way to spend time.

Collaboration Is a Spectrum of Relationships

It is not the same every day. In fact it is not the same every minute. I am awed to witness the flexibility that dance artists maintain in being able to make something, share it, let it go, come back to it months later, reconfigure it, and watch as the solo they helped to craft from their own personally made movement gets assigned to a different dancer. That is why rehearsal is not only about sweat or technique or how to lift another body. Rehearsal is also a time to come to terms with our emotional selves, our ambitions and competitions, our daily questioning about why we are doing what we are doing.

Choreographers Work at Being Challenged in Rehearsal

We develop ways for making things and then we follow them for a while. The content of a piece, the individuals in the company, the stage or site will affect how we rehearse. But each choreographer I know depends on certain central methods. Many of us are curious about the working practices of our colleagues. Our conversations often swing toward process, sending us home refreshed in our commitment to our own methods as well as willing to borrow new practices. I think this artistic borrowing is an essential form of cultural sharing, and most of us do both with deep curiosity and with great pleasure. I think that choreographers are good at this kind of sharing because we are so often asked to teach choreography as part of a touring package or as a form of economic survival at home. This affords constant opportunities to notice what is actually working and how it works, and to observe that these concepts are shared fairly regularly within the profession. When I introduce an approach that I have borrowed, I acknowledge its source to the dancers, although by the time it has been synthesized into a rehearsal period, it will usually have undergone a fusion with other ideas at play. We share cultural borders with our choreographer colleagues. The practice of borrowing changes us in many useful ways.

So one part of a conversation with choreographers might be about how they did what they did in one moment I observed in their work. What ensues is often a detailed description of a moment in rehearsal. And as they talk, I can attempt to picture what they are saying. This is not easy, since their words, actions, and personal shorthand might not be anything like my own. But if we persist, I can both "see" what they are saying even as I am translating and editing it into a form I can borrow. I slip into their process for a moment as a way to expand my own. And then I can't wait to get back to the dancers I am working with and try this new little structure on and see what we can accomplish.

Three Examples

Wayne MacGregor, the resident choreographer at the Royal Ballet in London and director of his own company, Random/Dance, told me how his work with neuroscientists has helped him see the patterns in his interactions with his dancers in rehearsal. Apparently, the scientists named seven ways he regularly works, and he is now busy trying to develop new ones. For example he said that he "sings" to his dancers to get them to try something. And as he spoke, he actually did a kind of "la la" rhythm. In my mind I instantaneously saw what a wild moment that would be in our rehearsals if I went in and gave them their directions with either song or just the rhythmic sounds. The short conversation and quick mutual comprehension with Wayne was sharing of a very high order. Having seen a TV special on Wayne's work just the night before, I could envision all the more clearly his actual practice because I noticed how physically close he was to the dancers as they worked. I realized that I could borrow that too. A practice like this may not quite qualify as a method, but it serves as a reminder to mix up any patterns of interaction I might have developed.

One thing that I love in the work of Margie Jenkins is how the more complex movement-moments still share a tender and human place with the simpler structures she gives us. She is highly accomplished with intricate movement, and watching one of her recent pieces, I admired moments of extreme physicality and beauty. One in particular caught my attention, one which the dancers had repeated more than once in the performance. The next day over coffee, I asked Margie how she made it, and she gave me the most involved description of structures for combining and recombining specific points of physical contact. To anyone listening from another table I am sure her words sounded like a foreign language. But I was busy seeing it all over again, and also thinking how I would translate what she was saying into something I could bring into my next rehearsal period. When I had a chance to try it a few months later, the resulting passage did indeed have some of Margie's magnificent and very physical intricacy, while retaining the character of the dancers who made it. She rehearsed her rehearsal for me, and then I re-rehearsed the ideas with the company. I am grateful for the information.

David Dorfman was the first choreographer from outside the orbit of the company, or beyond Washington, D.C., that I brought in to make a piece for us. Earlier he had re-mounted two of his existing duets for an intergenerational cast, and that had gone so well we decided to have him make something new. *Breaking the Plane* was danced on a stage covered with leaves and had a kind of heavenly surrealism to it by the time it premiered. Having a different choreographic process and sensibility in our midst was also, from my point of view, heavenly, although that may be true paradoxically because of David's humanity. What was so enlightening to me was to watch him wait. He didn't just wait for a second or two; he waited for full minutes at a time. And he didn't give people a break or send them out of the room or go to the corner. He just stood his ground, went somewhere inside his head, used us in his mind, and then returned with tasks, physical ideas, ways to proceed. As much as I wanted to borrow this amazing capacity of his, I found I couldn't. But on some days I try to channel him, and give myself a bit of time to sit back and let the molecules rearrange themselves in my internal environment and my external vision.

The idea behind these examples is not that I am going to be Wayne or Margie or David, or that I am trying to make the dancers in my rehearsals look like theirs. It is not the product or performance or outcome that we share, but rather the knowledge that our rehearsing processes are ever-shifting maps that we can willingly give each other to further our individual quests or the needs of our field.

Coda

A few years ago I met Martin Seligman, a professor at psychology at the University of Pennsylvania. What follows is an oversimplification of his work, but at the time I met him he was interested in investigating our human assets as opposed to our pathologies. An approach he took was to bring together an odd assortment of people to reflect on "genius." One speaker, Bob Scales, a former three-star general, talked about different kinds of genius within the military. He described a young man who excelled in Viet Nam because he could always somehow "intuit" which side of the hill to climb in order to safely lead his troops into and out of battles. As he explained, I thought to myself that this soldier was probably "embodying" the hill in his mind. That is, by becoming the hill, he could see or imagine what was lurking on the other side. I think of this kind of ability is a choreographic way of thinking, partly because choreographers need to be able to see in a full circle and realize there is always a back side as well as the front, and partly because you have to have the notion that by being something other than yourself you can get new information even while you are, of course, merely yourself.

I commented on this and thus set up a conversation about the relationship between the physicality of soldiers and dancers. This early exchange paved the way for a later one in which I was able to talk about the way we use rehearsals to move from imagination to reality, from theory to practice, and the speed with which we can organize ourselves because of skills gained in this process.

The general got very excited. I think he might have actually stood up, but I know he took the floor and stared to talk fast. He said that they were having trouble training soldiers using simulation activities because they somehow weren't real enough. He wondered aloud if rehearsing wouldn't do it better.

What's the difference? one might ask. Well, maybe no difference, really, but the opportunity of using new language brings with it the opportunity for reflection, examination, and then recommitment. It brings with it the possibility that by listening carefully to the implications of the new word, someone who had been asleep will wake up because of a small change or nuance. And if everyone wants to get to the innovation, the new idea, a better way, or just improve, well then anything that can push people to reconsider is worthwhile.

Of course in my mind there is a real difference between simulation and rehearsal because rehearsals are not pretending. They are 100 percent real and demand absolute commitment. It is a terrible rehearsal if people think it doesn't count. For one thing, someone will get injured if we are not all paying attention. And we won't remember what we built together, and we won't discover the underlying idea we have been working toward unless everyone is at full power. We can't get to the next step if we haven't all focused together with great integrity and full emotional and physical readiness. What profession wouldn't want that in its workforce?

Free Fall

My first job out of college was a teaching position at the Sandy Spring Friends School in the Maryland suburbs of Washington, D.C. I had always loved history, a legacy from my father, and I got the job because they needed a history teacher but wanted a dance program too. I was the perfect candidate. Actually, I could not have known any of this during the interview because the whole conversation between the headmaster and me took place as if it were a Quaker meeting. He just waited for me to talk, or maybe he would have talked had I let the silence last long enough. I am not sure. But I know I eventually talked about my love of dance and my desire to understand history, and somehow he hired me. I was just a few years older than some of my students.

Toward the end of the first semester, I decided to give the kids an assignment that I thought would open their minds to the mystery of history. I wanted them to see first-hand how truly difficult it is to know what has happened, and to have the opportunity to investigate the dilemma of ascertaining historical truths. So I picked a Friday and told them that on the following Monday I would collect a two-page essay describing what had happened that day. It would be, I said, a history of a Friday at the Sandy Spring Friends School.

Class started with much excitement on Monday. I decided to have people read their papers aloud. At the conclusion of the first few, the students were still expressing quite a bit of enjoyment over the variety of perspectives and even over the discrepancies. But by the time we were into the eighth or ninth essay, an unease had settled on the group. There was absolutely no agreement about anything. By the end of the hour, I had close to a rebellion on my hands. One student said on the way out the door, "Thanks for taking the rug out from under us. This is not just about history anymore, this is about life."

Welcome to the world of free fall.

I have often thought about that moment. To me there was and is liberation in the notion that all of us have our own experience that is truthful and unlike that of any other person. I hadn't considered that the assignment would in fact point out to these high school students that their natural way of seeing even the most standard activities of daily life was not, in fact, shared precisely by anyone else, and I hadn't expected the comprehension of that idea to scare them.

What I have come to see since this experience of almost forty years ago is that not everyone likes free fall or is prepared for it. The thrill comes to those of us with a long history of practicing and making things—most especially, making things in which methods emerge from process.

In my early days of choreographing dances, I used to marvel at the fact that we would begin a project with absolutely nothing. No script, no movement, no light, no costume, no character, no thing at all. And then by the end, we had accumulated, through a thousand small decisions, an experience that could be shared by a few or by many. We had willed into existence a whole world. Of course, because we work in dance and live performance, it was a world that would dissolve again each night. But that too led to the wonder I felt about the whole endeavor. And perhaps the very transience of the world has contributed to my belief in our capacity to make what is needed, let it go, and then make again. In other words, go ahead and pull the rug out because I will just put another one in when needed.

These early experiences prepared the way for the larger projects involving whole communities. Here too, nothing at the beginning, sometimes not even an idea. In fact, part of the making was figuring out what we would fill out the space with. Over time, with fits and starts and chaos and mistakes and tears and sweat, something would emerge. We might have focused a lot on the final event, but what actually constructs the liberation of free fall are the countless methods tested over and over with small variations. These methods became my parachute. The more I had amassed, the bigger the dive, the longer the drop, the more radical the experiences.

As I have come into my later years, I appreciate ever more this experience of free fall. It feels good because I can count on the methods I know to save me or at least soften the landing. But what is really thrilling is when the nature of the fall forces me to find new methods, new tools, new solutions, new processes.

Portfolio of Stage Dances

Woman of the Clear Vision (1975), a dance in which I portrayed both my mother and myself. Photo: Marte Birnbaum.

Memory Gardens with Sally Nash and Jeffrey Janowitz (1976). Designed by Ingrid Crepeau, the giant puppets each required three operators. Photo © 1976 Michael Hauptschein.

Elevator Operators and Other Strangers (1978): Pamela Lasswell, Bob Fogelgren, Colette Yglesias, Jim Patterson, and Marty Belin. To a song called "You've Got to Plié," office workers imagine a different kind of life. Photo: Dennis Deloria.

RSVP (1979): Thelma Tulane and Liz Lerman, with Paul Sarvis and Rima Faber, background. Thelma fulfilled a childhood dream when she became a regular performer in the early days of the Dance Exchange. Though her mother was in vaudeville, her grandmother had forbidden her to dance. Photo: Julie Wiatt.

Journey (1980): Liz Lerman. Using the text "Self-Accusation" by Peter Handke, *Journey* employed a method called equivalents in which each word is performed with a corresponding movement. This was the movement for "between." Photo: Anderson Associates.

In the Gallery (1981). Five years after the founding of the Dance Exchange, we were invited to perform at the Kennedy Center for the Performing Arts, where *In the Gallery* premiered. This dance featured a nude figure model, museum goers, and dancers embodying various aesthetic viewpoints. At the end of the piece an 80-year-old woman disrobes. Photos: Dennis Deloria (top), Dennis L. Albrecht (bottom).

Docudance: Reaganomics (No One Knows What the Numbers Mean) (1982): Liz Lerman, Helen Rea, Bob Fogelgren, and Diane Floyd. In some of my work combining movement and the spoken word, I would speak directly to audience members, acting as an intermediary between them and events on the stage. This was the case with the *Docudances,* a series of pieces about current events that earned us coverage in the *Wall Street Journal* and on *CBS News* and NPR. Photo: Dennis L. Albrecht.

E. Hopper (1984): Jess Rea and Charlie Rother. Visual art and the way that visual artists think has been an inspiration for many choreographers. This piece was based on the work of American painter Edward Hopper. Photo: Deborah Dunnell.

Still Crossing (1986): Jeff Bliss, Beth Davis, Don Zuckerman, Deborah Caplowe; Vanetta Metoyer, Charlie Rother, and Jess Rea on the ground. Commissioned for the centennial celebration of the Statue of Liberty, *Still Crossing* was premiered with the twilit New York harbor as a backdrop. Photo: Bob Fogelgren.

Sketches from Memory (1987): Seymour Rosen and Don Zuckerman. Working as an intergenerational company opened up many possibilities for narrative and imagery in the Dance Exchange's work. This was one of several father/son duets I choreographed over the years. Photo: Sally Daniels.

Docudance 1990: Dark Interlude (1990): Thomas Dwyer, Bea Wattenberg, Beth Davis, Boris Willis, and Charlie Rother (clockwise from center). In the wake of funding controversies at the National Endowment for the Arts, we examined the notion of obscenity. Photo: Michon Semon.

The Good Jew? (1991): Naaz Hosseini, Thomas Dwyer, Tom Truss, Amie Dowling, Boris Willis. *The Good Jew?* initiated a cycle of pieces that examined questions of identity, occupying me through most of the 1990s. Photo: Peter Schweitzer.

Shehechianu: Faith and Science on the Midway (1995): Kimberli Boyd, Bea Wattenberg, and Rome Quezada. We conducted extensive research to evoke some of the events and people of the 1904 St. Louis World's Fair. Bea Wattenberg portrayed Shifra, the Palestinian Jewess, while Kimberli and Rome reenacted the dance of the Princess Raja, which had been documented on a film that we discovered at the Library of Congress. Photo © Matthew Barrick/Barrick Photography.

Hallelujah/USA (2002). After creating distinctive pieces in fifteen communities across the country with the *Hallelujah* project, we gathered more than 100 participants to help recreate some of the work's key segments at the new Clarice Smith Performing Arts Center at the University of Maryland. Photo © Stan Barouh.

Dances at a Cocktail Party was created for the Tampa Bay Performing Arts Center's
American Music Festival 2002: "Bernstein, Broadway, the Bomb—The Age of Anxiety."
Intermittently, we've had opportunities to perform with live musicians. Here the
collaboration enlivened not only the dancing but the stage set as well. Photo: MJMazzola.

Small Dances About Big Ideas (2005) with Martha Wittman, Kevin Malone, Matt Mahaney, Ted Johnson, and Cassie Meador (top); Lesole Maine and Cassie Meador (bottom). Commissioned for the 60th anniversary of the Nuremberg Trials, *Small Dances* was a character-driven piece featuring such figures as Raphael Lemkin, the relentless activist who fought for recognition of genocide as a war crime. One of the requests in our commission from Harvard law professor Martha Minow was to return to the body as an aspect of genocide. This led to the "autopsy duet," portraying a forensic anthropologist and an ethnic-cleansing victim. Photos: Chris Randle (top), Enoch Chan (bottom).

Ferocious Beauty: Genome (2006): Gesel Mason and Shula Strassfeld (foreground) with Ben Wegman, Thomas Dwyer, and Elizabeth Johnson (background). Recorded and live-feed video were integral aspects of the choreography and essential elements in imparting the scientific content of this work. Photo: Andrew Hoxey, courtesy of the *University Daily Kansan*.

Ben Wegman at CERN. Photos: Amelia Cox.

Transdomain Practices

Calling the Ancestors

There were two of us asked to open a statewide conference on arts and education in Hawaii: Hula master Raylene Jackson, a beautiful woman in her sixties with hair down to her waist, and I, standing before a large room filled with expectant and passionate conferees. She went first and began chanting an ancient melody in an ancient language that quickly transported me and everyone in the room to a place that words cannot explain. "Bring in your ancestors," she translated. "Bring them into the room with you."

I began to call to mind my ancestors. I saw my parents and their parents and then those before them, all envisioned in the form of photographs—the only evidence I have of them—a flashing of faces in various sepia tones. Then Raylene asked us again to bring in our ancestors. I couldn't think of any more in my family line, as the rest were lost somewhere in nineteenth-century Eastern Europe and, before that, Spain (or so my father liked to say). So I began to think about my dance ancestors. I picked and chose from a company that included Isadora Duncan and Helen Tamiris, from the cowgirl in *Rodeo* way back to Marie Camargo, the first to shorten her ballet skirts. Still Raylene was chanting. So I moved to John Cage, seeing my connection to him through the intertwining of his art and his thinking. On to Marcel Duchamp, noticing that he entered my imagination from two places at once: the formal art side, where he practiced his sly form of transgressive behavior, and the community side, where I envisioned him playing chess in public, making art in whatever time and place he chose and inviting others to see it with a fresh countenance.

Raylene chanted on and now I was into it. Thomas Jefferson, FDR, and then Norman Thomas, the socialist who ran for president in my youth and whose picture hung at the top of the stairs of all the houses I lived in with my parents.

Finally Raylene stopped chanting and said quietly, "You are not alone, you never were."

There was absolute silence in the room even though it was now filled with thousands of souls.

It was hard for me to give my talk after that. I just know that in those few short moments Raylene managed to get me and everyone else in that room to realize the richness of our past and the diversity of our individual origins. We each belong to many domains, and although we may live in one, we have a history, need, and empathy for others. We are dwellers in the transdomain.

In Defense of Creative Research

....

When I Do This Movement, It Means This Word That I Am Saying

Once I had made the dance *Journey* in 1980, I had acquired at least one choreographic method that aided my interest in subject matter choreography. I
hadn't yet codified it, but I knew that if I took one word at a time and found
one movement or a series of movements to represent or simply parallel it, I
could actually convey ideas and give an audience an experience of movement
literacy at the same time. This was important to me as I felt that the generation of choreographers that I belonged to had left the general audience behind
as we pursued the interesting movement vocabulary that was to become our
hallmark. The sense of discovery that these innovative ways of moving made
possible was worthwhile, but the familiarity and comfort that comes from
recognition had been lost.

I would subject this "equivalents" approach to movements and words to
many variations and a lot more rigor in the years to come. But even at the
start, this technique gave me confidence to proceed in my investigations of
ideas and subject matter. It meant I could be even more fearless with research.
With the research came discovery, and with discovery came the realization
that the dances were a focal point for my own lifelong learning project. Now
I had a reason for going to bookstores, talking at parties to anyone who knew
anything, and seeking in conversations a link to whatever my current interest
happened to be. Now I found a place to put my ongoing relationship to current
events, as well as a place to connect the community stories I was hearing with
larger narratives or smaller details. And because the stage demanded rigor, the
expressive outcomes of the research had to evolve both in form and substance.

The nature of artistic research is unique to the researcher, the subject, and
the ultimate artistic entity that will contain the result. It is true that you can
say that one things leads to another, but it is really more accurate to say that
one things leads the artist to choose another. Oddly enough, as I observed my
own expanding set of methods, I began to notice that once again my artistic
tools and temperament were helping me forge a way of researching that was
broad, mysterious, rigorous, synchronistic, circular, and playful.

I Am Going to Consider Research as a Form of Rehearsal

A project can begin with something as small as an image, a passing statement, or a moment of curiosity shown by a commissioning partner. Anything beyond that is a void eventually to be filled with bodies, text, music, narrative, lights, costumes, and so much context.

My research began to demand its own time frame, which I found easier to maintain if I thought of the research like I thought about rehearsals. What made me start to see it within the light of art-making was the way my mind accompanied the research. If I allowed myself to be an artist researching, rather than attempting to be the scholar of my college years, I discovered a freedom, an agility, and an appreciable increase in the activity of my imagination. It was and is akin to a split-screen computer: on one side, images and abstractions of color or shape, and on the other side, words, stories, facts, statistics, concrete details.

At our first performance of *Docudance: Nine Short Dances About the Defense Budget and Other Military Matters* in 1983, we actually published a bibliography in the program. That drew numerous comments from the press, audience, and friends. I was surprised that it sparked so much attention. Without research, how did anyone think we could make the dances? People seemed to assume that if it is art, it must be exclusively personal expression based entirely on feelings or intuition—and therefore no research would be necessary. I suspect, too, that the stereotype of people who work with their bodies being all body and no mind led our audiences to think that we somehow just made it all up. It might be hard to comprehend that these stage creatures with their practiced bodies might also have a keen interest in the intellectual side of our subjects. It was a stretch to imagine that we might hold two ideas in our heads at the same time—and ask our audiences to do the same.

The Research Doesn't Show, But Sometimes Can Be Felt

I would also discover that audiences don't notice the research. That's because by the time a piece comes to the stage, all the variations and iterations of abstraction and translation have made the research much less obvious. The performance (usually) doesn't contain footnotes or source acknowledgements, and as makers we often can't remember how the material morphed as it led us down the rabbit hole of discovery. And if our audiences can't repeat the particular fact, idea, or sentence that made them think or feel while in the theater, then perhaps they have no way to absorb the notion of research behind the experience.

It was during the *Docudances* period that I began to really track my methods of working with ideas. The first of these current-events-inspired pieces, made in 1980, was about politics and art. In it I said: "How are we supposed to know how to make dances that are *about* anything after decades of avoiding it?" Two years later, while making *Nine Short Dances About the Defense Budget and Other Military Matters*, I noticed that I was beginning to answer myself.

I had a kind of brainstorming-for-the-body approach in which I made a long list of ideas on one side of a piece of paper and a long list of research opportunities on the other. Then I went to work, back and forth between ideas that included not just information but also music, costumes, images, poems. All kinds of things went into those lists because I didn't have to fulfill someone else's ideas about what constitutes real research. The research itself was different too: wandering in the stacks, talking at dinner parties, fingering fabric, looking at other artistic treatments of the same subject, finding and making weird associations with the morning news—it all counted. Eventually I put all of it under the improvisational microscope of rehearsal. The studio became the great analyzing and synthesizing element.

Like all brainstorms, some of it worked and some of it didn't. The editing was partly dictated by what ideas I could make stageworthy and what ideas remained obstinately unavailable to the structure I had established. Now, as I work under the construct of multiple outcomes for the same research, I am able to keep certain ideas around longer because they don't have to fit onstage. They may instead show up in a panel discussion, a workshop, an article, or online. But in my early work, it was the stage or nothing. Sometimes I loved an idea so much that I kept it on the stage well past its worthiness. Other times I could recognize that there was no making a good relationship between idea and subject, and despite all my attempts it was doomed.

Research Might Happen over the Dinner Table:
A Look at the Personal

After the political pieces, I went through a very long period of making dances that addressed the complexities of identity, sometimes as the sole focus of a work and sometimes embedded in larger contexts. I conducted research by reading and studying historical periods, with all that that can entail for an artist, and also by asking the dancers to investigate their own lives and experiences. The content resulting from these two approaches may have differed, but the artistic methods fed each other.

One particularly fertile period included our examination of the *senninbari*, which were belts given to Japanese soldiers during World War II as protective charms during combat. Each belt consisted of a thousand stitches, with each stitch made by a different woman. I was initially drawn to the idea by the communal sensation it aroused in me and because I wondered how the task of making the belts was accomplished.

The most I could learn from available sources was that sometimes women stood on the corner and collected stitches from pedestrians passing by. So when we went to Japan to create a community-based intergenerational project, I expressed my interest—and walked right into a very big controversy that crossed generations, nationalities, and aesthetic styles. Our questions brought up painful memories for the older women in the group. The younger women were careful, but nonetheless expressed their deep disgust about the war, the emperor, and the stupidity of anyone who would think a belt like this could save anyone.

Such intergenerational tension stringently tests this broader notion of research and points toward an even deeper value. Beyond providing information and artistic content, the act of asking, listening, and talking builds a framework in which disagreements can be held with respect and eventually with fresh eyes and ears. I asked if people would be willing to go home and talk within their families about this period and especially about the *senninbari*. I made time in the next day's rehearsal to listen to the stories—many, many stories. It was difficult for me to understand all the nuances as I listened through our brave interpreters. It seemed however, that the women did not just stitch. Sometimes they stitched in defiance. They pricked their fingers and put the blood into the belts. They wove their hair into the belts. Storytelling within families was ignited by the research for the dance, and the information changed the way we made the piece and the way it was danced.

Back on Campus, I Notice That There Is a Difference with This Research

Making both *Ferocious Beauty: Genome* and *Small Dances About Big Ideas* within the same period made me finally notice the amount of research in which I was engaged and to take note of how the research affected rehearsal, process, and product. The fact that we were on so many college campuses as we made these works also provided a useful context for comparing creative research to more academic pursuits, and pressed the question of how these two modes might learn from each other.

If the medium is the message, and if form and content reflect on each other, then one other aspect of Dance Exchange methodology has a big impact on the nature of research. This is the dictum that research yields multiple outcomes. This is a key contributing factor to the nimbleness we feel with the subject matter by the time we are finished, and why, I think, we have a certain improvisatory alacrity in expressing what we have come to learn. Our subject matter gets a thorough going over by virtue of the fact that we have a rigorous process for bringing ideas to the stage, a planning process for workshops, a writing-and-speaking process for program notes and panel discussions, and a reevaluation process for all of the above as we tour. And as we tour we discover even more by observing what actually catches people's attention. Since we have multiple forms of expression to choose from, we begin to see the particular advantages of all the possibilities, whether talking or dancing or video or participation or fast-paced discussion or writing.

Our constant immersion and shape-shifting through all these possibilities leaves me generally dissatisfied when I witness Powerpoint presentations, lectures, or Q&A panels. It is not that these formats are bad. It is just that alone they cannot do justice to the years of research undertaken by the person reporting, and they cannot convey the fullness of any topic to a younger, hungrier generation. How could they? But as long as we accord greater respect to certain academic orthodoxies than we do to other ways of sharing and disseminating knowledge, researchers and their audiences will pay a price in narrowness of impact and sheer boredom.

It was also during this period that I was asked to join a group of eleven choreographers called the Center for Creative Research, which was funded by the Mellon Foundation. It was convened by Sam Miller, long a leader and visionary in the dance field, who challenged us to think about our work beyond the performances and to notice the many ways we could engage with institutions of higher learning. As we thrashed out ideas at each gathering, and occasionally gave witness to each other's processes, the conversation of this group helped me to recognize that we were all doing research and doing it in ways that were both similar and unique. Knowledge about the practices of these colleagues has emboldened my own.

At the first meeting of this group, we agreed to each take ten minutes to share something about our artistic process. Some showed video, some talked, some read. But Eiko Otake moved the coffee table a few inches, then simply slipped to the floor and settled her body between some chairs and those of us close by. Then, over the next few minutes, she let us see the subtle shifts and changes in her body that only she can make. Slowly moving in parts and then as a whole, she rearranged herself among the furniture, which now loomed as large as continents in my mind as I observed her. I had seen Eiko and her husband, Koma, perform before, but always at a distance. The proximity here was truly breathtaking, and I learned and relearned in those moments what more I could ask of myself and the dancers I work with. I wasn't researching, but this was a field study.

I had a chance to meet other colleagues during two trips that I made to Europe taken within thirteen months or each other. On both occasions I met choreographers from several continents. I was intrigued to hear the term "research" come up occasionally on the first trip, then appear in almost everyone's conversation by the second. As I listened, I noticed many different meanings behind the word. On the one hand, some choreographers used the term to denote what they did in the studio, a way of asserting that the physical exploration of rehearsals constitutes a form of research. Others were using research to describe their study of other fields, motivated by the quest for knowledge that would aid in both choreographing and contextualizing the work they were making. And still others were using the word as a way to describe an investigation of the methods they were using to make dances. These choreographers were borrowing from other fields of study to see if it might affect their way of working.

Everything Counts while You Research and Make Something

I had my most recent encounter with this research business at the University of Maryland, College Park, by testing and teaching a three-week intersession course designed to connect history, dance, and physics. Connected to my developing work, *The Matter of Origins*, my subject was Edith Warner, a woman who ran a little teahouse near Los Alamos, New Mexico, and the ripple effect of Robert Oppenheimer's requisition of her services to feed the physicists who were there during the war years.

The problems started right at the planning stage. How was I to convince the various departments of the course's value for their students? Each wanted more of their own discipline represented. I was trying to get them to see that more of a less-familiar discipline might be of greater use to the students in the long run. I am bothered by still having to make this case, but I am almost always sharpened by having to argue.

In this situation I found myself talking about how to use the personal to both notice and engage, as well as to harvest methods of investigation. For example, I wanted the faculty to understand how navigating the personal, rather than avoiding it, could lead to interesting research methods. As an example, I wanted my students to understand the relationship between how they get to know a person in real life and how they might get to know a historical character. In addition, if they really noticed the way they discover their interest in another person—the steps, the different ways they communicate in texting, phoning, or e-mailing—then they might be able to harness these modes to a structure for a work of art that also requires an audience to get to know the subject, and sometimes the artist as well.

So on the first day the students were given some writings by Edith Warner. On the second day they were asked to think of questions they wish they could ask her if she were in the room. I tried to get them to not censor themselves. How do you get to know someone? Where do you start? Do you ask for family or personal history or what they had for breakfast or where they went to school? And what do these questions tell us about ourselves, about our subject, about the way we contextualize? I wanted students to see that they are constantly engaged in research in their own lives. We just don't call it that. And if we could figure out what we are doing, think how our studying might change!

The students were asked to make a project that had to have performative elements that communicated in some way what they had done during their research process. I wanted them to be able to make the research evident either in the performance itself or in some other means of their choosing. But they couldn't just assume that I would know what it was. They could use footnotes if they wanted to, but I expected more because I, too, was doing research and was curious about what new approaches might unfold.

Here are some of my notes from the first week of the course, with a few annotations:

Projects are mediation between your own interests and the research. The making of something eventually moves from the personal to the consideration of audience. This battleground between public and private is a very interesting landscape for learning about oneself, the subject, and ultimately structure and meaning. There are definite advantages to each side of this dilemma, and the compromise that ensues is very tricky, but very compelling.

It is useful to form categories as we listen to both questions and answers. This exercise of "naming" helps us evolve into our next step both for the subject at hand, but also if we want to be able to repeat any of the process we have begun.

So often the process itself is sparked so fast that unless we take the time to name it, the path is obscured later by forgetfulness or at least a lack of nuance.

In the same way of noticing how you might categorize, it is also useful to notice the images forming in your mind/imagination as you listen or talk. If I pay attention to this space, sometimes I am led to just the right image, and if I play with the image I can also extrapolate a metaphor, a structure, or an idea for rehearsal. (As one example, I asked the students to notice how Edith Warner noticed. The only way we could know this was to read her Christmas letters and short essays with that question in mind. There was a one sentence in which she says that she got the news about the atomic bomb and Hiroshima from Kitty Oppenheimer, who had come to visit her kitchen to get vegetables. This led to a discussion about the many ways that we get the news. That in turn led to a new set of research questions as well as a possible structure for a performance piece that could be based on a variety of news outlets, even gossip over a kitchen counter.)

Where Is All This Going?

All this thinking about research is offering me one more chance to claim the power of artistic practice and the role that artistically driven research process-es can play in life beyond the art world. To me this is no longer an experi-ment. Using artistic methods makes learning natural, a discovery, an engine for getting up in the morning or staying up all night. Using artistic process makes knowledge a combination of the known and unknown and makes the researcher an individual with vision, as well as a synthesizer of what has come before. So when my rabbi asked me recently what I thought we might do with the educational environment of the synagogue. I said, "Make stuff." Every-thing—the learning, the discipline, the research—follows from that.

In the end I have come to see research as an act of conversation. It is a com-panion. It is a refuge. It is a source of inspiration of all kinds. I do sometimes end up in an eddy, off to the side of the important stream I thought I was on. But that is where an artist is lucky. Because I can move the whole stream over to the little tributary if I think it worthy, and if I have enough will, I can bring my collaborators and audiences with me.

I love my postmodernism. I don't like the word for it, but I love what it is. For me it means to take things apart and put them back together in new ways, bring unlikely things together and see what you get. And when you do bring them together, put them next to each other in odd ways at random, sequence them out of rhythm or just plain guess, sit back and make meaning.

So I gaily move about the world of shipyards and science labs, schools and synagogues. At times I feel like Johnny Appleseed, bringing my little postmodern basket of tools that I hope plant seeds for new kinds of methods in old places.

At one of these, Temple Israel in Boston, I was working with the wonderful rabbi Elaine Zecher. As we watched some improvisation taking place in front of us, we whispered to each other on the side. I said something like, "I just love postmodernism." Elaine smiled slyly and said, "Fine, Liz, but actually you are doing petichta."

I asked her what that was, by now used to my own ignorance of Jewish tradition and looking forward to one of the many mini-lessons I get along the way of collaboration. But I was unprepared for what followed.

Elaine explained to me that there was a special form of Talmudic scholarship called *petichta*. This approach involved the usual Saturday morning Torah study but with a twist. Someone would bring in a story that had nothing to do with that week's Torah portion. The task of the students (probably many very learned men) was to link the story in the Torah to the off-hand story that had been brought to the table. Though I have since learned that petichta has a more scholarly and narrow definition, the spirit remains the same. It is postmodernism at its best, for sure.

I was reminded of how much that is lost through time can be resurrected, reused, reconstituted and thereby feel as fresh as the newest breakthrough in creative thought. That is why, when I teach people tools for creative practice, one of them is about reviving ancient traditions in new ways. Onward with petichta.

Postscript

As I was preparing this book I decided to check in with some people whose stories I have been telling all these years. Here, in true Talmudic fashion, is Elaine's response to the above version of the tale:

> Thanks for this. I am so honored to be part of the story. I love the concept. . . . [Regarding] Petichta, I wanted to give you the very scholarly definition so that you would have it. The general idea was to connect something from the non-Torah, non-Prophets section of the Bible, which is the Writings (Psalms, Proverbs, Ruth, Esther, etc.) with a Torah verse. That is the technical definition. In the broader definition it could be seen as taking two different ideas and creating a thread/river/pathway connecting them. It was also developed in the 500–600 CE . . . Talmudic times, since the Talmud was written down by the year 500. The other part that you will like is that it means "opening," which is so absolutely postmodern because we have opened ourselves up to the "re"newing/surrecting of which you spoke.
>
> I hope this helps.

Elaine

Fresh Readings: Reviewing Books on Tango and Nureyev

A key concept in transdomain practice is that of multiple outcomes emerging from the same research. A corollary to this is that ideas and movement get tested on multiple stages. So when the *Washington Post Book World* asked if I would like to review two books on dance themes, I jumped at the chance. I was interested to see if I would read a book differently, knowing I would be writing about it (I did read it differently, or at least paid attention in new ways). I was intrigued to have another way of going about criticism and felt that I might be freed from some constraints I would have feel if reviewing stage work by choreographer colleagues. There was some freedom, but there was also a new awareness of sensitivity, which I suppose would be a constraint for some but for me was more just something to notice. And finally, I was curious to see how I would make sense of movement as it is described on the page, and then in turn make it meaningful in the review. It is always the challenge: to make movement matter in worlds where it is impossible to see.

A few quotations from these articles may point to the reason I found the whole experience worthwhile. They also demonstrate the more complicated uses of reviews. As I am usually the person at the other end, I have at times rebelled at the way in which reviewers writing about my dances have used the act of seeing my work as a means of supporting their own interpretation of the world. After this experience I can say, "Why of course." In the following excerpts one can see how the selection process alone gave me, the reviewer, an opportunity to expose, educate, provoke—whether that was the author's intent or not.

In this excerpt of the review of *The Art History of Love*, Robert Farris Thompson's book about tango, I followed the author's thread regarding the use of folk forms. The last sentence in this paragraph is obviously more about my point of view than his, but I was grateful for the opportunity to make it and, even better, to do so in the *Washington Post*:

> Mr. Thompson's points of reference are diverse and illuminating. In assessing the contribution of the great Astor Piazzolla, he introduces a very

interesting comment made by the composer Bela Bartok during a lecture series at Harvard, in which he says that composers could respond to folk music by either quoting the tunes or examining the elements of those tunes—modes, patterns and ornamentation—and therefore create something new. With this enlightening parallel, Mr. Thompson helps us understand the rigorous way in which artists borrow, fuse, synthesize and learn from each other. It is critical for the general public and for policy makers to understand, that when cultures are clashing, sometimes it is the artists learning from each other that makes understanding really possible.

This idea is taking on even more resonance for me as I consider the role of America in a postwar Iraq and in other areas of the world where we will, I suppose, remain as an occupying force. I find myself asking often, what role could artists play if we were to spend real time in these extremely complex situations. As even our military commanders seek to recruit more civilians (they usually mean engineers and farmers, I think), it is interesting to imagine a role artists might play, whether sharing the truth through stories; exchanging artistic methods, tools, techniques; making evident the underlying humanity of each person . . . I could go on.

One other except from this review allowed me to champion the dancers themselves. I took enormous pleasure in noticing something that perhaps another would have missed entirely:

> Because tango is a dance form that has straddled art and life, because some of its best proponents were never on a stage, and because according to Mr. Thompson the elements that led to its birth were so widely and fervently pursued, many of its great practitioners might have been left unnamed. But not in Mr. Thompson's hands. One of the most startling aspects of this book is the time the author takes to name names. He tells us their stories, their habits, their contributions and most especially their styles. Though this litany at times approaches the point of fatigue, dance practitioners will feel validation in reading about so many amazing artists. This book is an honor roll to brilliant dancers, poets, and musicians, people of imagination and passion. It is a paean to all the feet, hands, hips that went before us, to all the dancers who saw, borrowed, stole movement that they loved to see, had to do, needed to try in order to make their place in the world matter. Mr. Thompson makes sure we see their value.

The second review I wrote, on *Nureyev: The Life* by Julie Kavanaugh, presented more treacherous territory for me as it laid bare some of the worst aspects of the ballet world. I tried to find ways to affirm the best of that universe:

Reflecting on Nureyev's sad twilight, darkened by his growing frailty from AIDS, we can easily forget what this remarkable innovator accomplished. At his best he insisted on a male presence in a world of female sylphs, and into the bargain brought his female partners along as real people and not mere swimming swans. He broke the barriers between ballet and modern dance, producing a bountiful cross-fertilization of choreographic concepts. He demonstrated a capacity for curiosity and research that set a standard for his field. He helped hasten the inevitable destruction of the high art/low art polarity, introducing a commercial, pop-star mentality that continues to sell tickets for enterprising ballet companies to this day.

But in fact, the images portrayed in this story were far worse than my own trivial experiences in my youth. And so I said:

It is the ballet world that is left to take the hit for capitulating to a star's incessant abuse of the people and systems that bring art to the stage. The reader wonders how this all could be. Hardly anyone, it appears, stood up to this spoiled creature—which is how friends, colleagues and power-brokers all seemed to see him, as a beautiful animal whose magnetism would be lost if confronted.

The book made me sad. Writing about it helped me find the origins of my grief and connect Nureyev's story to the big picture of art, artists, and the way our thinking about them culturally can hinder the best outcome of their genius.

There is really nothing special in these observations. The implication that each of us reads or sees or experiences a story, a book, a work of art differently is nothing new. Having a platform in which to state ones' reflections was new to me, and I can feel its power to push my thinking even now, a few years later.

Ruminations and Curiosities: A Series of Anecdotes and the Questions That Follow

As I write this, I am teaching a creative process class at the Bates Dance Festival. I hardly ever use the word "creative." Over the years I have found that it has too many bad connotations. It makes many people feel less than themselves, and for reasons that are difficult for a teacher to overcome. But perhaps I've thrown the proverbial baby out with the bathwater. By avoiding the word "creative," I may have stopped seeing the power of the word "creation." This is odd, as making things is the most important single thread in my life. But then I am always happier talking about "making" as opposed to "creating."

When I began to work in religious settings, I noticed that creation was a big part of how people pictured God. For some who struggled with God concepts, creation offered a positive way to think about godliness. Reluctantly, I recognized that ideas about making things were a useful part of the conversation about creation in faith communities. I also saw that this put me back in a crazy loop around understanding the power of creativity as a force in an artistic life.

Growing up, I hadn't really liked the creation story as told in *Bible Stories for Young People*. During the thousands of hours of dance training—in those days, first ballet and later the classical moderns—I didn't much think about the relationship between the way people consoled themselves with meaning and the sweat of becoming a dancer. Even though I wandered between the intensity of a Reform Jewish education and the orthodoxies of the art world, it would be many years before my own work in religious settings would spur me to ponder how the act of making dances might also shed light on the act of making a world. Most recently, as I have pursued encounters with scientists, I have begun to catch the links with yet other spheres of action: passionate physicists smashing particles in order to complete their own truth about how the universe begins, artists obsessively creating over and over, and every tribe in every era making for itself a story of creation. In this crack of light opening into my world, I see counterpoints and mirror images between art, science, and religion. The thousands of rituals, prayers, speculations, missions, practices, philosophies, theories, and all the joys and trappings of varied disciplines have a lot to say to each other as each field strives to comprehend the nature of beginnings.

Going back and forth between worlds has become a passionate way of working, for me and the artists of the Dance Exchange. We have evolved many processes to move a conversation between various disciplines, lines of work, and ways of being, and I chart these under various rubrics in my mind. One of them is what I call "overlapping inquiry." It might be best understood as a vast Venn diagram that layers the content of questions, the method of questioning, and the means by which answers lead to further questions. All these are compared, contrasted, and used as a way of making connections and meaning. In that spirit of overlapping inquiry, I offer the following ruminations from my perspective as a choreographer and teacher, starting with this idea of creation.

Why is creation so powerful? Why do we risk so much to try making something again? Why does it matter so much to artists, scientists, and people of faith how it all started?

There is such a desire among so many to bridge differences of faith, geography, race, and gender. The Dance Exchange often gets asked to make that happen. Over time we have found some methods that serve most circumstances. One of them begins with the idea that we get to know people in their own way first. We meet them on their own ground, in their own settings. We listen to their stories, their perspectives. We may ask each of them similar questions, but we are eager and curious to hear their particular answers.

It was like that in Tucson. In the spring of 2000, as we were working on a multiyear project we called *Hallelujah*, I found myself in the Arizona desert with a film crew and my colleague Peter DiMuro, who was at the time head of the project. Leading up to this moment, we had met many, many different people from different communities. Sometimes they had heard of each other, but mostly in quite general terms. Of course the Native Americans knew of the Jewish community, and likewise, the Jews knew that Native Americans lived among them. Truly, that was about it.

But there we were, out in the very hot sun with religious leaders from these two different communities: Rabbi Billy Lefkowitz, from the Conservative branch of Judaism and head of the Tucson Jewish Day School, and Daniel Preston, a Tohono O'odham tribal leader and medicine man. We wanted to understand how these two men and their people—from faiths born on opposite sides of the world—viewed this environment. These two talked about how the desert was an essential part of their peoples' history and ritual. The spirit of the creator was everywhere, they agreed. Then the rabbi said that God was still creating. That it was our job to take part in this ongoing act by appreciating every breath and every morsel we ate. Then I thought I heard him say that if we ceased this participation in creation, God would die. The Tohono nodded his head and said, "Yes, that is why we do the dances, the ceremonies." But what brought them to their absolute and utter connection was the power of a word, in this case "Adam," or "O'odham," meaning man of the earth, people of the earth. Two distinct cultures from two disparate worldviews, linked in the yellow dirt by a word.

Why do people feel better when they feel a connection? Why does an act of mutual agreement change the way we feel inside?

A few weeks later we captured these statements on video as we opened the Tucson version of *Hallelujah*, an evening-length work called *In Praise of Ordinary Prophets*. The two-thousand-seat house was filled with people from many different communities across the city. The stories we would tell that night came from Latinos, Jews, Native Americans, Catholics, academics, artists, folklorists, endless categories of human hope and endeavor. The second act was to open with a blessing from Daniel Preston. He had received permission from his people to appear onstage with us and to tell his stories. His section was to begin with the blessing while a group of older dancers encircled him with a blend of contemporary and gestural movement devised from the words he spoke. Just before the curtain opened, he came over to me and said, "I just want you to know that I am not going to perform."

I was shocked. All the hours building trust, building an understanding, and building a bridge from theater to community and back again, suddenly lost. "Daniel," I said, "you have to go on. We practiced so hard for this moment."

"Oh Liz, I am going to go on," he responded. "It is just that I am not going to perform. I am going to do a blessing."

Thinking of all the dancers onstage, I said, "Well if *you* are doing a blessing, then what are *we* doing?"

I suppose up to that point I had not felt a need to make a distinction between performance and prayer. Sometimes the same, sometimes different, I knew in that encounter that I had experienced many nuanced moments where the language for these actions was inadequate to describe the uniqueness of the felt event.

Daniel's comment has informed my thinking ever since. Before this moment I had often been the recipient of blessings and had recited thousands of them in the context of religious practice. But I had never quite accepted or been able to comprehend what a blessing actually is. How incredible to think that dancing for an audience might be a blessing that goes in two directions at once.

How are prayer and performance alike? Is a blessing a prayer? Is a performance a blessing?

Leading up to the *Hallelujah* tour, I had spent some time teaching several intensive weeks in a program we called Moving Jewish Communities. Generously supported by the Righteous Persons Foundation, this Dance Exchange institute was designed as an opportunity for dance artists to come together to study and share techniques for using dance inside communal activities such as worship, study weekends, religious school classes, and holiday gatherings. At one point in the week, we developed a series of choreographic studies onsite at a synagogue in Washington, D.C. I was interested in getting the practitioners to see that site-specific activity was a key element to changing the attitudes of temple members about art, prayer, and their buildings. As we worked, it became clear that that we were crossing the lines between dance, performance, and ritual with careless abandon. I wasn't worried until one group did a participatory experience that led to a lot of weeping and hugging: dancers stood in a circle, holding the Torah and crying about how they—as women—had never had a chance to do this in their pasts. At first I mused on how so much of dance is more interesting to do than to watch. But as the dance continued for what seemed an agonizingly long time, I began to get uncomfortable as I thought we were descending into a sloppy acceptance of feeling over form where old wounds would reopen as a means of celebrating victimhood. I was curious to see how the dance/ritual, which was the word I gave it as time slowed down, would end. It didn't. It just stopped when the last person had her turn.

The artist in me was unfulfilled. I suggested that if they raised the rigor of the dance *as art*, by finding an ending and moving the remembered injury forward to a new place, they could deepen the quality of the *religious experience*. I was met with anger and utter disdain.

Why was I unfulfilled and why did I feel such deep discomfort? The struggle to understand why we dance is a big enough question. But the question of why we dance *for others* is even more fraught. Who is the dance for? What purpose does it serve? My own sense is that the context helps us find a particular answer in a particular moment . . . not the same answer for all time. (The classicist might insist there is only one answer, and that indeed might be the definition of the intention of a classical or even orthodox ideal—in dance or worship.)

One thing that might shift the context is the intent behind the choreography. I remember the frustration of a student who was training at the Dance Exchange about our methods for working with older people. I kept demanding more of her, and she finally said in exasperation, "I am a good person, and what I want to do is a good thing. Isn't that enough?" And I had to tell her gently that, no, it wasn't enough. A double standard that allows one level of rigor for performance and a lesser one for teaching or community engagement or worship is not acceptable. Even an old person, or a congregation, or God needs the practitioner to be reaching for excellence. ("Ah," you are thinking, "what is excellence?" That too might be variable, but it does exist.)

When people dance in spiritual settings, the feeling, healing side of our natures may dominate. But we *can* demand both nurture and rigor. This is a very important idea to me, though it can be difficult to achieve without constant practice. In the case of my Moving Jewish Communities students, increasing the rigor might have deepened the ritual, turning what looked like indulgence (at least to someone standing outside their circle) into a process for creating new understanding for participants and witnesses alike. Perhaps my students were in fact busy revising their expectations about performance—much as I had been doing since my early days at Children's Hospital. New contexts may reveal a need for new standards. For many years I thought that I had one set of standards for my theatrical work and another for work in community. But over time I have come to see that there are at least three values I hold regardless of where and when a dance happens. The first is that those involved are 100 percent committed to what they are doing. The second is that they know why they are doing it. And the third, perhaps the most difficult to discern, is that something is being revealed. Maybe my irritation with my students that day in the synagogue was a nagging awareness that their form of commitment and mine were so different. How were they using inquiry? Who got to experience the revelation?

Does performing a ritual require some awareness of form, beauty, and audience?
Should a ritual take you on a journey to someplace new? Are you supposed to be trans-
formed or is it enough to be comforted? Is ritual just for those doing it?

My questions about ritual, performance, and prayer have continued as have
my experiences in the religious world. In the fall of 2006, I was invited to
be the Rabbi Sally J. Priesand Visiting Professor at Hebrew Union College in
New York City. This appointment involved teaching thirty future rabbis and
cantors. I had planned to teach a course to let these clergy discover the potential of their bodies in relation to ritual objects, to use ensemble techniques
to build congregational life, and to play a little in the choreographic world
of text and movement synthesis. I anticipated questions about the use of the
body in prayer and the power of performance as an aid in intensifying the
worship service. All of this happened, but what emerged as the true questions
surprised me.

My students worried about the flow of the service. They felt they had to
be "really good" at keeping the feeling of the experience going without a moment of transition or a break for an explanation. They fretted over how to
do this when their congregants didn't necessarily know the sequence. They
practiced and choreographed experiences that were meant to please the professionals, not necessarily their true audiences. I tried to get them to see that
their congregants liked seeing them as human beings and wanted them as
teachers, not just as impresarios for God. I told them that flow was overrated.

Is flow overrated? Why do we think the lyrical is more spiritual? Can we trust an
audience or a congregation to make sense of things that at first may not seem to "go
together"?

These future rabbis and cantors wondered how they could lead prayer if
they weren't praying, and they found it very hard to pray when they had to
lead. I encouraged them to rethink what prayer was and to consider that—by
being in an authentic relationship with their congregants—they *were* praying.
To stop to make sure everyone is on the same page is a holy act, not merely a
transition, if in fact they believe that having everyone reconnect at the same
time with the same prayer actually matters. I felt like I was coaching dancers in repertory, trying to help them find the value in performing in present
time as opposed to simply making a virtuosic run-through of choreographed
movement.

Improvisation requires paying attention. What is the nature of internal connec-

tion to external demands, and what does this tell us about artistry, spirituality, or leadership?

In my own work in congregational settings, I have come to rely on a concept I call "big story/little story" as a way for people to connect their personal experience with the larger narrative with which they interact from week to week during worship. For instance, working with the ancestral prayer called the Amidah, I might ask the question, "Who in your life has made it possible for you to be here tonight? The babysitter, or maybe a grandfather who helped you find the beauty of your faith?" Through memory or reflection on immediate events, by telling stories and having conversations as people pair off or form small groups, we draw out some images that represent a personal connection to the bigger idea of the prayer. Images become movements that we sequence into a dance that everyone can do from their position in the sanctuary. We may add music, and ultimately we reattach the movement to the prayer or story where it originated. That is when things really start to explode as people discover how the gesture for their own story supports the telling of some oft-spoken prayer or oft-heard passage from the Torah. That moment of connections becomes the spiritual experience people seek.

So I was surprised to find out that my clergy students were very reluctant to get into personal stories as a collective activity and especially to put narratives from their own lives into the mix. Telling them privately, to just one other person, and then disguising the images inside an abstract dance was okay. But to actually make their experience public was uncomfortable, scary, and forbidden. As we explored the discomfort, I came to see several reasons for the feelings this structure had aroused: as clergy they worried that their congregations might "commodify" the story and use it as a weightier form of gossip.

They were reluctant to enter the personal because they were unclear about how to set their own boundaries. They worried that being personal would lead the congregation to feel like a therapist. And they felt that by getting personal they might lose their professionalism—a phenomenon that I'm discovering is not unique to the field of religion.

Can we only be authentically personal in therapy? Does this caution result in leaders becoming isolated in their leadership?

I found my students' concerns about these risks to be disturbing, even shocking, and sad. And I realized that here again I was presented with a commission, a role for artistic process as a tool for people in their own everyday lives. As artists, we use the personal all the time. But we don't *only* use the personal and we don't use *all* the personal. We set limits and create abstractions, variations, and translations as means of furthering our own understanding and then furthering the communication of that understanding. Without the personal we are lost in a world of generalities. With too much personal we are lost in sea of indulgences. Oh, but then there is discipline.

Partnering and People

....

It is ironic that I enjoy being by myself. As my husband, Jon, likes to say, we each like our own company, which is a good thing since we both spend a lot of time alone. Alone time has a particular quality. It reminds me of a big dog rummaging happily through familiar and unfamiliar habitats. Our old golden retriever would circle around and around, searching for just the right spot, and then flop down for a nice long daydream or a good chew on some bone that needed a little more attention. Growing up, I could do just that with my dolls: rejoin the game I had left on the floor up in my room and feast for hours on some odd combination of talking, acting, and ruminating. Alone has a certain comfort. But then we also have our still-adolescent four-year-old hound dog, and it is just as easy to speculate on her kind of alone craziness: bounding with ridiculous new energy toward anything that is calling. Coming from any direction, opportunism overtakes her and she is gone in a frenzy of excitement and pleasure. Either way, by now I know, as do the dogs, how to follow the scent and pursue the trail without knowing the end. I like all of that.

But as much as I like the alone time, I spend most of my work life in dialogue. What follows is a brief look at how that practice has been informed by partners and people and by tricks of the mind.

Irene Eckstrand

It all started in water. I was in the shallow end of a pool at a funky spa in West Virginia, the end that mothers stand while the children splash around and try to swim. The next Thanksgiving we returned to spa, exchanging my husband's storytelling prowess for a weekend of rest in the woods. I was in the pool again, and the same children, including Anna, were splashing around, now a little older. I think it was on the third Thanksgiving that I realized the same mom was also standing there, and so we began to talk. That is how I met Irene Eckstrand, a biologist working at the National Institutes of Health. Like our evolutionary ancestors, we too soon stepped out of the water and began taking long walks, which led to deeper conversations on the relationship of our working lives, including the beauty and rigor of art and science. As I was developing Ferocious Beauty: Genome, *Irene and I met for coffee every few months. That is where I made the conceptual leaps I needed in order to make sense of what I was learning from the laboratories of the scientists and from our own laboratory of rehearsal.*

At the heart of transdomain practice is this concept: apply your ideas and thoughts from one place where you're working, or from one group of people you know, to another. Then let the rehearsal process or the stage or the event be the mediating space. Let the spark move into a new arena and see what happens.

With partnering comes the confirmation of ideas already developed, as well as challenges and interruptions. It comes with doors flinging open on new thoughts that don't even have a house yet. It comes with a lot of wrong turns, good humor, bad taste, and messy, messy ordeals. It can be flirtatious or fatuous, stimulating or sedating, irresistible and irritating. But I persist because most often the encounter yields some strange or brilliant or first-time-ever idea, vision, or experience that moves the whole enterprise forward. Usually I retain a position to be able to stop the worst of it. Not always, in which case the misery is vast, the sleepless nights many.

Most projects require a research period. When the research requires meetings, and when the early meetings are conversational, I often feel like I am going fishing. The talk can be quite passionate, but it has a whispering quality as people get to know each other. I am searching for a hook, looking for the connection that will drive the partnership. It is important to know if this is a person I can spend time with because I know what lies ahead will be demanding, confrontational, communal. Will we be able to get along, share ideas, take criticism, and learn from each other?

But when it comes to ideas, a hook is not enough. It is more like casting a net. I throw out my ideas in a broad and loosely knit construct that includes stories, questions, and histories both personal and public. Then I wait and listen. Eventually I gather in my net to see what has happened to this data and begin to discover what "catch" matters in this place, to these people. Then the next round of conversation will begin.

Bob Harriss

When I met Bob Harriss of the Houston Advanced Resource Center as part of a planning process for a project at the University of Houston, I met someone who was also conversing by casting a net. He too was searching and throwing out ideas and waiting to see what he caught. This was a revelation to me and helped me observe and name an additional quality of open-mindedness: deep curiosity about another field, a capacity to experience and reflect in the same time frame, and a willingness to let new ideas affect ways of thinking whether the subject matter being discussed is crucial or just merely interesting. A few months later, in a performance experiment that came out of this earlier fishing expedition, a group of us—dancers, artists, and environmentalists—came together to drink tea in an art gallery, a barrel of oil as the centerpiece of the main exhibit. Bob stated his definition of resilience as "our capacity to absorb impact," and dancers embodied the idea with swift, intense duets on the hard concrete floor. The audience had an immediate opportunity to investigate the premise of impact and absorption and the challenges of renewal.

Dancing is a good metaphor for partnering. More accurately, the history of dance provides numerous metaphors because of all the variations in what dance partnering looked like, felt like, and in the technical ways in which it has been accomplished. There have been changes in the rules, in the physical capacity of dancers, in the meaning of the touch and the lifts, and recently in the very big question of who is leading and who is following.

My first memory of a lift was in the studio with Florence West. I was probably about twelve and was thrust into the work with the older dancers because I was almost good enough and because Florence's temper had made her lose another body. She had me there to fill in. She had a few women of varying ages in the group and one man. His name was Wayne, and he was kind of a mysterious presence in the studio as we all saw him but had no clue about him, at least those of us in the younger classes. She told me to run to Wayne. I did, and the next thing I knew I was up and over his head, around his back and then just as suddenly on the floor again. I was shocked. It was fun, but I had no idea how it had happened, what he had done, what I had done, and absolutely no way to repeat it. Luckily, Florence either didn't like it, changed it later, or I was just a momentary stand-in for someone else. It didn't happen again, for which I was grateful. As fun as it was, I didn't like losing control, and for the longest time that is what I thought I had to do if I was going to be in a duet that included any lifts at all. I would eventually learn otherwise, but mine was a long process to discovering what partnering really entails.

As I learned to partner more effectively while dancing, I saw that the way we talked about dance partnering proved to be excellent language for partnering in other ways too. I came to notice the weight-sharing involved in the relationship between choreographer and dancer, the question of who is leading when an artistic director and managing director make decisions for the organization, the way gravity plays a role in our collaborations with presenters, the power of touch as we work in communities. The experiences that grew out of these myriad partnerships form a backbone of my work. Along the way I have had great teachers who have steadfastly worked with me to improve my communication, my vision, my personal development, and the art that emerged from these. These people may not have been technically teachers, but by partnering with honesty, we were all able to discover something, including meaning.

The Dance Exchange doesn't have a booking agent. Rather we are like a partnership factory in which a whole bunch of people are building relationships that lead to appearances by various artists in a host of settings. Some of these connections are so strong that when a person we have worked with moves to a new venue, we go along too. In these cases, we've sustained long-distance relationships over time, giving presenters the opportunity to mix with new artists as our company changed personnel, and introducing us to institutions and communities as our partners settled into new jobs. This model has its own challenges. Nothing stays the same, even good methods. We have all had to unlearn perfectly good processes and develop new ones to better match the times, the community, and changed personnel.

Ken Foster

It is difficult to describe the excitement of learning with people over time. Presenters like Ken Foster, who are also wondering about the wider role art could play onstage and in the community, have become partners in conversation and a kind of experimentation that carries a lot of risk but leads to concrete ideas. But no matter how theoretical we would get, Ken always worried about the people we were working with in his community of Tucson, Arizona. Were they going to get enough supper, and could they get to the theater okay, and would their families feel welcomed, and was the green room going to be big enough? Many of our methods were advanced in Tucson as we returned for multiple residencies over the course of several years.

So when he took a new job at the Yerba Buena Center in San Francisco, I was delighted to continue our relationship. Ferocious Beauty: Genome *arrived at*

Yerba Buena as its third stop on our tour. It was very new. The performance went fine, but with a new work and a long tour ahead of us, I wanted feedback. I asked Ken directly. And I got quite a bit, much of it the kind that makes me say to myself, Damn, I thought I solved that, but I guess I didn't and it means I have to go back to the studio. Touring requires unique partnerships, and I treasure the ones where love and confrontation go hand in hand. Shared history can sometimes lead to repetition, but it can also insist on innovation.

There is no getting cozy. Oh, occasionally the bed in the hotel is actually absolutely right, and the water pressure in the shower pulses correctly for a tired body. And surely we find the restaurant with food we like and then go there every day and order the same dish. We can pretend to find comfort both personally and professionally, while still maintaining boundaries that make making art together possible. It is real work to build the environment that pushes each to their own best qualities while ensuring that the whole is moving too.

But we cannot get cozy, and I think this is a good thing. Different communities have different standards, and we bear the brunt of this whether we are teaching or talking, performing or participating in local events. The criticism can be subtle or harsh, in our face or behind our backs. But we hear it, and I always reflect on it later. It will lead me to rethink a character or a phrase. It will demand of me that I attend to the way I said something. And then I can decide anew which is the best way to do that thing the next time.

Lately I have observed how even the best of local theater companies, entrenched in their own communities, play to their home audience. They are beloved, and the in-jokes fly through the script and across the lights. This clearly has its benefits for audience and performers alike. It is like having your regular seat at synagogue or your regular place in technique class. The world looks familiar, and your perspective is a reminder of what you know.

I can't help but feel that the touring life forces ongoing examination that allows me to "grow" the work. Of course, we customize wherever we go, and that makes what we do a little different from a touring Broadway show performed eight times a week.

But as I sit here, just completing one of the longest periods of travel in my personal history, I am still committed to the rough nature of being on the road. I want young artists to have the same chance. Make the work, take it to strangers and find them puzzling over it, then rework it and take it to some other strangers and find them asking different questions, and then rework again. It is a true dialogue and there is nothing cozy about it. The strange audience, the unknown critics, the hypercritical peers can all be turned into demanding partners of the mind.

Dan Zemel

Even as I write these lines about coziness, I realize that I have my patterns too, and they lead to my own brand of cozy. That is why I like being around my rabbi, who once said, "If it ain't broken, break it." Okay, I even like the coziness of the words "my rabbi," and I am so lucky to have this particular one in my life. Dan has the rare capacity to be both open to new ideas and totally blunt. He brings a brilliant mind, an oblique sense of humor, and a complete passion for making moments truthful. We have been experimenting together for almost two decades now, and although the method of our meeting may be worked out, the outcome of our conversations is always transformative (a word he would never use).

Nothing is possible without the dancers. They are amazing. Each of them brings distinct hopes, histories, convictions, and the accumulation of thousands of hours of physical labor. They need such tending and such care, demanding from me a willingness to think about each personally and professionally, while still keeping a distance that makes making-together possible. It is real work to build the environment that pushes the best qualities of each while ensuring that the whole is moving too.

Martha Wittman

Martha Wittman came to the Dance Exchange after teaching for thirty-five years at Bennington College. She was, in fact, my teacher, and it is always a beautiful thing to tell audiences of this history. Anyone who wants to truly understand how a dancer can accomplish being contemporary through seven decades should study Martha. Most of us can't help but portray our early dance training in whatever we do. Martha somehow manages to be able to be both modern and postmodern. This is an easy transition between two words on a page, but just about impossible to accomplish with the body, the forms are so different. If someone were to research her transition, among the things that would be noticed is her fierce relationship to practice; over and over she does the steps off in a corner quietly while others are working, but even while doing that she has her eagle eye on the young ones, and if asked can give outside direction that is deep and inescapable.

As our collaborative relationships grew over the years, I have come to be able to read the warning signs, see the need for personal intervention, and ask for help from others to carry on the complexity that emerges from shared artistic activity. The biggest changes have come as I have pushed partnerships forward to include the dancers on so many levels of art-making and organization-building. Early on I realized that they complained less if they were in on the decision making, and so dancers serve on our board of directors, lead projects, attend casting meetings, and help decide what work we accept and what we don't. That inclusion has its cost, but the Dance Exchange has gained a roomful of invested participants and leaders in design. And with that investment comes some curious and contemporary ideas, both emerging from their heads and expressed through their bodies.

It changes who you look for if you want people to participate so much in the making and share so much of themselves with each other. Certain training issues may have to be untrained, such as when you guard your creativity and when you share it. And they arrive with such variety and ability that there is really no protocol or system other than working together to see if the environment is mutually supportive. You get wild ones who need to breathe more, you get squeaky ones who tell you what is going on all the time and let you know if you slip up. You get very individualized ones that even in as open an environment as the Dance Exchange require you to make the situation more flexible. You get the ones that stay a short time because they have so much on their minds they can't rest, and you get the ones who realize that they can keep on growing into a million different jobs and ways of being, and so they stay for a very long time, bringing their own imprint squarely into the multitude of processes that are emitted by the work.

Sally Nash

When I have a particularly sticky issue or when I need a real scrubbing of my brain, I get in the car and drive two hours to see my friend Sally Nash. Our fathers knew each other back in Wisconsin, and we grew up knowing that there was another dancing daughter somewhere in the state. But we didn't meet until I came to Washington, D.C., where Sally became a member of the first company of the Dance Exchange. Eventually she moved out to the Virginia countryside, became a Feldenkrais practitioner, and built a dance company out of back-to-the-land folks and named it the Last Minute Wood Company. She made unique dances bearing the mark of her originality, precision, and absolute authenticity. Now she is painting with the same commitment. She is my teacher in her regard for honesty, and we tackle our minute differences as if they were chasms. After a few hours, I get in the car and drive home.

One of the thorniest issues in partnerships is how we acknowledge the gifted among us as well as assign blame when things go wrong. We are not all equal in all things. We have tried so many different structures to aid us in these issues. Once in rehearsal I gave an assignment, and in reviewing the results, I thought one partnering pair had done a phenomenal job. As is our practice, I had others learn what this pair had devised, and it became our opening sequence. As the dance progressed, I left that sequence intact so that when the piece premiered, it still looked much like it had the first time we had seen it.

I was approached by one of the pair that had made the sequence, who asked that she be given a special mention in the program. We have a general clause in all programs that thank the collaborators, but nothing specific to each person's contribution. I told her that if we gave her a special acknowledgement, then I should probably thank the dancer who cracked the joke just before we broke into small groups to solve the assignment. After all, maybe it was her laughter that freed her to make the excellent phrase she had choreographed. It's a problem. She did contribute more, but I saw no way to particularize what she had done unless they all got a special mention. Oh yes, partnering . . .

Thomas Dwyer

We have a lot of nicknames for Thomas Dwyer. Most people might not find them flattering, but I think he does. He is old school. His military background, the poverty of his youth, his mother's love, his coming to dance later in life all add up to a completely unique individual and partner. If I want young dancers to come to see the meaning and reasoning and persistence it takes to remain a movement artist, all if have to do is bring them into an extended relationship with Thomas. You learn a lot, and if you devote yourself to going to this kind of school, the return is extraordinary and powerful. He brings a level of loyalty, commitment, devotion, and plain hard work that sets a bar beyond the capacity of those of us living in modern times. We just try to keep up and look for the wry smile that speaks to our success. And meanwhile, audiences are treated to a one-of-a-kind image: an old man dancing with fury, athleticism, and tenderness.

Of all the personal and Dance Exchange philosophies that I draw upon, the one that most underpins this discussion of partnership and collaboration is that of permeable membranes. A quick review: making distinctions is a creative act. At its most basic is the simple awareness: "I am not you." And while we are at it, I am not my mother, or my daughter, or my organization, but these things are all a part of me. This has big implications for identity. I am fully a woman, and always a woman, but I do not make all my decisions based on that fact or those facts that make that true. There are so many categories, including my Jewishness, my artiness, my friendliness, and on forever. But what I love and know is that I can have these permeable membranes that allow me to slide between worlds and people and ideas, as well as put up barriers to these very same universes. With skill I can move through a lot of potentially conflicting relationships and overwhelming influences but still emerge intact and clear-headed. Nothing is revolutionary in this understanding. It is pretty basic to most theories of identity and collaboration. The difference is, I guess, that I take a lot of delight in the versatility of the design and in the surprising outcomes that spring out of these oddball pairings that we can accomplish because we can always redraw or create new boundaries.

Although the dancers are key collaborators, I have been nudged into strength because of other dance artists whom I consider my friends, my colleagues, my competitors, my muses, my wake-up call. It is funny how it happens over time. Being for a few years in touch with someone and then losing contact for several years seems to be the pattern. It doesn't diminish what we learn, but rather speaks to our skills as interlopers.

Jawole Willa Jo Zollar

I first met Jawole Willa Jo Zollar of Urban Bushwomen when I was invited to share the program with her at a benefit in New York City. It was snowing, so I had a hard time getting out of town; one inch on the ground in Washington brings everything to a standstill. I arrived and found my way up to Harlem to a cold theater but a wonderful group of people. I was performing parts of Nine Short Dances About the Defense Budget and Other Military Matters. *I remember telling the audience that if anyone wanted to shut down the nation's capital, all they had to do was make it snow. And I remember talking to Jawole nonstop in the wings and backstage and afterwards. Then and since, we have had wide-ranging dialogues about the trade, the art, the field, the companies, the female in us. I really do not have the words to convey the quality of what she voices, except to say that Jawole is fearless. Our conversation has barely ceased since that moment some twenty-five years ago, except that we carry it on now in taxi cabs, airports, and swift exchanges as we travel our parallel but unique journeys.*

Is there a downside to all of this partnering? There are certainly tradeoffs. I don't always get what I want, and I am not always sure I know what I want because I wait a while to synthesize the signals around me. I have probably overcorrected for all the authoritarian decisions I had to work under. Perhaps it is time to march myself down to the other end of the spectrum. And so I turn to my lifelong friends and companions to help me think, feel, comprehend what is happening to me.

Elliot Maxwell

A walk is a rest for my restless mind, especially when I have a provocateur along with me. Elliot Maxwell and I started walking when he carried his baby daughter in a pack in front of us. She is now a post-college young adult making her way in the world. Her father and I keep walking and talking about many things, but especially about how things come together in this world. It sounds vague but it isn't. His recent move into open-source philosophy and practice proves a vivid trading ground for conversation about how ideas and movements spread, who owns them, in what order, and well . . . how things come together.

The partnering, sometimes evident, sometimes mysterious, bustles along. Inquiry, confrontation, disagreement are evident everywhere. And then it is back to the studio to find the ways in which these discussions bear fruit in the work itself. Dancers have ways of seeing and noticing that are so different from those of even the best theoreticians, and the translation processes I invoke to make more sense out of these flourishing ideas pushes the movement process too. How we have evolved as a culture that somehow dismisses the extra-sensory use of the body as a reckoning place is beyond me. I would have little to contribute to my talking friends if I didn't have my physical moving workplace, where I can sort out and reflect.

Coda

It is difficult to spend time reflecting on relationship and not talk about my husband. I have maintained over the years that my partnership with Jon Spelman is private. It is also a bit of a mystery. Sometimes we look at each other and say in agreement: "Who are you?" He is a terrific sleeper, and I am not. So when we vowed on our wedding day to pay attention to each other, I know that on the worst of my sleepless nights I can wake him up. His quiet listening and gentle words make entering the next day possible. And he's funny.

I had been asked to speak about creativity at the American Bankers Association's big conference, but I had also been placed on the "spouse" track. So everyone was surprised when over fifty bankers showed up for the session. We covered a lot of ground that day, including making a dance that was performed by the bankers, first to music and then to the mission statement of the organization. Here is the rest of what we did.

First I asked them when they had been creative in their work lives. Since I think all things begin with our understanding of our own experience, I wondered how they thought about creativity. It was clear from their answers that their own view of creativity was so narrow that there was little that they could do as bankers that would fit into a creative framework. It was also clear that their concept of creativity was freewheeling, structureless, and indulgent. In other words, it lacked the rigor that they themselves prize so highly in their own world. By the end of the session we had come to this point of awareness.

Creativity is about:

1. Rattling around in other people's universes. It is done through unexpected partnerships, unexpected connections, unexpected juxtapositions.
2. Embracing paradox and allowing two ideas in your head at the same time. Either/or thinking limits our ability to shift positions, change points of view, see other solutions.
3. Recognizing that creativity and originality are not the same thing. Creativity is in abundance when we understand evolution, diversity, and theme and variation.
4. Framing larger to get out of the personal. And nothing is too small to notice.
5 Turning discomfort to inquiry. Saying no is a wonderful moment of learning, if we understand how to mine our uncomfortableness.
6. Making or adding meaning. Creativity is exercised this way, but we also know that we can subtract meaning to move the parts around.

Toward the end of our session, one of the bankers raised his hand and said somewhat belligerently, "Okay, Liz, I see what you are saying, but at the end of the day, all the numbers have to add up." And I said, "Right, and on some days, all the dancers' arms have to end up going in the same direction at the same time." And so we come to one more item in our list.

7. Creativity means hard work, discipline, hours of sifting, sorting, rejecting, and being embarrassed for thinking such ridiculous thoughts that finally precede the really good idea. And sometimes that really good idea is about everyone being the same every time we perform.

Docudance: Nine Short Dances About the Defense Budget and Other Military Matters (1983). Photo: Robert Sugar/AURAS Design.

Politics

Two Assertions

It may look as if the artist is behaving like an activist, when actually all she is
    doing is building a world in which she can live and work.
It may be useful to reflect on the difference between tradition and convention.

A Return to Inquiry

What do we mean by "social" and what do we mean by "action"? If we change those words to "art in the world," does it change the outcome? What do we mean by art that values being part of the world, or in the world, or affecting the world? Does the meaning of art change if being social and being active are part of art's reason for being? How does moving from purity to subject affect the art and the artist? Why do people think that as soon as there is subject matter there must be a message? Why do people think that art with a message is didactic? What is didactic, and how is calling something that a tactic to silence others? Why do we think that art with a message is only art with a social message? Why do we confuse message with subject matter? Looking at the subject matter of art in your lifetime, why do you have trouble with the oppression stories? Isn't anger a useful byproduct of the theatrical experience? In what role do you put the audience when you tell sad stories, or scary stories, or victim stories? Isn't empathy the major outcome of any art? Without empathy, how can people actually change? What do we mean by change? How does change happen? What is the rehearsal for change? Do we consider the moment of change to be the only moment of value? Who is doing the changing? Why is change valued? What is wrong with contentment? Does merely pointing out a problem make art useful? Is usefulness actually useful? Isn't art useful for itself? Is the problem not with art but with our own patterns around it? And is the problem with patterns not within the pattern but within our unwillingness to rethink? What is wrong with taking refuge in an unthinking approach to whatever we are doing? Could you be confusing unthinking with intuition? Is intuition good in your mind and unthinking bad? Are bad and good constructs that can help us in these situations? Why is making stuff the answer to everything? How come saving the world through art is still something worth believing in? Do you really think that art matters as much as food? And why do I still love the theater?

Activism, Professionalism, Purity

....

Once, years ago, I was on a panel with choreographer Bella Lewitzky, one of the great exponents of modern dance on the West Coast. We got to talking about our shared concerns. She told me that she loved teaching and doing teaching residencies, but that she never put them on the same resume as her concert work. She was of the opinion that the concert promoters would like her performance work less if they knew about her teaching passions and successes.

Once I was talking to a research scientist, who was also a practicing doctor, about how to regulate the applications of the genomic revolution and other issues in science. He said that scientists needed to be involved in the process of establishing the regulations. I asked him if scientists were rewarded for being on such committees, whether in the university or by the government. He said the opposite is true. They lose status, salary, time, and research money, he told me.

Once I was in a meeting with some fishermen on the coast of Maine. We were there to learn about their stories in order to make a dance about their lives. They talked about how they wanted to be involved in regulating themselves in light of the environmental issues facing the industry. But they said that it was politically impossible to do so because their fellow fishermen would consider engagement akin to defection.

Once I was talking with a geneticist who works in marine biology. I was learning about the ocean, about the ecology of life forms in the ocean, and about his passion and love for the great whales. Others had already told me about his work with the whaling industry and other ways he has been active. He said, in passing, that he keeps his activism separate from his scientific research, because otherwise his research would be suspect. He also said that he loves both worlds, and that each needed the other.

Since starting the Dance Exchange in 1976, I have always believed that we needed to keep one foot in the community world and one in the concert world. We know that these worlds inform each other, allowing us to challenge ourselves to attain higher and higher standards as well to meet the particular needs of each project. But over the years I have seen how this very exciting and dynamic way of working can be perceived by others in my own profession as compromise. It seems that some would preserve the idea of artistic purity as practiced in the studio and onstage as the epitome and high point of an artist's existence. I wonder to what extent this way of life limits our possibilities and leaves the world at large bereft of connection, skills, and actual tools.

It Is Easier to Be against President Bush Than It Is to Change Small Dynamics in Our Own Field (Even in the Arts Where We Think We Are Radical but in Fact We Are Not)

It was an unusual opportunity. I was asked to come to the North Carolina School for the Arts to give a lecture as part of the Kenan Writers' Encounter at the Thomas S. Kenan Institute for the Arts. I was to be the last speaker in a series that had gone on for five years and had included folks such as Angela Davis and Brian Greene. It was tantalizing, as I was in the throes of writing this book, and I thought it would be fun to read both something publicly for the first time and something from an older work. The reason I was looking into my earlier writing was that Ellen Rosenberg, who had invited me, had specifically said she was interested in women who were old (she didn't exactly say that, but she meant it when she described something like having had a long life in the field) and who had managed to stay visible.

So I did my *I Ching* thing with my old book *Teaching Dance to Senior Adults*, by which I mean that I just opened the book to a random page to see if it presented anything worth revisiting. It opened to a very innocuous-looking paragraph headed with these words: "Seating Arrangements." I didn't expect much to be useful there, as I was seeking something to fit the topic of my talk, "Redefining the Radical."

But to amuse myself I read. I am glad I did. Almost every sentence was about change, small but real change. Most of this particular change was wrought by the simple radicalism of putting a modern dance technique class into a home for senior citizens. But it reminded me that it is easier to make art and stand up and yell about, say, President Bush than it is to operate in your own world and change something in which your family, colleagues, or friends totally believe. I know this because there is always a moment in the choreographic process when I feel that being true to the piece will put me at odds with someone I care about.

This is what I found. The paragraph opens with this sentence: "Since the first part of the class is done while sitting, it is necessary to have plenty of room between each chair so that the arms can be held out from the side of the body."

Chairs in a technique class? It is true that in modern classes we often sit or lie on the floor. But never in my student history had we sat on chairs. I suppose nowadays we are used to Pilates demonstrations and TV exercise programs or infomercials that promote the use of chairs. But in 1975, when I began my work with older people at the Roosevelt for Senior Citizens center—known affectionately as the Roosevelt Hotel—in Washington, D.C., such images hardly existed. Now we are used to all kinds of fitness directives, including little diagrams in the airline magazines show us how to keep our blood flowing while sitting. It makes me aware of how far we have come.

The text continues: "The problem with this is that people feel far apart from each other."

A place for feeling in a technique class? My first reaction on reading this was a kind of surprise to remember that even as a young teacher I must have perceived that my older students had feelings and that it was important to support them as they experienced a wide variety of emotions during class. It strikes me now as a wild observation to have made. Although I mostly loved my dance classes growing up, on reflection I think that much of the time I experienced an expectation that feelings were to be left outside the class. With the exception of Martha Wittman, whose gentle but insistent pedagogy pervaded her classes at Bennington College, I remember loud voices counting the music, along with a general message that "you are wrong, so fix it." Maybe some of my teachers formed some of their methods with the thought that students had feelings, but I can't remember any of them.

Next sentence: "Occasionally people may want to hold hands as part of a chair dance, and the distance precludes this."

Holding hands? To be fair, I started having people hold hands in technique class before I ever went to the Roosevelt Hotel. I did it in my classes at George Washington University because I wanted the students to touch each other, and I wanted them to try to learn how to actually see something while dancing as opposed to carrying on the glazed-over look that comes from working so hard with inner focus. I found if they held hands while they did their pliés, they usually did them better and with less stress. But at the Roosevelt, holding hands took on a different dimension. There, holding hands in dance class might be the only time that week that some of my students experienced touch. I made it a staple of the class.

It was also rehearsal for standing exercises during which I might want them to support each other as they rediscovered their balance.

"Once again the teacher must decide, with feedback from the students, what makes the most sense." A technique teacher seeking feedback from her students? Indeed I did learn from my students, at the Roosevelt and elsewhere. And it became clear to me that it was just easier to make this process transparent than to try to guess what was working for the people in the room. Listening to many voices also demanded that I learn to support differing opinions. By trying to pay attention to all the individuals in the room, I discovered ways to synthesize the many into one or to select a few as examples while still acknowledging the whole group. It began to breed a new kind of tolerance in myself, allowing for more discussion and chaos in situations where before silence and a highly structured protocols had been the rule.

"At the Roosevelt, people have chosen to keep the chairs close together and to stretch their arms in different directions."

I think one of the most significant notions in art and community is that we can use artistic process to help us understand and negotiate issues in our lives. Rather than settle for a lowest common denominator, you can teach people to practice theme and variation. Then they can help themselves to staying involved, participating and continuing their own exploration. At the Roosevelt, the students decided that being close was more important that doing a movement in precisely one way. They had learned theme and variation, and they knew how to improvise, be flexible, and adapt.

A brief discussion of setting the chairs in a circle follows, and then come these sentences: "This way, everyone can see the teacher and each other. This is important since there are several times during class when it is necessary to follow people other than the teacher."

One of the discomforts I brought with me to the Roosevelt from my modern dance teaching was that I knew there was a lot of knowledge in the room whenever I faced a class of dancers. But somehow the setup of a conventional technique class meant that I was the one given permission to see, to comment, to fix. I was trying to find ways to get other people in the room to share what they knew with each other. Since so much of teaching dance involves watching and noticing, it seemed especially important to get more eyes on more bodies. It was at the Roosevelt that I got to figure out a series of methods for doing this.

The next paragraph addresses some of the dancing issues that emerge if you sit in a circle. The most prevalent of these is the problem of left and right. It is quite difficult to teach a group of beginners about left and right while in a circle. As I say in the book: "No amount of discussion seems to remedy the situation. What is worse is that often participants end up feeling stupid because they cannot get something as basic as left and right. This situation can be resolved by designing dance movement in such a way that it does not matter which arm goes up."

I love this. So the final part of this innocuous section is to suggest that the actual movement vocabulary can change, can *be* changed to support the group's evolution as dancers.

And then, just to be absolutely clear, I remind the reader that if it is important to get the arm right, the move right, or the notion that only one movement will do, then teach *that* and your students will get it. Just don't sit in a circle.

Looking back twenty-five years, I can see how I used the senior center as a means of changing my teaching, giving myself tools, and informing my classes with my values. I can also see how my students taught me and how lucky I was to be far away from the telescopic eye of my profession so that I could work in tune with my own ideas and my art form as I defined it. This was gentle, incremental change, which I then applied to the classrooms where I was teaching professional dancers. But now I recognize that it was radical to the bone.

A Job Swap and Slow Banking: Two Op-Eds

··

Some mornings I just wake up angry, probably from watching too much cable news the night before. I get up early and go to my desk. I think I am going to tackle my ever-full e-mail inbox. Instead, inexplicably, I begin to write. Often, on certain ornery, cranky days, the words come out feeling like an opinion piece for the paper. (Of course there are hardly any more papers, so maybe I should write one about that.) Here are two pieces written in the year that the U.S. economy fell apart.

A Proposed Job Swap to Save American Capitalism

Do Wall Street executives deserve big bonuses during hard times? Does increased arts funding have a place in an economic stimulus package? I'll leave it to others to debate these controversies. Meanwhile I'd like to make a modest proposal to solve some of our economic problems: let's do a job swap. We'll put the corporate executives to work as artists while the artists run Wall Street.

Since their first task will be getting economic markets back on solid footing, I'm convinced that artists have the perfect resumes for their new jobs. Here's why:

1. Artists work ridiculous hours for no pay. And most of the artists I know will keep working until they get the job done right.
2. Artists do not need fancy offices. In fact, they usually work in the worst part of town . . . until that part of town becomes fancy because the artists are there. Then they have to move because they haven't paid themselves enough to afford the new rent.
3. Artists throw everything they earn back into the store—which is *why* they haven't paid themselves enough.
4. Artists do not need financial incentives. Artists do the work they do because they love it. Or because they believe in it. Or because they think it is a social necessity for our communities. Or because they know that when people make poems or pictures or dances, our best human spirits emerge.
5. Artists do not expect to get anything if they do a bad job. Except maybe a bad review.

6. No artist gets a bonus because there is never enough money at the end of a project. If there is anything left over, they will start another project.
7. Artists keep very tight budgets. They know how to spend the same penny over and over (*not* by cooking the books, but by pinching, recycling, borrowing, bartering, and plowing their economy-airline frequent-flyer miles back into their next project).
8. Artists have a rightful reputation for fresh ideas combined with a capacity for self-evaluation that borders on recrimination.
9. Artists play well with others, having evolved highly efficient collaborative techniques in the service of their visions. But they are also very independent, delivering great things even when they work alone.

Meanwhile, in their new capacities as painters, poets, cellists, and choreographers, our Wall Street executives might be experiencing a combination of culture-shock therapy and ethical boot camp. Artistic practice may force them to discover what they really believe in, because the combination of introspection, discipline, and craft that fuels an artist's work (oh, and it *is* work) puts people in a very demanding state of truth. Doing what artists do every day, some former executives might find themselves in overcrowded classrooms, excited to share their practices to help young people discover that they actually can learn. Others might be sparked to help communities solve problems by bridging differences through the unique power of their art forms. Those who have been lucky enough to get funded for their work will likely be staying up nights, filling out multiple forms to document the exact use of every penny they have been granted. All will find their moral compass tested as they balance the demanding loyalties of pursuing personal vision and creating value for an audience.

The job swap I propose might have a final payoff: with artists in charge of Wall Street, you might even see people donate to the cause because artists know how to inspire others to participate together, to work for something that matters, to build on the intangibles of the human experience, to make a difference.

Imagine that kind of Wall Street.

Slow Banking

I want a slow banking movement. Like the slow food movement, it would be small, local, and efficient. Here's why:

In my first job after college, teaching at the Sandy Spring Friends School outside Washington, D.C., I earned a very small amount of money as the school also housed and fed me. But I proudly opened my first bank account independent of my family back home in Milwaukee. The small bank in the town of Sandy Spring gave me a little black book to note my deposits, which I did in pencil and which they approved every two weeks when I deposited my check.

Three years later I moved to New York City to check out the hyper-professional dance world and to test my wares among peers. I went to the local bank near my extremely funky apartment on Second Avenue and Third Street across from the Hell's Angels, who shared that end of the block with me. I took my little deposit book to the major bank on the corner and presented it to the people there. They just laughed. Well of course they did; it was so unofficial. Nonetheless, I was quite surprised. Didn't my money count? Then I realized that I would never be known to them the way I was to the tellers and managers in Sandy Spring.

I wanted the bankers to know me and my fortitude and what it took for me to save every paycheck. I wanted them to know that if they screwed up, it was my life that went with them. I wanted them to realize that even though I was a young dancer, I had dreams that I intended to fulfill and that I needed them just to keep my money safe. I wasn't asking them to make me a fortune. I only wanted to be sure that when I needed my hard-earned savings, they would be there.

How difficult is that?

If we did have such a movement, I am sure we would not be in the economic meltdown we are currently enduring. Because not only would they know me, but I would know them too, and I, and thousands like me, would not have let them make such horrendous mistakes.

Pushing Back: A Rant in Three Movements

I am at heart a reformer, not a revolutionary. Over the years, I have often wondered why. I suspect the comfort of a middle-class upbringing made it especially hard for me to throw everything out. But also, I have been sufficiently lucky—or cursed—to understand at a visceral level that there is almost always something useful, even beautiful, in what one wants to change. Moreover, I suspect the heavy dose of ballet and classical modern techniques in my very young life stripped away any revolutionary zeal I had in me, since I was enough of a success early on not to seek alternative paths in order to get to dance at all. But if I've lacked the will to push things over, I've gained a lot of momentum by pushing back.

Push Back 1: Orthodoxies and Institutions, Ballet to Postmodern

Ballet wasn't there quite from the very start for me. Impulse came before image, and I was already dancing around long before I saw any pictures of dancing. And when I did start responding to images, they were not of ballet. In a *Life* magazine article about UCLA, I saw two Asian American co-eds facing each other, jumping high in the air, legs tucked under them, hair flying back and away. I was captivated by their beauty. I wanted to be them. I was four years old.

But soon enough, as it does for so many of us, ballet came to dominate my mind's-eye picture of dance, and even those physical impulses. How did it start? When did all the images become pink? I got a clue much later in life when I wandered into the Kennedy Center gift shop and noticed that, except for one Alvin Ailey poster, absolutely every dance-oriented book, toy, or tchotchke in the store was ballet-centric. I suspect that, even with parents who treated dance as a big-tent affair, my dreams became those of a young ballerina because that was the expectation in the world around me.

I often meet parents who say to me that their daughters want to be ballerinas, who tell me how much the girls love it and how hard they work. But something in their tone tells me that these young dancers are struggling. It might be a weight issue or the fact that someone else's daughter is this year's

Clara in *The Nutcracker*. I'll usually say something like, "Be sure your daughter knows that if ballet doesn't work out, there's a whole world of dance eager to take her in and help her find her way." I am met by a wry smile that seems to signify that that will never happen. Either the parents feel that the alternatives are a comedown, or they suspect that their daughters will perceive my assurance as a feel-good ploy, a consolation prize rather than what it is—a potentially rigorous and challenging role: that of making dance a real part of a whole life, not just part of the tween fantasy.

How does ballet's position at the top of the hierarchy get established so clearly and with such tenacity? What is it about the professional dance world that makes the possibility of anything other than ballet and the most classical of moderns seem inferior?

I loved my ballet classes. I can count maybe three times out of many hundreds that I didn't want to go. I hardly ever minded missing the rest of life at that time. I have very strong memories of being at the barre, the standing leg aching as we did one more set of repetitions before turning to the other side. The barres at Florence West's studio made of copper that turned our hands green as we held on and sweated and attempted to get our legs ever higher, our backs ever more supple, our feet ever more pointed. I was pretty cheery during all of this. Until when? What happened that began to change it all in my head and in my body, and what happened that made me complain, question, push away?

Two things shattered my little world simultaneously. During three summers at the National Music Camp at Interlochen, I encountered not just competition but unfair results emerging from favoritism and unwritten rules that seemed to defy the obvious. Although I held my ground through hard work and a lot of crying, I never really reestablished my belief in the essential beauty of dance and dancing. Meanwhile, back home in Milwaukee, my position as one among the favored in the eyes of my teacher was usurped by the arrival of a new young ballerina.

Were issues like this worse in the ballet world? Probably. Did they reflect the strange neuroses of my teachers? Yes. Were my teachers worse than others? Probably not. Was the system flawed? Yes. Does it have to be that bad? No.

I recognize now that reality was setting in. My teachers were only human, and they had their own pressures to deal with. I couldn't see that, and at the time such things were not a matter for discussion. If I questioned the situations

I found myself in, I was told, "This is the way it is done" or "Get used to it, because you cannot control these things" or "If you can't take it, get out now."

Though I couldn't name it, I began to suspect that something else was possible. There *was* an alternative to either accepting or getting out. It would take years of testing to figure out what it was.

Turning toward modern dance as my teen years progressed, I encountered a new set of challenges. I recognize now that I was coming of choreographic age at an odd time, during the transition between modern and postmodern. It would take a few years for the insights of the Judson innovators, Twyla Tharp, and the second-generation Merce Cunningham school to reach the midwestern lyrical mover that I had become. By the time they found me at Bennington College in Vermont, I was beginning to question the whole deal. Maybe it was the institutions of the dance world revving up in a mystery I couldn't fathom or find. Maybe it was the coldness of the form. Maybe it was the meanness of the stars. Maybe it was the clubiness of the indoctrinated. Maybe it was the lens of my own naivete that made me shake my head in confusion and disgust.

But just maybe it was the movement itself: fun to do, hard to watch. The audience person I was couldn't get it, even while the dancer I was got caught up in the intellectual game of it. It would take many years for me to harness the inside information and joy of dancing purely to the ideas that mattered for me. But as a very young and unsophisticated seventeen-year-old, I was lost at sea without a story to tell or an image to hold.

A final impediment to my career in the ballet world was the fight to control the body and keep it rail thin. Looking back I can see no reason why anyone should have helped me with this, although at the time I was clearly looking for some guidance. I don't know how much my own discomfort with not fitting in pertains to my slightly frumpy body. (This issue remained potent enough for me that a decade later, when the Dance Exchange printed its first nondiscrimination clause, we included the word "shape" along with the required list of race, religion, and ethnicity. The inordinate amount of positive feedback this inspired is probably a measure of the silence we were breaking.)

So what was the movement style of this modern-to-postmodern bridge period in which I struggled? What were the aesthetics, processes, and values that a student was supposed to grasp? And how much did they affect me as a dancer and future choreographer, really? This much I think I could have stated as the prevailing expectation: you need to find your own form of movement invention, but the result has to look enough like the accepted ideas of movement at any given time. And the "look" of this movement came from the minds and bodies of our teachers, who themselves learned from one of the masters. This is the part that is hard to understand. I knew you were supposed to have fresh ideas about dancing, "ideas" actually meaning new steps. But they had to be recognized as fresh to the right people. As time went by, it would often seem that mine weren't. And without fresh steps nothing else about the choreography could be recognized as innovative either.

Dancing is such an experiential form of being-learning-doing. I could feel the world changing. I could sense it in every muscle and understood things in a way that words could not encompass. But years later, when my father said to me, "Don't confuse the beauty of Judaism with the tiny institutions that synagogues have become," the whole picture of that phase in my growth and discontentment became clear. His words made it possible to see that Bennington College was merely a frail institution unable to keep its practices in line with its ideals. I knew what that felt like, and I knew somewhere that it was fixable. But it would take a long time to get over the constant hurt, to pull myself up again and talk myself into trying it over another way.

What happened? How did I respond to this world and what action did I take, or not? I can tell the stories again but even in the telling I will come off as defensive, which I hate. Perhaps it's enough to say that as soon as I was in a position to be a guide to others, as early as in my twenties, I was saying, "Teach the class you wish you were given. Treat your students the way you wanted to be treated. Challenge and ask for sacrifice in the ways you would have responded had you been pushed." And, to myself: "Make a laboratory of your own where mistakes can flourish."

Push Back 2: Hierarchies and Prevailing Values

Hierarchy becomes a problem when it imposes right and wrong without fresh thinking, causing those left out to feel victimized and those on top to get by on entitlement. Both victim and entitled end up crippled. But the erosion of our calling can be seen and felt all around us, especially if we dare to break the collusion of relationships formed from either being on the inside (by way of media attention, grants, unquestioned aesthetic assumptions, shared values) or the outside (on account of political perspectives that breed blame, unquestioned aesthetic assumptions, shared values). You know you are in a hierarchy when the person at the top pays a visit to the bottom and gets covered by the media. The reverse is never possible.

There are hierarchies hidden like extra dimensions in the folds of everything we do. I was musing recently about the Dance Exchange's decision to give up trying to perform in New York City every year. About a decade ago, I realized we could either afford to pay dancers' health insurance or have a regular season in the Big Apple. We chose the insurance. Once I was off that treadmill, I was able to notice a few things: there is a hierarchy of venue, a hierarchy of reviewer, a hierarchy sustained by which paper or magazine or blog sends the reviewer, by which page of a paper the review appears on. I could easily have spent my life fighting to get to the top of these. That's the thing about hierarchy: we know it, live, experience, and want it even though it does not always represent the most important fight or the true battle we want to win.

Training has its problems too. What questions are we supposed to be asking? By defending the pure and protecting the learning we all received from our own beloved teachers, we blind ourselves to the needs of present time. In the end, we are caught saving what might have been useful twenty years ago and give birth to a generation already behind.

I only heard Rabbi Harold Schulweis speak once, but his words hit me hard: "Idol worship is the act of honoring the part more than the whole." And so we end up valuing what we can measure, which puts undue emphasis on technique, turning the tool into the master. We need to rearrange our thinking about this word "technique" and define it as giving a body range, giving a mind a set of flexible methods for questioning, giving our communities a vast array of experiences to help them sift meaning out of individual and communal life.

We lose the potential joy of orthodoxy when we allow that orthodoxy to take over as the fundamental reason for everything. It would be useful if we could understand how to honor the past, the tradition, the knowledge of our predecessors, and still be able to be in this moment, to recognize that this is our time.

I have always said that teaching dance to old people once a week was a simple antidote to the necessity of narcissism. How hard is it to give up ninety minutes a week (and that includes travel out of the studio and into some other universe)? How hard is it to go out and give a little of self and of what one knows? How hard is it when the return is so great? And how is it possible that that one act is somehow deemed treacherous or the actor a traitor to the field? How ridiculous it is to think that we have tainted the profession when we share what we know beyond the walls of the profession.

I was asked recently in an interview if I thought my work was still radical. It was a good question. I found myself saying something like this: in our country at this time, the body is still a radical canvas. Our confusions about our feelings for ourselves and each other, our extreme habits of care and abuse, our struggle over decent health care, our ongoing platitudes and name-calling over gender and race, our hopes and fears about the future of our biological selves—all of this means that art that starts and ends with the body itself has the potential to make a revolution in awareness and change. However, I said, sometimes I think it is the dance profession itself that keeps us from our radicalism. The dancing can get in the way of the body.

I think choreography is big. I think it is way more than the steps themselves. In fact, the steps themselves are the smallest aspect of what choreography really is. To build an environment so all can do their best, to imagine something from nothing and then pursue the inquiry with compassion and without compromise, to discover the best old and new ways to express the truth, to dispel the tension around competing loyalties, to arrive at the right decision, to market, to research, to sell, to cajole, to pressure, to conceive, to push, to finish, to celebrate others, to design the look and feel of an experience, to structure an entity out of the raw material of movement and sounds and images that lives on a stage and communicates to an audience . . . it is a big job. The steps are one small part, but to be constantly judged by the steps alone is not only painful for me but a disgrace to the field as a whole. No wonder it can sometimes seem that no one cares.

Push Back 3: Political Movements

One of the Dance Exchange's managing directors once said to me: "Let's just think of the Dance Exchange as a tent, and that we'll put a lot of different things under it, but only what fits." And I said back: "Well, be sure to leave one flap open, just in case."

I am claustrophobic. About all kinds of things. Not just about space, but about ideas too. And so I have had a terrible relationship with political movements. I have tried to belong but have found it impossible. In my first year of college in 1965, I made it through one meeting of the campus's Students for a Democratic Society chapter. One. I found the meeting boring, with the men showing their peacock feathers, the conversation lacking nuance. I left.

And although my family background and my artistic intentions put me in contact with many politically progressive opportunities, over the years I have found myself consistently on the outside. At its most extreme, the explanation may be that I have been unwilling to submit my thinking to someone else's rigid agenda and unwilling to tie my art-making to a foregone conclusion. At its most simple, I may not be a joiner.

To be fair, I have had wonderful long nights in deep discussion with many brilliant people who care about the same things I care about and who work tirelessly for ideas of justice, free thinking, and a more equitable economic system. I agree with them, most of the time. But what I have not been able to do is make my art speak for these notions unless it has grown out of an artistic process that is open to complication and welcoming to ideas that might be unpopular.

I think it is this kind of dilemma that has made many artists immune to demands that they produce work with political themes. And yet I am drawn over and over to history, to stories, to questions that tumble into the realm of social realities. What I have tried to do is find a way to use my performing art to raise questions and allow for emotion as these questions emerge and un-fold. And I have tried to find unique ways for factual information to make its way onto the stage. But mostly I think the power of dance performance comes from audiences having to sit for a certain amount of time, which forces them to face a portrayal that might at least afford a chance to think about a tough problem. I have also used my community practices as a means of bringing unlikely sides together to try to see things in a new light. Here I am sure that art has a big and useful role to play and, if done right, does not jeopardize or confuse product and process.

I am not saying shy away from political subject matter. Quite the opposite. I am only hopeful that the subject gets subjected to rigor of all kinds.

For a while it seemed that when I spoke to political or community groups I talked about the power of art. And when I talked to arts groups I talked about the power of community. Somewhere in that weird bridge-like margin I can sit and see the world. The flaps of the tent are wide open.

Small Righteous Angers

....

Small righteous anger leads to small dangerous thinking.

The first time I noticed the problem was at a retreat for choreographers held at Jacob's Pillow. We were all gathered as part of some funder or organizer's idea that we in the dance field should be talking to each other more and that a few days together would be a good thing. There were other gatherings that summer as well, including one for presenters. Now that I am thinking about it, I believe that the choreographers were divided into two groups: those of us interested in community practices and those who, I suppose, were not. I am not sure how these categories were characterized, but just the fact that there was a division started the righteousness. Somehow, some of us were already feeling dissed.

Much of the actual activity during our few days in Massachusetts was terrific. There was a lot of sharing of tools, a lot of wisdom about survival, making stuff, the dancers we work with, and a million side tracks that were all fascinating. And these activities did indeed build solidarity. They once again revealed the yearning for connections that makes human beings be constantly surprised by simple facts that are at once obvious and hidden. For example, when one choreographer used a method for introductions to a community and everyone else in the circle had happened upon the same notion in some form or another, the head-bobbing and acknowledgement that swept around the circle made everyone feel good.

Another kind of solidarity comes from trashing others. This too seemed to breed among ourselves as we sought validation. And this thinking also bred thinking about taking action that was far from helpful, and maybe downright problematic.

In this case, it was the funding game that "privileged" the presenters and made everyone in the room dependent on selling their wares to a group of people who held the power—the power not just to make our work evident by its performance but actually enable us to survive, because without the work there are no rehearsals, no next piece, no opportunity to continue. So many discussions gained energy and agreement by first denouncing the system and then blaming the presenter.

I participated. But then a kind of creepy feeling emerged, not just for me, but for some of the others too. So we began to push for solutions. Couldn't we partner with the presenters to face the wider financial problems confronting our field? This idea came up at the same time a rather pleasant fantasy swept the room in which the artists were given the money and the presenters had to go to a convention and wait in their booths in the exhibition hall until the artists came around and picked them.

In one moment an image flashed in my mind: a series of concentric circles of power emanating outward so that the farther out you went, the more powerful the person or the function. I saw that we, the choreographers were doing battle in our heads with the very next circle, the one we could see from our back doors. In fact, really, we might want to take on something farther out from that. It would be daunting, but perhaps in the end more worthy than the conversation we were having, which seemed spiteful and fueled by grief.

It is hard not to remain a victim. The scars are difficult to heal. It becomes a framework for seeing and re-experiencing the world. I see it in my artist community and I see it in my Jewish community. So one morning I woke up and wrote:

Victim's Bill of Rights

1. I can be angry at small things and always be right.
2. I can seek out the small hurt and renew my righteousness.
3. Because I was wronged, it is up to the other person or thing to make it right for me.
4. I have the okay to pass on my hurt and my right feelings about it to anyone I want to, especially those coming after me.
5. My experience of history is the most valid, and so my understanding of the present is also right.
6. I have been wronged so many times on this subject that no matter how small the hurt, it can never be fixed.
7. My uniqueness is in part due to this hurt, so don't fix it or I will become like everyone else.

Let me be clear lest this be misunderstood or misused out of context: there are conditions that oppress people and victimization is a real and terrible thing, but victimhood does not have to be a constant and singular way of being. It can be an informative frame and a generative tool for action, rather than a way of life. Here again I discover myself finding solace in the idea of multiple perspectives, and in the knowledge that we are each many things.

Power defined by wealth, status, or unfettered choice provides a context for so much of what we do. Our recent work with scientists, where the perception is that the collaborations favor the scientific community, has led to an often-repeated experience. It might occur in a discussion that has brought together a group of science and art folks. Perhaps we have seen *Ferocious Beauty: Genome* or have been involved in a workshop or are planning some event. At some point, one of the artists or a person in the audience stands up and says: "Okay, I see how much art is doing for science, but what is science doing for art?" Usually the question or statement is accompanied by applause from at least half of those present. Usually there is a feeling of one-upsmanship in the moment. Usually the person sits down with a lot of sass.

And usually I take a deep breath and have to work through something akin to licking a wound, rewinding a film, smiling through tears (none of this really, because I do it fast and in private—under the face, so to speak).

I have lots of answers at this point, but I wonder where the question is coming from. It doesn't usually speak to the subject at hand but rather seems to be part of a long battle for recognition, and the seeming one-sidedness of the collaboration we're discussing makes the person who posed the question feel a long-burning resentment again.

I want to say that the whole project is art. Science is contributing the way love contributes to a dance about relationships and domestic turmoil, the way history contributes to a dance about war or race, the way women contribute to a dance about sisters. I want to say that I get stuff from the scientists every day, including how to organize the Dance Exchange, how to fundraise, how to think about time and memory and speed and velocity, and the millions of tiny encouragements that keep us going, like friendship.

But I don't think that is what they are looking for. I think they are in a cycle of non-acknowledgement and are lashing out at the nearest potential perpetrator. They are not asking why art is relegated to such a small place and why that makes them feel small and what they might do about that that is different from the way art is reflected in this project.

In its most recent iteration, the question was raised at a discussion at

Hampshire College. But this time, since I knew the questioner and honored her thinking, I strived to get to a deeper place myself in the dialogue. What emerged was the sense that maybe the only way we are able to really start this science–art collaboration is to realize that the two disciplines are unequal to begin with—unequal in status, resources, and public perceptions of actual need. If taken from the point of view of power, art is in service to science from the start. But since I am so accustomed to hiking the horizontal, so used to meandering through permeable membranes, I hadn't noticed, except when comparing wealth and resources. I try not to measure much by that or live my life by that, because if I do I am doomed to small righteous angers every day. And who wants that.

Nani, bulky love practitioner. Photo: Liz Lerman.

Bulky Love

To the Attendance Monitor at
Sligo Creek Middle School

Anna Spelman was absent from school on Friday because she went with her father to the National Storytelling Convention in Jonesboro, Tennessee. This is an annual trip for the two of them. They get very important personal time together and reconnect with storytellers from around the world. They also continue to advance their conversation about aesthetics, narrative, point of view, and performance.

Anna will do the homework she missed.

Sincerely,
Liz Lerman

Motherhood: Stories and an Interview

I need family. Yet I always rejected the idea that the Dance Exchange was a family. I didn't like the references to my being "the mother." (I let only Marvin Webb—a dancer whose infectious cheer was unstoppable—call me Big Mama, and even then I permitted it with some chagrin.) It wasn't only that I had a family at home, or in Wisconsin, or scattered about with cousins and nephews and nieces, but that I just didn't want to carry the burden of all that hope and nourishment and battling that family seems to inspire in us. Sometimes the metaphor creates hostilities and hardships that are too much to bear. I know that, more than once, the intensity of my capacity to nurture has outstripped my ability to lead well, choreograph better.

I met Jon Spelman, then as now a storyteller, writer, and performer, when the Dance Exchange was only five years old. He was at that time preparing to leave the company he founded, the Florida Studio Theater. He joined me in Washington, and together we have made a life, a home, a family, a daughter. We jokingly say "married (at this date of writing) twenty-nine years, together fourteen" in order to account for the immense amount of time we spend away from each other because of touring and residency work. Always I carried this image of myself flying through space, connected to earth only by the slightest tether held by Jon and Anna and the animals and whatever house we happened to be living in at the time. Otherwise, I am sure that the centrifugal force of the activities of my brain and body would have sent me into the far universe.

Two sections follow: one is a very brief set of stories from when Anna was a baby, describing her impact on me and the dancers at the time. The second is a fake interview I did with myself when I was on a writing retreat at Bellagio in 2003.

I hope that these writings convey that by living a completely conventional life at home, I was able to lead a totally unconventional life in the world. And by going to PTA meetings and meandering through the halls on Back to School Nights, by helping with homework over the telephone, by missing the performances of my husband and the recitals of my daughter, I joined thousands of other Americans in a struggle to keep whole with the things that mattered even while I was pursuing the things that mattered.

Baby Anna Stories

When she was just a baby, everybody wanted to take care of Anna. I thought this was a fine idea. I believed that she just needed to be held and played with and, to some extent, it didn't matter who was doing it. We were on tour. I was busy. One of the dancers took her for a while. We were near a beach somewhere. I went looking for her and found that the dancer who had taken her had given her to another dancer. So I went to find dancer 2 but instead found Anna, by herself on the sand. Dancer 2 had simply put her down and gone away. I completely lost it—couldn't believe it. But dancer 2 hadn't realized he was responsible for her. He thought dancer 1 was. Anyway, this led to a policy about Anna. If you had her, you were responsible, and if you were tired of her, you had to give her back to me or to *someone*.

Seymour, one of our older dancers, noticed that Anna was getting all of the attention. He said he wanted some. So we instituted Baby-for-a-Day. Once a week we picked someone who could be the baby for that day. We all cooed, touched, bubblah-ed all over the person. We liked this so much that we added other days. The one I remember best was Generalization Day. You could say anything stereotypical about anyone or anything. We laughed a lot. Much of this off-handed humor was due to Beth Davis, a dancer who was great to tour with. This phenomenon of special days lasted only a few months—we got tired of it—but while it lasted, everyone seemed to enjoy being the baby.

Every now and then I would feel very bad about leaving Anna at home while I was on tour. I was miserable. It was okay while I was working. But at night in the empty hotel rooms, I could barely stand it. During one period I embroidered a lot: beautiful things on little dresses for her, just to stay connected. But it was the dancers Bea Wattenberg and Judy Jourdin, both grandmothers by then, who helped me the most. Each in her own way would find a private time to tell me it was okay. Bea used to say that my daughter would hate me whether I stayed at home or not, so I may as well do as I liked or needed. Judy would just tell me calmly that Anna would love me no matter what, or something like that. Both of them loved to babysit when Anna was with us.

We had a big tour of New England when Anna was under a year old. While at Dartmouth, I had committed to performing two different programs, including *Russia: Footnotes to a History* in which I danced the prologue. I remember running "home" to the hotel and nursing Anna and then running back to the theater and dancing—all this in the bracing New England fall air, with my asthma kicking in as it only does in the cold.

In that same winter, and again in New England, we arrived at a theater during a snowstorm. We got out of the cars in a parking lot covered in black ice. Charlie Rother, one of our older dancers, was holding Anna. He slipped and fell, and they both went down. I wasn't sure who to worry about more, as I was several hundred feet away. What an odd sensation that was. They were both fine.

We were in Philadelphia in a new hotel that had opened in Chinatown on the day that Anna turned three. We had a great birthday party for her. All the dancers came to our room and had party hats and presents and cake. It was a big day for Anna. She had, up to that point, refused toilet training, telling me she would use the bathroom when she was three. So that morning I had gently reminded her that this was the day she was three, and it was time to use the toilet. She did, and that was that. One would think that as a choreographer I had an understanding of timing, but it was Anna who kept showing me the way it works in real life.

I Interview Myself

So why did you decide to have a baby?

I think I always assumed that I would be a mother. I worried a little when I met Jon because the first night we talked he told me he didn't want kids. At that time, I smiled inwardly, thinking, Ah, that will change. But actually it didn't. It took a lot of work on our part to get the point where we knew we could do it.

But did you have any concerns about work?

I had some. In the dance *In Praise of Animals and Their People*, I talk about how I lost a rather big booking because I was pregnant. And later, I actually acknowledged the dilemma when I gave a talk at a conference of community-art-school administrators and had Anna with me. I was speaking in a large hotel ballroom and mentioned that my daughter was in the corner of the room drawing. I said not to worry about her, that I had designated one person to watch her and that I hoped they wouldn't think me less professional for bringing her. The audience applauded. One woman approached me afterward to say that she had brought her child but had left her upstairs for fear of losing respect. We understood each other and the moment, but I took no pleasure in my own decision to bring Anna into the room. We simply acknowledged that the pressures on each of us as mothers were many and varied.

But the wanting to be a mother far outweighed these kinds of adjustments. I also knew I had to wait until I thought the Dance Exchange was strong enough for me to bring on another concern. When Anna was two and I was thinking of wanting a second child, Jon and I had one very brief conversation about it. He said I would have to go part-time. I said I still had too many questions to go part-time. He said he could watch one but not two. And I made up my mind right in that moment. Only one. I think it is one of three big regrets in my life.

So was it hard?

It was hard the day I circled the company and said I was pregnant. The only person at the Dance Exchange who already knew was Bob Fogelgren, the amazing magician who managed our operations and touring. I had told him at Dance Theater Workshop, just before I went onstage for my last performance of my go-go piece, *New York City Winter*. But I waited until I was past the first trimester to tell the others. When I did, one of them said, "Why do you want a kid? You have us." I laughed. But he was right in a way. Becoming a parent changes the way you feel about the company.

The person who warned me about this was Margie Jenkins, another choreographer with her own company. When I got pregnant, she said, "Plan to never come back. Plan to come back right away. Plan to feel differently about the dancers. You will have a real family now. And they don't." It was very good, but complicated, advice.

Here is the really difficult part—and I am saying this not because I am an artist. It is true for all parents: you are never in the exact right place again. What I mean is that when I am choreographing and I am so happy, I am not totally happy because I am not at home with Anna. And when I am with her and we are having a blast, I am also missing work. But this was much truer when she was young. Now either I have learned or I just know that my time with my daughter is great and my time with the company is great. Period. Not so much loss. But when Anna was a younger child, this tension would drive me crazy.

Sometimes I was happiest when she would come to the theater. We would set her up in my dressing room, and she would settle in with books, drawing stuff, crafts and music, whatever. She didn't like to watch, but we loved being with each other. Sometimes when I wasn't performing, she would sit with me in the wings and we would be together while I watched. This made me very content.

Later, as she matured into her teen years, she came to understand some of what is hard for me at work. She is a great ear, and a great comfort. In my imagination, our conversations are always happening as we are driving, and Anna is in the back seat as she was when she was little. And I hear this wise voice helping me think it through. Very amazing.

So how did you handle it all?

First of all I had help. We decided that in order for me to work, I needed to be sure that Anna was well covered. I can compartmentalize—a useful skill for a working mother. It was while I worked at Children's Hospital that I learned how to be intensely involved in something, leave it, go into something else very intense, and not to let one bleed into the other.

But in order to create the structure that would both separate and knit together my work and home worlds, I needed good help. First we hired a young dancer, recently graduated from college, who came well recommended from a dance presenter in South Carolina. I really liked her and wished she hadn't left so soon. She got caught up in some competing loyalties with her work, her dance, her marriage. But her time with us was enough to teach me how great it was for Anna to have other folks involved in her upbringing. I have very strong memories of rehearsing while Anna was on a blanket on the floor, the babysitter nearby (even of nursing and rehearsing at the same time, somehow). Then off they would go on some little excursion, maybe just around the block. Once I came home, and she told me that Anna had pulled her hair and that she had pulled Anna's in response, making her cry. Anna never did it again.

Next we hired JoJo Earnshaw, who stayed with us until Anna was in middle school, adjusting to the varying needs of our situation as Anna grew and Jon traveled less. At first, JoJo and Anna went everywhere with me. Their travel expenses were a line item in the Dance Exchange budget. This was one of the great, important things having Anna taught me about the company. If I thought things through, separated the institution from myself, and then approached the board about what was necessary for me to continue to work, the organization was often able to accommodate my family's needs. At that time, my salary was incredibly low, but the Dance Exchange covered the cost of Anna's touring for years.

Once, Jon and I were in residence for a weekend at the conference for the Children's Museum Network. We stayed at a fancy hotel in Asheville, North Carolina. I was to give a keynote, and we both did workshops and some performing. Anna was along too. She was about ten. The organizers loved that the family was there. They kept saying it was helping them keep their goals in mind. That was a lovely way to acknowledge the fullness of life, and a very rare moment indeed.

In that keynote address, I talked as I usually do about spectrum thinking. And then I added some new ideas I was having about integration. I had thought originally that I was integrating powerful functions of art from opposite ends of the spectrum, and somehow they would create new ground for making art at a point in the middle. I was beginning to see that that wasn't possible, that the challenge was more about constantly moving across the spectrum, back and forth. A little like rocking on your sitz bones. If you do it long enough and with small enough oscillations, eventually you find the center. But you don't really stop moving.

I said that I think this is true about working and being a mother. It is never really integrated. It is always a little like moving big or tiny distances on the spectrum. One woman challenged me. She asked if I really thought that and said it made her sad. And I said, "Well, of course there were small moments of integration, but they're very small." We did not reach an agreement.

Now I am not sure that integration matters. Having both is wonderful. Having to choose is sometimes hard. And whenever you choose, you make either a wrong choice or a different choice. But I love my multiple worlds, and I am not sure I want them all together at the same time anyway.

. . . .

I still lose sleep over my daughter . . . not because she is crying and teething in a crib next to me in a strange hotel, but because she is living her life.

It might be important to say that Anna has vetted what I have written here and agreed these words could be public. This is the sort of thing she has done with her performing parents since she was old enough to convey her wishes. She has personal courage, an independent mind, and a generous disposition.

Representation Found and Lost

It is all symbolic. Nothing really represents anything else unless we agree to accept certain conditions.

When Anna was a baby and just developing language, we had a delightful period of time before all of her letter sounds were secure. She particularly liked the sound of the letter B, and she used it for her own entertainment in its purest form. She could spend long minutes just basically moving her lips in a steady stream of B's. Then she began to play with emphasis—loud, soft, long, short. After a while, these experiments began to mean something to her, which we in turn were able to understand. At first they meant whatever she was pointing at. But then through a long series of fits and starts and stops, she began to point only to things that actually began with B: baby dolls, the color blue, balls and bananas. And so she learned that B could actually represent something particular. The playing subsided as she began to work on the new sounds that followed her beloved B, but her first words mostly began with that letter. We were surprised that her first sentence did not. That occurred while she was sitting on her little bike seat behind Jon, the three of us out riding at dusk, and she pointed skyward and said, "Moon behind tree." It was definitely representational and mystical all at once, a rare aesthetic feat.

Representation: a complicated idea with multiple dilemmas. In dance, the idea of representation somehow became so very tainted that the joy of trying to understand and employ its nuances has been lost on several generations of dance makers and performers. The initial culprit was probably bad interpretive dance: the kind that was made in response to "Pretend to be a tree." For me the issue is not *being* the tree. The issue is the pretending, and that pretense rightfully made audiences squirm. In addition, as in other styles that lose their authenticity through cliché, the easy and simplistic representational approaches to subject matter very often gave viewers a narrow path of reinterpretation that was not just boring but precluded any possibility of fresh understanding.

My own experience of representation is that through varied approaches to an idea I discover what really matters to me and how best to get others to understand what I am pointing at. Sometimes it stops right there. But I also find that the "play" of the idea is akin to abstracting it slowly over time. I see that something can stand in for something else as the form takes shape. If Anna goes from B to ball, sometimes I find myself going in reverse.

One consistent theme in this book is the use of artistic practices in life and the awareness of how that use emboldens art-making back in the studio. Some of this crossover comes from the simple fact that certain behaviors already exist in both worlds, such as giving and getting feedback. Oddly enough, as vital as this act is, it is very difficult to come by in the professional art world, which is one of the reasons I developed the Critical Response Process (CRP). This is a four-step, guided structure for sharing feedback on artistic work-in-progress that I formulated in the early 1990s. As I have facilitated, taught, and written about CRP over the years since then, I've noticed how often its principles prove useful in everyday communication and how those uses suggest a fresh set of variations on the process. Since the spread of interest in CRP coincided with my daughter's teen years, it was perhaps natural that I experienced an interplay between feedback as practiced in the dance studio and the feedback that was happening at home.

I admit to practicing some ideas with Anna. Or perhaps it is more accurate to say that by being Anna's mom, I had an opportunity to notice relationships between parental feedback, critical response, and just plain family life. For starters, I found it useful to look at my daughter and her friends as if they were artists. Whether or not they were studying art seriously, it seemed helpful to equate their traits and behaviors with those I had observed among dancers, choreographers, and other arts colleagues: opinionated, bold, fragile, looking for distinction among peers, trying to hold onto rules and trying to break rules, finding a voice, and telling it like it is, especially to their close elders. Like artists, teenagers often profess originality when they actually need to practice a lot of repetition and theme and variation. Their declarations may sound new to them and old to their parents each time, but it is the nuance, the change in tone, the angle of the voice that tells the tale, and I discovered that my ability to hear and see the small variances in these repetitions actually made a difference in our communication.

I like to say that CRP is feedback for anything you make, and the making of a life is what you get to watch as a child grows up. Step 1 of CRP asks those responding to art to state what is exciting, meaningful, interesting, evocative,

or memorable about what they have observed. This notion of thoughtful observation and comment is, of course, central to parenting. As parents, though,
it becomes a challenge to not say too much, to not overburden a child with our
associations and pleasure in their advances. In facilitating CRP, I often empha-
size in Step 1 that "nothing is too small to notice," and one thing Anna made
clear is that the more particular I could be, the better. This intensified as she
grew older. As is true of many artists, just saying "that was good" or "this is
interesting" was not enough. It was if she was measuring me and my choice
to take the time to read, look at, listen to, and notice some of the little items
she placed in my path.

The Critical Response Process operates with participants in three roles:
artist(s), responders, and facilitator. With Anna in what corresponded to the
artist's seat, I found I had to be thoughtful about which of the other two roles
I was playing. I discovered that she was often less interested in my willingness
to see meaning in the "other side" of the story she was telling. It seems that
my daughter did not want or need her mother to be a neutral facilitator of
her life. At least when she was in the heat of reliving the story, she was more
apt to want me to see her meaning than to teach her something by pointing
out some other meaning, especially the meaning that might exist in her an-
tagonist's actions. So a parent is not the same thing as a facilitator, at least not
in our household. At times I was able to notice that we were in one of those
moments, and that by shifting roles we could actually have a different conversation. But I had to be careful not to abandon my chief role and Anna's most
important need: that of Anna's advocate and listening mom.

I tried to follow Anna's lead in other ways as well. When she invited me into
her room to help her with her homework, she wasn't giving me permission to
tell her to clean up her room. That would have led to a fight: no homework,
no cleaning, no moment of closeness between parent and child. I think of this
discipline as similar to Step 2 of CRP, which invites artists to pose questions
about their own work. The responder's job is to answer them truthfully, but
to stick exclusively to what is asked. The idea is to help with the homework
but not to bring up another subject unless asked, and certainly not to bring
up some old subject that has been a source of discomfort on other occasions.

Figure out how to do that in Step 3, which is where responders get to ask
questions but must follow the discipline of phrasing the questions neutrally—
that is, in a way that does not reveal an opinion behind the question. I have to

say that sometimes Anna got tired of the questions, particularly of the endless internal reworking of experience that asking questions can elicit. It didn't matter whether the questions were neutral. It mattered that she could simply stop thinking. But when she wanted to work through how she was going to handle something that had come up with her friends, more often than not the activity of chewing over the nuance of language was accepted with grace.

The fourth step of CRP offered me a chance to play with language. Here's where responders may state opinions, but must request permission first: "I have an opinion about X; would you like to hear it?" It hardly ever worked to follow this standard script at home, as that mostly led to eyes rolling back in the head and an exasperated sigh. What did work, though, was to paraphrase the basic question with something like: "I am going to be a parent for a moment. Is this a good time?" Or "I need to talk about something that has an opinion in it. Now or later?" Or "Is this the time for me to tell you what I think?"

Of course she would sometimes say, "No. Not now." But more often she would respond by stating her own limits: "Yes, but just one thing, not a whole slew of them." Or "Yes, but only for one minute." Or "Okay, maybe, but what is the main idea here?" I loved that she set her own terms in this, and I also liked how it made me work to say my own piece carefully and essentially. The power of letting someone know that an opinion is about to be delivered is a great way to move conversations ahead without getting sabotaged by ill will that is easily avoided. The opinion is still offered and, I would posit, is better received when folks of any age have a chance to prepare to listen.

Did Anna feel "handled"? I don't think so. By this point in our lives, these ideas were so embedded in my way of being that it felt more like I was just being me than that I was trying on CRP. We didn't fight too much in the sense that voices got raised or doors slammed or people got hurt because of flying epithets. Did we challenge each other? Yes, a lot. And this I loved about her teenage years. Her ability to give me feedback was one of the things I treasured most in this period of her life.

We all want and need criticism from people who are willing to challenge our behavior or our assumptions. The way Anna and I spoke to each other—whether to register problems, state the need for change, or express disappointment—helped to form each of our riverbanks. We were strong streams moving ahead but getting nudges from the outside that affected our path, our intensity, even at times the whole direction of our lives and relationship.

Bulky Love

....

I am going to try to explain yet again why some of us love movement. I want to try to make it clear that it has value even though it is hard to measure. I want to make it impossible to be dismissed ever again. I am so sick and tired of people calling the work that my colleagues and I do "touchy-feely"—as if something were wrong with touching and feeling. Actually, I don't think they really mean that touching and feeling are bad. I think they are using this popular phrase as a code, a quick and easy putdown for something much worse. They are saying that this activity has no intellectual value and therefore it is a waste of their time. That is why I am always trying to *let the rigor show*.

But lately I have come up with an additional solution to this casual but powerful language of confrontation. It introduces another way to remind people of the value of things we cannot accommodate with our minds alone. I call it Bulky Love, and it is how our golden retriever lives in the world. Love, or something akin to it, absorbs our dog completely. It emanates from her toward most living and nonliving things (except for white plastic bags, which for some reason terrify her). She greets all and everything with such openness and curiosity that she brings out the same qualities in others. In fact, when Anna was younger, we often told her to "be like Nani" as she went off into new situations.

The next time someone challenges me about why dancing matters or why the experience of art matters, I am going to ask them if they have or ever had a pet. And then I am going to ask them to describe that experience.

I know it is hard to put into words. We cannot explain why we spend hours of our days and nights talking to our animals even though they can't quite understand us, making sure they are comfortable even though they can figure that out for themselves. There is no rational reason to spend large amounts of money on their health and upkeep. We keep doing it. Now there is research that shows kids score better on tests if they read to their cat or bird, and that the elderly feel more connected if visited by someone with a dog. This is good. But it isn't the reason we keep our animals. There is something more, and words and statistics cannot account for the experience.

And that is what happens with dancers when they move. The nature of it is almost impossible to name. The accounting of time and money and intensity is not measurable. We do it, and we share it, whether there is an identifiable need or not.

But it is real and total and worth it, and just like our relationship to animals, it is steeped in ancient history and thousands of years of experience. It is wrapped tightly in our DNA, and we would not call ourselves human if we let go of it.

Ferocious Beauty: Genome (2006): Thomas Dwyer. Photo: Andrew Hoxey, courtesy of the *University Daily Kansan*.

Epilogue

Field Note

Choreography is a way of thinking. It is a way of gathering evidence, laying out the pieces, organizing the trail. Choreography is a way of seeing the world, the things that move against each other and then back into their own places. Choreography can happen in less than a second as a vision appears, then later in time as the vision is made real. Choreography is watching a person rise out of a chair and seeing in that action the awkward beauty, the purpose, the muscles at work. It is recognizing when someone needs to be told what to do and giving them directions. It is noticing when someone has the skills and talent and capacity and will to move forward, then allowing them the space to do so. Choreography is time-based, but the time shifts. Choreography is a medicine chest, a Torah scroll, an acupuncturist's needle, a beat, a bell, a bullhorn.

The choreographers I know are great talents but even greater thinkers. They have come to understand that learning is a verb. They can talk about personal discovery and collaborative process with compassion. They are an experimenting breed, practicing their craft and their growing methods all the time, engaging whoever is around, including their own kin. They comprehend action and make it real in thousands of variations. They do their work whether the world cares or not. Mostly it doesn't.

The way that choreographers organize minds, bodies, ideas, money, institutions, people, and their own lives untangles a natural process for practical use. Because we are very practical. We are also funny, sad, hard, hard-working, and very independent. We resemble cowboys and wrestlers in our feistiness, seamstresses in our ability to piece together unity and connection when it is needed.

At some time in our lives we were very physical. We might still be. We have probably redefined what physical is and have made that awareness a source of deep pleasure or nuanced consternation. Choreographers have a curious relation to their bodies and to the bodies of the people they work with. Some focus purely on the drive to define and extend what the human body can do. Others seek to extend what the human body can say, some with quiet subtlety and some by juxtaposing movement with media, stories, light, sound. All exert imagination, active minds at work, and the recognition that we are born with a body that will teach being and beauty and that will let us admit to the ugly, profane, and impossible in our world.

On Being Nimble

It is a rare opportunity to work with choreographers from other parts of the world, so I jumped at an invitation from Emma Gladstone at Sadler's Wells in London to participate in a gathering they call the Big Intensive. We spent the first day working with our Critical Response Process as well as with tools for collaborations between dancers and dance makers. English was our main language, with some translating going on in the margins of the circle as we worked. So I was surprised to see the British choreographers huddled during the lunch break trying to figure out my use of the word "nimble." Some combination of my accent and the placement of the word within a sentence made it difficult to understand. Also, I had apparently used it often enough that they felt they needed to understand what I meant.

In retrospect, the episode got me thinking about how being nimble is a skill, a technique, and an outcome, all in relation to hiking the horizontal. I realized that nimbleness is a way to describe what happens to artists who arrive at Dance Exchange one way and leave another. They gain a certain kind of agile intelligence, both of body and mind. They can translate quickly and make unlikely but deep connections in the way they see, listen, and move. They shift between leadership and followership with little concern for status, and they move with authority in new settings while still honoring local traditions.

It Starts with Distinctions

I find the making of categories tantalizing. I like the names I come up with after I've described a border. It is a powerful act of creation: deciding what to separate from what and how to name the now-formed group(s). Beyond the personal, in the wide world, this separating and naming is an act of real power. That is what identity movements are in part about: the right to place oneself and one's group in a proper light with proper name(s) and then to secure the right of mobility beyond the category by choice. Inclusion and exclusion become dominant activities, and the persons who uphold those decisions are indeed powerful.

Nimbleness in Personal History

I have a mental image of a filing system residing in my mind where I keep the personal memories, stories, and experiences of my life. This image is based on my actual filing system: a series of manila envelopes with their headings sloppily written in pen, pencil, and colored markers. Some headings are crossed out, some envelopes re-used, bent out of shape. They are in a variety of containers including boxes and mesh-wire desktop systems, and in loosely organized piles that live in various parts of my study. I keep some general categories, such as Family (further subdivided by particular names and more general groupings like Nieces and Nephews), and these are sometimes divided again by eras. I also have big divisions, like the Dance Exchange and its substructures, Writings, Choreography, and Finished Projects. There are a lot of files.

In my parallel mental system, my memories and my life experiences are filed somewhere in my brain, and like the real files, they require upkeep. I have to clean them up, combine, throw out, re-title, and move the pieces around. Of course in the life of my mind, the speed of this shifting is breathtaking, and I am not always aware I have done it. But when I stop to think about it, I can see the value of renewing my understanding of where I have placed an experience. Sometimes, because of what is happening in the present, I find I have to rearrange an experience's placement in my history. This, I think, leads to nimbleness.

An example of this re-categorization occurs when some of us become parents. The personal memories of our own parents come under more scrutiny. For example, in our earlier lives as children, we might have taken the experience of yelling parents and put it in the mental file called Screaming Mom and Dad. But when we discover ourselves yelling at our own offspring, suddenly we return to our memory and think more kindly of our parents' folly. I still keep the category Screaming, but I might change the tone of it. Or I might copy the story and build a second file under the heading Where Does the Anger Come From? Oddly, when we place it in a new file, we find it has a whole different set of companion stories, and this is when the shifting in our understanding takes place. Where Does Anger Come From? resides with stories about rules, experiences about jealousy, and even meditations on submission. The fact that our parents yelled a lot gets a new context or at least an additional context. And context is everything when it comes to nimbleness, to multiple perspectives, to nuance.

I like this copying, re-filing, and moving the memory around. I am not sure whether this copying is like making photocopies in multiple generations, where the story fades and distorts over time. I suspect it is more like a digital system, where the copy simply lives in its various dimensions unchanged by repetition, shining with its many facets, illuminated by its new neighbors.

But what I have come to see is that my capacity to re-file my own history gives me a certain freedom from it. I like the various meanings the same memory might fulfill, and I enjoy noticing what is happening in my current situation that makes me consider this old friend again. Perhaps the fact that it doesn't reappear consistently or in relation to the same moment is what is liberating. Multiple perspectives allow for and actually breed more tolerance, not just in the concrete world, but in the world of my memories too. And they certainly free me from having to feel the same way about some early childhood experience, or act in the same way because of it.

Of course all of this doesn't change history. But this persistent sorting does seem to make it possible to change the meaning of history. And that leads to nimbleness, or what I think of as a merry slide between past and present. The nimbleness comes from practice, and the practice always yields something curious to muse about. It also means the files get a going-over every now and then. And that too may yield certain liberation, like a good spring cleaning.

Nimbleness from Image to Physicality

A dancer's training is complex, varied, vivid, and incredibly time-consuming. We grow our physical bodies though so many different approaches. In my case, the path—beginning with a "creative modern" class that gave way to classical ballet that gave way to classical modern that gave way to postmodern eclecticism—certainly traversed myriad forms of pedagogy.

One of the inconsistent consistencies was the use of imagery. Some teachers lived by this method: "Stand as if a balloon were lightly rising out of your head; place your feet into the floor as if their roots dug down fifteen feet . . ." and so on. Other teachers communicated in strictly physical terms: "Stand with your head directly on top of your neck which is aligned to your spine" or "Spread your toes wide and use your whole foot against the floor." For me there was usefulness in the imagery as well as in the more anatomical descriptions; years later, I continue to be inspired by both of these ways of working. More specifically, I have found that the better I am at sliding between the two, the more opportunities I can find for discovery, whether about choreography, performing, or comprehending the material. Something in this process of moving between image and its poetic cousins, and in the more anatomical and simple, descriptive language of sheer physicality, allows for new comprehension of the material at hand.

So how does this work? Probably the form that is easiest to explain is something I call "scripting a gesture." Gesture shows up a lot in contemporary choreography because it is interesting, human, has great potential for narrative, and because it is recognizable to audience members. They enjoy the familiarity of a gesture that is just sitting there, particularly when it appears among the more generalized movement that characterizes much of stage dance.

So imagine a gesture that looks like someone has made a fist. If I asked, "What is this?" or "What does this look like?" the answers would probably be something like, "Somebody is angry" or "Grabbing." Or a story might emerge: "A person is having a tantrum and wants you to pay attention." These are all possible, and they fall into the category of narrative. So if I said, "Okay, right, but what is it? Can you describe this without using words that need further explanation?"

So you work the gesture. Do it slowly and see what language can be applied to make it purely physical. I might say as I watch: "The fingers gently curve toward each other, then touch the center of my palm, and then press." I might further organize my response for choreographic purposes and say: "Edges curve toward a center, then press or push against an obstacle."

What is curious is that this language can serve as a very interesting improvisational script for the body in motion. This is great for our rehearsal process. But the words might also inform the subject. Let's say anger was an underlying emotion in a piece. In that case, the idea of pressing against the center, which itself might be an obstacle, might lead back to meaning. And that is what I think being nimble is about. Sliding between poles that some might find incompatible and then, by translating one to the other, discovering new meaning in the process.

Nimbleness in History

At the end of Anna's junior year abroad, I went to visit her. She had just spent a semester in Barcelona, and we decided to take a car trip: we took ten days traveling around her beloved Spain. The long ride and the sights gave us ample time to converse about the insistence of history and the way it both ennobles and impinges on the present. We got into the subject big-time when in Cordoba, because the city allows you to see its history everywhere. We visited both a statue marking the birthplace of the Jewish scholar–philosopher Maimonides and the famous Mezquita, which made clear the Muslim influence throughout the country. We also saw where Ferdinand and Isabella first began to issue the decrees that led to the conversion, expulsion, and death of the Jews in Spain.

Anna began to argue, with some frustration, about how so many of her Jewish friends seem to be Jewish when discussing anti-Semitism but not much at other times. I told her two stories, the first taken from the dance I made called *Shehechianu*, in which I wondered how we could honor our history without letting it determine our contemporary actions. In fact, the piece ultimately asked whether we needed to step out of history in order to save ourselves in the present. The second was a story from my childhood. I was about eight. A neighbor boy bit my arm. I cried. I went to tell my mother, but she wasn't home. I sat on the curb waiting for her so that I could show her. She took a long time. The bite mark was disappearing. So I bit my arm again. I needed the wound to show.

How does history set the agenda for the present? And for how long do we have to do battle over these old hurts? Anna and I both bemoaned this aspect of our condition.

And then I said that this is where we need to hold two ideas in our head at the same time. This is where we need permeable membranes. This is where we need to call up some authentic form of respect at both ends of a horizontal spectrum. All of these ideas make it possible to acknowledge the dreadfulness and beauty of what happened, and to also acknowledge that now is now.

This requires great imagination, great fortitude, and a lot of nimbleness.

Back to Emma Gladstone in England, but now a year later. We are listening to Ruth Little, a dramaturge from the Royal Court Theatre, take a roomful of international choreographers through a reading of first scenes from a variety of plays. She is discussing the atmosphere, the tone, the very first image as a way of studying text and of preparing for first rehearsals, which is the subject of our gathering. I am sitting next to Emma and whispering to her that I am translating many of Ruth's ideas and language into dance terms. We have an intense discussion on the side. Emma is challenging me in the best sense of that word because she isn't sure translating is such a good idea. She is afraid, I think, that it might lead to a literal equivalency that would not enlarge our capacity but rather reduce it.

Later, we attack the problem again, this time with a pen, paper, and a thinking grid, which is a format I use to spark my own brain and map multiple meanings inherent in translation. To organize the exploration, I line the top of the page with terms and images that Ruth used to describe one of the plays—things like centrifugal force, fog, paranoia—and I make a list down the left side of the page with categories for dances—things like costumes, set, kind of movement phrases, music, personal memories. I am hoping this last idea, memory, will allow us to explore quickly an unlikely connection from our own experience and put that into the brew.

I want to express the importance of making room for waste (with a sly idea that waste is never really that because it will be recycled for later use, or because it is a form of "muscle-building"). If you try to be too efficient too fast, rejecting iterative play, almost all attempts will be simplistic. What makes this particular exercise so valuable is that it affords the sheer joy of thinking itself. I am most likely not going to actually use these ideas; I am just expanding the pathways of the brain by intersecting and overlapping unlikely images at the same time. We try it together by linking a memory with the term Ruth used in reference to Georg Büchner's play *Woyzeck*: centrifugal force. Emma starts talking about the rides at the fair, where the spinning gets going really fast and then the floor drops out. We have a good laugh as we imagine for a moment how that might be a set or how the floor could drop out from under a paranoid character or how the whole "dance" could be done with the movers plastered against the wall the way it is in a fair ride. This dance will never be produced except in our heads, but I have to believe we are both more adept at translating from idea to representation and back again just by virtue of the practice. Nimbleness: swift brain-work moving between forms, images, disciplines, and problems that by now we know aren't problems but puzzles.

Hiking the horizontal can be exhausting, exhilarating, time-consuming. It defies total congruence and agreement among friends and allies. It forces us to decide on excellence in each moment, to apply what we know to be true to the particular circumstances we find ourselves in, as well to bring our best historical judgment to bear. The horizon stretches far away not in one direction but in many. I like that. It gives me hope. After all, we have our tools, our methods, our partners, our commission, our insights, and our vast capacity to make stuff as we go along.

Liz Lerman; Judith Jourdin and Kimberli Boyd, background.
Photo: Lise Metzger.

Appendix

Works Choreographed by Liz Lerman, 1974–2010

In choreographic terms, hiking the horizontal has meant that the dances sometimes have changed to suit new circumstances, appeared in multiple iterations with more than one title, or borrowed sections from one another. It also has meant that some dances have been made with extensive collaboration from particular Dance Exchange colleagues, above and beyond the role the dancers normally play in developing movement and narrative content. With all this in mind, it is not an exact science to make a list of choreographed works. What follows is my best attempt, with choreographic collaborators noted where their leadership was especially significant.

Title	Premiere Performance	Date
The Matter of Origins	Clarice Smith Performing Arts Center at Maryland, College Park	2010
Darwin's Wife	Center for Education and Culture, Sapporo, Japan	2009
613 Radical Acts of Prayer (collaboration with Cassie Meador)	New Jersey Performing Arts Center, Newark	2007
Ferocious Beauty: Genome	Wesleyan University, Middletown, Connecticut	2006
Man/Chair Dances	Omaha Symphony Orchestra, Holland Performing Arts Center, Omaha, Nebraska	2006
Small Dances About Big Ideas	Harvard Law School, Cambridge, Massachusetts	2005
The Mad Dancers (play by Yehuda Hyman, co-directed and co-choreographed with Nick Olcott)	Theater J, Washington, D.C.	2003
Hallelujah/USA	Clarice Smith Performing Arts Center at Maryland, College Park	2002

Title	Premiere Performance	Date
Dances at a Cocktail Party	Tampa Bay Performing Arts Center	2002
Uneasy Dances	Tampa Bay Performing Arts Center	2002
Hallelujah: In Praise of Paradise Lost and Found	Power Center for the Performing Arts, University Musical Society, Ann Arbor, Michigan	2001
Hallelujah: In Praise of the Creative Spirit	Bates Dance Festival, Lewiston, Maine	2001
Hallelujah: In Praise of Beauty and Disorder	Walker Arts Center, Minneapolis, Minnesota	2001
Hallelujah: In Praise of Constancy in the Midst of Change	Flynn Center for the Performing Arts, Burlington, Vermont	2001
Hallelujah: Stones Will Float, Leaves Will Sink, Paths Will Cross	Skirball Cultural Center, Los Angeles, California	2001
Hallelujah: In Praise of Fertile Fields (collaboration with Martha Wittman)	Jacob's Pillow Dance Festival, Beckett, Massachusetts	2000
Hallelujah: In Praise of Ordinary Prophets (collaboration with Peter DiMuro)	University of Arizona, Tucson	2000
Hallelujah: First Light	The dock, Eastport, Maine	2000
Hallelujah: In Praise of Animals and Their People	Lisner Auditorium, George Washington University, Washington, D.C.	1999
Hallelujah: Gates of Praise	Lisner Auditorium, George Washington University, Washington, D.C.	1999
Getting to Hallelujah	Garde Arts Center, New London, Connecticut	1998
Moving to Hallelujah	Skirball Cultural Center, Los Angeles, California	1998
White Gloves / Hard Hats	Garde Arts Center, New London, Connecticut	1998
Pas de Dirt	Garde Arts Center, New London, Connecticut	1998

Title	Premiere Performance	Date
Fifty Modest Reflections on Turning Fifty	Gammage Auditorium, Arizona State University, Tempe	1998
Shehechianu: Skin Soliloquies	Lansburgh Theatre, Washington, D.C.	1997
Fresh Blood	Queens Theatre in the Park, New York	1996
Light Years	Intelsat Headquarters, Washington, D.C.	1996
Nocturnes	Lisner Auditorium, George Washington University, Washington, D.C.	1996
Shehechianu: Bench Marks	Lisner Auditorium, George Washington University, Washington, D.C.	1996
The Music Hall's Shipyard Project	Music Hall / Portsmouth Naval Shipyard, Portsmouth, New Hampshire / Kittery, Maine	1996
Sustenance Dance (collaboration with Michelle Pearson)	Mayfair Festival of the Arts, Allentown, Pennsylvania	1996
Portsmouth Pages	Music Hall, Portsmouth, New Hampshire	1995
Room for Many More (collaboration with Kimberli Boyd)	Chicago Historical Society	1995
Shehechianu: Faith and Science on the Midway	Lansburgh Theatre, Washington, D.C.	1995
Flying Into the Middle	Joyce Theater, New York, New York	1995
Safe House: Still Looking (site-specific)	Friends Meeting House, Wilmington, Delaware	1994
Safe House: Still Looking (theatrical version)	Cowell Theater, San Francisco, California	1994
Spelunking the Center (collaboration with Tom Truss)	Kennedy Center for the Performing Arts, Washington, D.C.	1993
This Is Who We Are	Marvin Center, George Washington University, Washington, D.C.	1993

Title	Premiere Performance	Date
Incidents in the Life of an Ohio Youth	BalletMet, Columbus, Ohio	1993
The Awakening (collaboration with Kimberli Boyd)	McKinley High School, Washington, D.C.	1992
Untitled (site-specific)	Kennedy Center for the Performing Arts, Washington, D.C.	1991
The Good Jew?	Israeli/Jewish American Dance Festival, Boston, Massachusetts	1991
Untitled	Meredith College, Raleigh, North Carolina	1991
Short Stories (version 2)	American Dance Festival, Durham, North Carolina	1991
Short Stories (version 1)	The Barns at Wolf Trap, Vienna, Virginia	1991
Anatomy of an Inside Story	Dance Place, Washington, D.C.	1990
A Life in the Nation's Capital	Dance Place, Washington, D.C.	1990
The Perfect Ten	Serious Fun! at Lincoln Center, New York, New York	1990
Docudance 1990: Dark Interlude	14th Street Danscenter, New York, New York	1990
May I Have Your Attention Please!	Union Station, Washington, D.C.	1990
Five Days in Maine	Maine Festival, Portland	1989
Floating Hand	Dance Place, Washington, D.C.	1989
Reenactments	Kennedy Center for the Performing Arts, Washington, D.C.	1989
Ms. Appropriate Goes to the Theatre	Dance Place, Washington, D.C.	1988
Atomic Priests: The Feature	Dance Theater Workshop, New York, New York	1987
Sketches from Memory	DAMA Theater, Washington, D.C.	1987
Atomic Priests: Coming Attractions	DAMA Theater, Washington, D.C.	1987
Black Sea Follies	Lenox Arts Center, Lenox, Massachusetts	1986

Title	Premiere Performance	Date
Still Crossing	Liberty Dances in Battery Park, New York, New York	1986
Russia: Footnotes to a History	Museum of Contemporary Art, Los Angeles, California	1986
The Transparent Apple and the Silver Saucer	Sidwell Auditorium, Washington, D.C.	1985
Space Cadet	Washington Project for the Arts, Washington, D.C.	1984
Ives & Company	National Portrait Gallery, Washington, D.C.	1984
E. Hopper	Dance Place, Washington, D.C.	1984
Second Variation on a Window	Dance Place, Washington, D.C.	1984
Pavane for Two Older Women	New Music America / Old Post Office Pavilion, Washington, D.C.	1983
Variations on a Window	New Music America / Old Post Office Pavilion, Washington, D.C.	1983
Docudance: Nine Short Dances About the Defense Budget and Other Military Matters	Marvin Center, George Washington University, Washington, D.C.	1983
Songs and Poems of the Body: In the Text	Dance Place, Washington, D.C.	1982
Docudance: Reaganomics (No One Knows What the Numbers Mean)	Dance Place, Washington, D.C.	1982
Songs and Poems of the Body: In the Gallery	Kennedy Center for the Performing Arts, Washington, D.C.	1981
Current Events	Dance Place, Washington, D.C.	1981
Journey 1–4	Washington Project for the Arts, Washington, D.C.	1980
Fanfare for the Common Man	City Dance / National Mall, Washington, D.C.	1980
Pollution Dances	McPherson Square, Washington, D.C.	1979
Who's on First?	City Dance / Warner Theater, Washington, D.C.	1979

Title	Premiere Performance	Date
RSVP	O'Neill Choreographers' Conference, Waterford, Connecticut	1979
Bonsai	National Arboretum, Washington, D.C.	1978
Goodbye Wisconsin	Dance Exchange, Washington, D.C.	1978
Still Life with Cat and Fingers	Dance Exchange, Washington, D.C.	1978
Elevator Operators and Other Strangers	Dance Exchange, Washington, D.C.	1978
Ms. Galaxy and Her Three Raps with God	Baltimore Theatre Project, Baltimore, Maryland	1977
Memory Gardens	Washington Project for the Arts, Washington, D.C.	1976
Woman of the Clear Vision	Hand Chapel, Mount Vernon College, Washington, D.C.	1975
Approaching Simone (choreography for play by Megan Terry)	Washington Area Feminist Theater, Washington, D.C.	1974
New York City Winter	St. Mark's Danspace, New York, New York	1974

"Influence, Inquiry, Action"
Portions of this article originally appeared as "Dancing in Community: Its Roots in Art" in 2003, published online at Community Arts Network, http://www.communityarts.net.

"The Roosevelt, Dancing"
Portions of this article appeared previously as part of "Art and Community: Feeding the Artist, Feeding the Art," in the anthology *Community, Culture, and Globalization*, edited by Don Adams and Arlene Goldbard and published by the Rockefeller Foundation Creativity and Culture Division in 2002.

"The Shipyard, Dancing"
Portions of this article appeared previously as part of "Art and Community: Feeding the Artist, Feeding the Art," in the anthology *Community, Culture, and Globalization*, edited by Don Adams and Arlene Goldbard and published by the Rockefeller Foundation Creativity and Culture Division in 2002.

"Dancing on Both Sides of the Brain: An Essay in Text and Movement"
This article was originally published in *Movement Research*, where it appeared under the title "By All Possible Means" in a special fall/winter 1994/1995 issue devoted to the relationship between speech and movement. This version has been updated to include reflection on work created since the article was first published.

"Choreographing Space"
This essay was originally written on commission from dance writer/editor Cathryn Harding and is published here for the first time. My thanks to Cathryn for her guidance and encouragement in its development.

"My Favorite Night at Temple Micah"
Parts of this essay originally appeared in the article "Bodies of Faith" in *Faith and Form*. 37, no. 3, 2004. Reprinted from *Faith and Form*, www.faithandform.com.

"Ruminations and Curiosities: A Series of Anecdotes and the Questions That Follow"
This article was originally published in *Journal of Dance Education* 8, no. 2, 2008.

"A Job Swap and Slow Banking: Two Op-Eds"
The op-ed entitled "A Proposed Job Swap to Save American Capitalism" was first published on the Community Arts Network: www.communityarts.net.

Index

About the Author

Liz Lerman is a choreographer, performer, writer, educator, and speaker. She founded Liz Lerman Dance Exchange in 1976, and has cultivated the company's unique multigenerational ensemble into a leading force in contemporary dance. Liz has been the recipient of the American Choreographer Award and the American Jewish Congress "Golda" Award, and was named 1988 Washingtonian of the Year by *Washingtonian* magazine. In 2002 her work was recognized with a MacArthur Fellowship and she has also been awarded the National Foundation for Jewish Culture's Achievement Award. She is the author of *Teaching Dance to Senior Adults* (1983) and the coauthor of *Liz Lerman's Critical Response Process* (2003). She attended Bennington College and Brandeis University, received her B.A. in dance from the University of Maryland and an M.A. in dance from George Washington University. She is married to storyteller Jon Spelman.

Library of Congress Cataloging-in-Publication Data

Lerman, Liz.
  Hiking the horizontal : field notes from a choreographer / Liz Lerman.
    p. cm.
  Includes bibliographical references and index.
  ISBN 978-0-8195-6951-6 (cloth : alk. paper)
  1. Lerman, Liz. 2. Women choreographers — United States — Biography.
  3. Choreography — United States — Philosophy. 4. Modern dance — United
  States — Philosophy. I. Title.
  GV1785.L435 2011
  792.8'2092—dc22
  [B]

                        2010038870